Final-Offer Arbitration

Final-Offer Arbitration

The Effects on Public Safety Employee Bargaining

James L. Stern
University of Wisconsin

Charles M. Rehmus
University of Michigan

J. Joseph Loewenberg
Temple University

Hirschel Kasper
Oberlin College

Barbara D. Dennis
University of Wisconsin

Lexington Books
D. C. Heath and Company
Lexington, Massachusetts
Toronto   London

Library of Congress Cataloging in Publication Data

Main entry under title:

Final-offer Arbitration.

Includes index.
1. Arbitration, Industrial—United States—Case studies. 2. Collective bargaining—Firemen—United States—Case studies. 3. Collective bargaining—Police—United States—Case studies. I. Stern, James L.
HD5325.F5F56   331.89′041′36330973   75-10525
ISBN 0-669-00022-1

Published simultaneously in Canada

Printed in the United States of America

International Standard Book Number: 0-669-00022-1

Library of Congress Catalog Card Number: 75-10525

Contents

List of Figures and Tables

Preface

Historically, government agencies have been thought to be reluctant to fund research about controversial industrial relations problems. Congress has blessed research into manpower problems, but when one turns to the question of strikes and alternative methods of dispute resolution, there is a mixed reaction. It is contended on one hand that social scientists can contribute little to policy formation in this field. On the other hand, there appears, by implication at least, to be the attitude that research in this field may contribute too much and may be supportive of positions that are adverse to those advocated by some politically powerful groups.

We are grateful to the U.S. Department of Labor for its willingness to support research into what we believe is an important contemporary problem and hope that the Department will continue to allocate funds to the study of collective bargaining procedures in both the private and the public sectors. We recognize that the findings of this study are controversial, but express the hope that those who find support herein for their own long-cherished prejudices and those who find just the contrary will distinguish between what is reported as fact and what is reported as probability and possibility.

We attempt to describe and analyze what has transpired in the field of dispute resolution for public safety employees in Pennsylvania, Michigan, and Wisconsin in the last few years and in the course of our presentation report and evaluate the views of the labor and management negotiators and the neutrals who have participated in the procedures that have been adopted. On the basis of these data, we estimate future trends and speculate about possible consequences of transferring various procedural arrangements to other bargaining situations. While it is recognized that such speculation involves extrapolation beyond the limits of the data, we hope that in so doing we encourage the reader to make his own determination of the degree to which the limited experience reported upon in this study provides an adequate base for generalization.

The authors were able to undertake this research project because of the financial support granted by the Department of Labor through its Labor-Management Services Administration. We wish to thank former Secretary of Labor James Hodgson and Under-Secretary of Labor Richard Schubert for their encouragement in this effort and to express our appreciation to Herbert Lahne who served as the Department's contract officer for this project and helped us in many ways. The views expressed herein, however, are those of the authors and should not be construed as the official views of the Department of Labor. The authors also wish to acknowledge the helping hand of their home institutions—the Universities of Wisconsin and Michigan, Temple University, and Oberlin College

—for providing a hospitable environment and general support for the project.

In addition, we wish to thank the Johnson Foundation for hosting and co-financing the conferences of mediators and arbitrators at the Wingspread Conference Center in Racine, Wisconsin. Conference participants found the atmosphere to be particularly pleasant and appreciated the thorough planning and hospitality shown by Leslie Paffrath, the Executive Director of the Foundation, and staff members, Rita Goodman and Kay Mauer.

The authors also wish to express their appreciation to David B. Johnson, Dean of International Studies at the University of Wisconsin, and Commissioner Morris M. Slavney, Chairman of the Wisconsin Employment Relations Commission, for organizing and chairing the conference of arbitrators and mediators.

The chapters in this volume have been written by different authors, with a minimum of interference on the part of the others. James L. Stern (Professor of Economics, University of Wisconsin) was the principal investigator who designed and organized the project and wrote the introductory, Wisconsin, and concluding chapters. Charles M. Rehmus (Director, Institute of Labor and Industrial Relations, University of Michigan) directed the Michigan study and along with Anita Schoomaker wrote the Michigan chapter. J. Joseph Loewenberg (Professor, Temple University) directed the Pennsylvania study and wrote the chapter about the Pennsylvania experience. Hirschel Kasper (Professor of Economics, Oberlin College) performed the regression analysis comparing the results of arbitration in the three states and wrote the chapter on that topic. Barbara D. Dennis (Editor, Industrial Relations Research Institute, University of Wisconsin) wrote the summary of the conferences of mediators and arbitrators and edited the entire volume.

Many other people helped in a variety of ways, and we wish to express our appreciation to them and to publicly acknowledge their assistance. Edward B. Krinsky (Assistant to the Vice-Chancellor and participating faculty member of the Industrial Relations Research Institute, University of Wisconsin) designed the questionnaire that was sent to arbitrators and wrote the summary of responses that is included as the third part of Chapter 5. Thomas A. Kochan (Assistant Professor, New York State School of Industrial and Labor Relations, Cornell University), designed the interview schedule that was sent to management and labor negotiators in the three states.

Research assistants who interviewed labor and management negotiators and coded questionnaires and performed many other necessary functions in connection with the Wisconsin study included Jeri Darling, Neil DeClercq, June Gertig, Brian Heshizer, Stephen Rubenfeld, Norman

Solomon, and Joseph Tremiti. Solomon and Tremiti, assisted in the later stages by Heshizer, performed the regression analyses and used data from the Wisconsin study in their M.A. theses in industrial relations. Clerical and other assistance were provided by the IRRI staff—Bette Briggs, Susan Dean, Jeanette Fegler, Sandra Offerdahl, Debbie Mrugala, and Gladys Rowe.

Anita Schoomaker collaborated with Charles Rehmus in writing the Michigan chapter in addition to serving as a one-person staff throughout the Michigan project by interviewing, coding, and performing other research functions as required. Rand Smith also served as a research assistant and interviewed many labor and management negotiators and assisted in analyzing their responses. Clerical and coding assistance were provided by Sue Sincich and Gerry Saunders.

Paul Boehringer supervised the distribution of questionnaires and coding of returns in the Pennsylvania study. He was assisted by Sanford Balick and Frank Paul. Barbara Heer provided administrative and clerical support throughout the project.

James Allen of the Madison Area Computation Center of the University of Wisconsin wrote the necessary programs for the regression analyses in Chapter 6. Mark McDaniel of Oberlin College and Alan Ponak of the University of Wisconsin also assisted in the running of the regression equations.

Finally, we wish to acknowledge our indebtedness to the labor and management representatives, independent attorneys, mediators, and arbitrators who answered detailed mail questionnaires. Without the cooperation of this group and particularly those management and labor representatives among them who also took time from their schedules to permit us to interview them personally at some length, it would have been impossible to carry out this study. Though their opinions are reported anonymously, we hope that they will find them to be a fair reflection of their views and that they and others will find this report useful.

Final-Offer Arbitration

1 Introduction

In the years to come, arbitration may be considered an essential part of the public sector bargaining process and may play the same role that the strike has traditionally played in the private sector. Its availability and judicious use may be seen as a necessary stimulus to successful bilateral negotiations in most situations. Today, however, both expert and public opinion are divided into three camps. First, there are the public sector traditionalists who still see bargaining as a threat to the sovereignty of public management and an impingement on the merit principle as well as the civil service system. They tend to believe that the last word should be management's, possibly subject to third-party advisory opinion in the form of factfinding and thereafter to legislative review if an impasse still prevails.

The second group is made up of the private sector traditionalists who believe that it takes the threat of the strike to make bargaining work and that this maxim applies to both the public and private sectors. They believe that if public employees have the right to strike, there may be even fewer public sector strikes and those that do occur will be easier to settle because they will not be illegal.

The third group could be flatteringly called experimentalist, pragmatic, and eclectic or even labeled less favorably as interventionist tinkerers whose ideas rest on uncertain grounds. This group believes there must be a strong third-party procedure—established by legislation—that is able to render binding verdicts on either party. These interventionists think that such settlements, rendered by one form of arbitration or another, will be more equitable to the interests of the parties involved, more satisfactory to each of them in the long run, and more in keeping with that nebulous concept, which all three groups invoke, called "the public interest."

One variant of these positions is put forth by individuals who would legalize strikes of nonessential public employees, permit strikes of more essential employees if there were safeguards to protect the public, and prohibit strikes in some instances where there were no safeguards. This last category of employees would be given the right to invoke binding arbitration unilaterally. The establishment of different procedures for different groups of public employees, which is dependent upon the essentiality of the service provided, leads to consideration of the application of public-sector-type legislation to such vital areas of the private sector as privately owned transportation systems.

The purpose of this study is not to provide scientific evidence to demonstrate the superiority of one of these positions over another, since to some degree, this is a matter of personal values. We do, however, illuminate the operation of bargaining under binding arbitration so that exponents of all three views will have further evidence upon which to draw in reassessing their positions. The states of Pennsylvania, Michigan, and Wisconsin have seen fit to give primacy to arbitration as the means of resolving disputes between municipal employers and bargaining units of public safety employees. All of these statutes are relatively new, and all were sought by organizations representing the employees involved. An examination of the initial experience under these statutes provides us with an opportunity to examine the effect of arbitration on bargaining processes and outcomes in three separate jurisdictions.

Each of the arbitration systems differs from the others in many important aspects. For example, the function of prearbitration mediation ranges from the heavy emphasis given it under the Wisconsin procedure to no role whatsoever in Pennsylvania, with the intermediate position being in Michigan. Another varying aspect is in the procedures for selecting arbitrators in the three states. The statutes in Michigan and Pennsylvania differ from Wisconsin's in that they provide for tripartite arbitration panels on which one neutral and one representative of each party serve; and the occupations covered by statute differ slightly from state to state, but apply in all three to firefighters and police.

The essential difference, however, which stimulated the interest of the researchers and led to this study, pertains to the form of arbitration favored in each state. Pennsylvania, the first of the three states to adopt arbitration, opted for conventional arbitration under which the arbitrator is free to adopt compromise positions on each issue that he is asked to resolve. Michigan originally followed the same pattern but subsequently provided that, on each economic issue, the arbitrator must choose the position of one of the parties and is prohibited from adopting a compromise position.

To some observers, including the Michigan legislature, this change is regarded as an important one. On the other hand, it can be argued that in multiple issue cases, the arbitrator's power to fashion a compromise is not greatly restricted because he may achieve this same result by adopting the position of one party on one economic issue and the position of the other party on the next economic issue. Even so, the Michigan procedure may facilitate mediated settlements to a far greater extent than conventional arbitration.

The Wisconsin legislature replaced a system of factfinding with recommendations with one giving preferred status to a procedure that although considered by some writers as "either-or" or "all-or-nothing" arbitration, is identified in Wisconsin as "final-offer" arbitration. Under this procedure, the arbitrator must select the position of either party in its entirety without modification. Although the statute permits the parties to substitute conventional arbitration for final-offer arbitration if they so agree, final-offer arbitration is used when such agreement is not reached and, in actual practice, has been used in all but one of the cases heard during the first two and one-half years that the statute has been in operation.

In the opinion of some skeptical scholars, the Wisconsin procedure smacks of gimmickry and encourages gamesmanship rather than good-faith bargaining. Supporters of final-offer arbitration claim, however, that it increases the pressure on the parties to take realistic bargaining positions and to settle their disputes through direct negotiations without use of arbitration. Also, in those instances when arbitration is used, final-offer arbitration limits the freedom of arbitrators to introduce their own prejudices and thereby shackles to some extent the power of what are referred to in Wisconsin in a disparaging manner as "itinerant philosophers." (In all fairness to the reader, it should be noted that the authors of the Michigan, Pennsylvania, and Wisconsin chapters of this volume have served as arbitrators and therefore are included in this group so unflatteringly characterized.)

The co-existence of conventional, final-offer-by-issue, and final-offer-by-package arbitration as well as the application of these three arbitration systems to the same occupations—essentially public safety employees—provide an opportunity to study the effects of their procedural differences on the bargaining process and on the outcome of bargaining. By examination of the statistics on the frequency of the use of arbitration, estimates can be made as to whether there is in fact a different degree of reliance upon third-party decisionmakers associated with the different systems. Ascertaining whether bargaining outcomes are affected by differences in the arbitration procedure is also possible as is, to some degree, determining the relative magnitude and direction of the effect of these differences.

Such information has direct policy implications not only for other parts of the public sector, but also for such segments of the private sector as the transportation industry—an industry where the use of final-offer arbitration has been contemplated by the President and the Congress of the United States. To provide a basis for evaluating such implications, the three arbitration systems as used in Pennsylvania, Michigan, and Wisconsin are analyzed in Chapters 2, 3, and 4, respectively. In Chapter 5, a summary of the views of mediators and arbitrators about the different arbitration procedures is presented, and in Chapter 6, regression analysis is used to compare bargaining outcomes across the three states. While individual findings are summarized at the end of each chapter, Chapter 7 sums up the findings of the study as a whole. It is important to note that because different authors wrote various chapters, the reader will encounter differences in emphasis and interpretation from chapter to chapter, which are also discussed and evaluated in the final chapter.

2

The Pennsylvania Arbitration Experience

Pennsylvania Act 111 of 1968 was one of the first statutes to grant public safety employees the right to settle collective bargaining impasses through compulsory binding arbitration. This chapter will include a brief history of the legislation, the experience under the act, the reactions of those who live with it, and the law's impact.

Review of Act 111

Understanding the status of collective bargaining for police and fire-fighters in Pennsylvania prior to 1968 develops an appreciation for the manner in which Act 111 was passed and for its provisions. This section presents a brief background of events leading to Act 111 and summarizes the terms of the act itself.

Background to Act 111

Legislation providing public safety employees in Pennsylvania with access to binding arbitration for interest disputes followed a lengthy period of other measures that employees found wanting. In the strike-prone years following the end of World War II, the Pennsylvania legislature adopted a bill specifically denying public employees the right to strike.[1] In lieu of the strike, employees were permitted to bring impasses to a tripartite panel that could engage in mediation and factfinding. Employees soon found that public employers felt little pressure from the panel's determinations. Meanwhile, a bill of the state legislature granted binding arbitration to public transit employees in the Pittsburgh area.[2] Public safety employees, who did not favor the strike as an impasse procedure and some of whose organizational constitutions did not sanction strikes, were encouraged to push for similar legislation. Their efforts met with success in 1959,[3] but the victory proved short-lived. The legislation was immediately engulfed in legal challenges. The Supreme Court of Pennsylvania ruled that the legislature violated the state's constitution (Article III, §31) by delegating power to set municipal salaries and otherwise apportion public monies; therefore arbitration awards were not binding on the public employer.[4] The effect of the court decision was to render panel determination advisory once again and thus, to all intents and purposes, ineffective as an impasse procedure. However, the court signaled the only way that binding arbitration would be legally acceptable, namely, by amending the state constitution.

The process for amending the constitution in Pennsylvania requires passage of the proposed amendment by two separately elected legislatures and then a popular referendum.[5] Mustering their political forces and accumulating a special fund, the police and firefighter organizations proceeded to follow the amendment route. Typical of their effort was the referendum on Constitutional Amendment 9-A held in November 1967; the campaign to pass the amendment was waged under the slogan "Support your local police and firefighters." The vote in favor of the amendment was four to one, the largest majority ever gained in a constitutional amendment referendum.

The enabling legislation for the constitutional amendment approved by referendum was passed in the following session of the legislature. The bill was drawn up by a lawyer representing the police after extensive discussion by leaders of the police and firefighters about its major elements. All efforts to amend the bill in the legislature failed. Municipal forces did not organize any major coordinated attack on it, perhaps because they did not feel threatened by its provisions or because they were confident that the courts would once again repudiate enforcement of arbitration awards. On June 24, 1968, Governor Raymond P. Shafer signed Act of the General Assembly No. 111, and public safety employees in Pennsylvania finally had access to compulsory binding arbitration.[6]

Provisions and Scope of Act 111

A review of Act 111 reveals its origins and intent. Almost the entire statute is devoted to the mechanics of the arbitration process and its results. The act, which is reprinted in Appendix A, provides that bargaining representatives designated by at least 50 percent of public police and firemen "have the right to bargain collectively with their public employers concerning the terms and conditions of their employment. . . ." Negotiations start at least six months prior to the beginning of the fiscal year. If a settlement is not concluded within 30 days (or if a law-making body does not ratify a negotiated agreement), either party may initiate arbitration proceedings. The tripartite board of arbitration consists of a representative from each of the parties and a neutral chairman selected by mutual agreement or from a panel of Pennsylvania residents submitted by the American Arbitration Association. An award issued by a majority of the tripartite board is final and binding, and "no appeal therefrom shall be allowed to any court." Each party is responsible for the costs of its representative to the arbitration board, but the public employer is also responsible for the costs of the neutral chairman and the administrative and other costs of the hearing. A timetable covers all phases of the arbitration process from the nomination of the representative arbitrators to legislative implementation of the award.

Act 111 is revealing for what it does not contain as well as for what it does. Compared to other statutes authorizing collective bargaining, it has little or nothing to say about such matters as representation procedures, bargaining unit composition, administrative agencies, unfair labor practices, impasse procedures other than arbitration, or restrictions on the scope of bargaining. The absence of these subjects is not by chance; rather, it underscores the fact that the bill is the product of employee organizations that were concerned primarily with securing ready access to and iron-clad results from arbitration.

Act 111 covers all publicly employed police and firefighters in Pennsylvania. More specifically, it applies to the state police; to police and firefighters in Allegheny County, which is the only county legally authorized to have public safety employees; [a] and to police and firefighters in the hundreds of municipalities throughout the state.

Many municipalities are small and have no police departments with full-time employees. The number of policemen who potentially could be covered by Act 111, however, is significantly larger than the number of firefighters. Not only are police departments generally larger than fire departments, but, more importantly, the tradition of volunteer fire companies remains strong in Pennsylvania. Even municipalities of 50,000 persons may be served by volunteer companies. Thus, comparisons in absolute numbers of Pennsylvania police and firefighters engaging in negotiations or arbitration are meaningless.

Experience under Act 111

This section deals with various aspects of the experience under the act including negotiations, arbitration, and legal challenges to the act and to arbitration awards.

---

[a] Counties other than Allegheny have sheriffs, but they are part of the court system and have only civil duties.

Data Sources

There is no central agency for administering Act 111 or for collecting data on police and firefighter collective bargaining in the state.[b] The information-gathering problem is compounded by the fact that there are more than 2,500 recognized municipalities in Pennsylvania. Thus, the information presented in this chapter has been derived from previous studies, from outside sources, and from questionnaires and interviews conducted in connection with the project.[7]

An initial brief questionnaire was sent to management representatives in 756 municipalities: all municipalities with a population of 5,000 and above; a 25 percent random sample of municipalities with a population of 2,500-4,999; and a 10 percent random sample of municipalities with less than 2,500 in population. Almost two-thirds (482) of these questionnaires were returned, with roughly equal distribution in each of the above population categories.

All management respondents who indicated they had negotiated an agreement or received an arbitration award were sent a lengthy questionnaire for additional information. Police and firefighter representatives in these communities were sent comparable questionnaires. Almost 40 percent of these questionnaires were returned in completed form. Response rates were generally higher from collective bargaining participants in larger municipalities.

Finally, 30 interviews in 11 jurisdictions were held with employer and employee representatives to gain insight into bargaining arrangements, experiences, and influences.

Collective Bargaining Negotiations

The responses to the initial questionnaire indicate that collective bargaining for public safety employees is pervasive. All 212 municipalities that engaged in collective bargaining did so with their police forces, but only 40 municipalities bargained with firefighters as well. While it is possible that smaller communities have no full-time police forces and therefore are in no position to negotiate under Act 111, the evidence suggests that even

---

[b] The American Arbitration Association (AAA) enters the operation of Act 111 only if the parties have come to an impasse in negotiations and then only if the partisan arbitrators are unable to select a third neutral arbitrator. The AAA has no way of knowing how many parties utilize arbitration machinery without resorting to the AAA's assistance. Moreover, a careful check of AAA records indicates that some cases submitted to the AAA are grievances processed under Act 111 rather than interest cases.

if only municipalities with full-time police employees are considered, collective bargaining is more likely to occur in larger than in smaller communities. Every community with full-time professional firefighters negotiated with its firefighters, which is a reflection again of the size of such communities and also of the firefighter organization.

Assuming respondents to the initial questionnaire were representative of their population category, one can derive the total number of current collective bargaining relationships between municipalities and their public safety forces in Pennsylvania. According to this computation, there are approximately 460 such relationships, of which fewer than 15 percent involve firefighters. The derived figure on firefighter bargaining is low, however. In 1969, 67 such relationships had been identified, and it is unlikely that any decline in bargaining among firefighter units has occurred subsequently.

The extent of negotiations has risen dramatically since 1968. Only two-thirds of such municipalities, essentially those above 10,000 in population, negotiated with public safety forces in the first year of Act 111. By the end of 1969, however, almost the identical percentage of major municipalities were engaged in collective bargaining with public safety forces as in the latest survey. Any additional bargaining has therefore come in smaller communities.

The majority of all public safety agreements since 1968 have been one year in length, but there have been numerous exceptions. Only about one-fourth of the parties involved in municipal-police bargaining reported that *all* agreements were for one year. The response from municipal-firefighter relationships was similar. Of the remaining parties, approximately one-half had experience with but a single multi-year agreement.

There is no such thing as a typical negotiating pattern. What occurs depends on bargaining history, existence of other bargaining units in the jurisdiction that are negotiating at the same time, circumstances surrounding a particular negotiation, and the personalities present at the negotiations table. In cases where one or both of the parties are determined to utilize arbitration, "negotiations" may be completed in one brief session. "Good-faith" bargaining cannot be measured in numbers, for even numerous or lengthy sessions may be a charade.

On the other hand, in many cases, parties have engaged in 5, 10, or 15 sessions lasting up to 5 hours each in an effort to reach agreement. Not all of these efforts succeeded, but the attempt was sincere. Over time, some of the early theatrics and abrasive aspects have lost their initial effectiveness. One negotiator for police reported, "In the past when we submitted our demands, a city negotiator would yell 'No' to everything and then we walked out. It was all over in 40 seconds." Negotiators have had to learn that bargaining takes time:

The city's first counterproposal was mostly "No"; but we have learned that when they say "No," they don't really mean a final "No" but "No for now." Often they say "No" one day and then come back the next and say they thought it over and now it is "Yes."

Parties that have developed a successful record of negotiating agreements have learned that it is generally wise to limit reports of progress to the press, municipal council members, and bargaining unit members.

Continuity in the leadership and negotiators on both sides also facilitates bargaining and the collective bargaining relationship. When there has been turnover in office or when new negotiators have entered the scene, it takes time to develop a smoothly functioning bargaining relationship. If one side experiences a more frequent turnover in leadership than the other, the result is likely to be an imbalance in skills and self-confidence. Eventually the weaker party may look elsewhere for assistance in negotiations.

If one side uses professional negotiators, especially lawyers or outside consultants, the other party may soon feel it necessary to employ legal counsel to participate in the negotiations. The suspicion is that without such help the negotiations may become one-sided and the less professional negotiator will be out-maneuvered. In such cases the result may be that both parties depend on persons outside the immediate relationship to negotiate contracts.

In an effort to remove some of the political influences from collective bargaining in the public sector, public employers have shifted responsibility for negotiations from members of the municipal council to appointed officials, such as the municipal manager. Only in the larger cities, however, is there a full-time employee whose sole responsibility is labor relations, and even then, negotiations may be carried out by elected or other appointed members of the municipal team.

A noteworthy feature among a number of Pennsylvania police organizations is that the same lawyer has represented the organization continuously and thus has, to all intents and purposes, become a part of the bargaining relationship. In such cases, the lawyer tends to enter the negotiations from the outset and control them from the formulation of demands until the conditions of employment have been set.

Firefighter organizations, on the other hand, generally select negotiators from their own ranks and use legal counsel to review proposals and contract language rather than to conduct negotiations. Only if negotiations reach an impasse does a firefighter organization tend to employ counsel for presenting its case at the arbitration hearing.

In any bargaining relationship, conditions that impinge on the likelihood of a negotiated settlement may change from one round to the next. General economic conditions that are recognized by both sides—such as national wage guidelines—may narrow the range of possible settlement. Conditions that are unique to the particular relationship may also prevail. In one situation, the firefighters were threatened with a reduction in force as the result of a consultant's report to the city on fire department manpower allocation. Shifting the primary goal of the firefighters from a dramatic increase in wages to shorter hours over a long-term agreement permitted a negotiated agreement following several arbitration awards. In another case, a police force found itself ahead of similar groups to the point where it was attracting an unusually large number of applicants for vacancies. Management was faced with its first negotiations for blue-collar employees. The police and management realized that a negotiated settlement would be useful and feasible. Whether the experience with negotiations will serve as precedents for bargaining in future rounds remains to be seen. What is clear is that parties can bargain a negotiated settlement if they want to.

All of these factors contribute to the attitudes of the parties toward each other, an important factor in whether a negotiated agreement can be reached. Overall, police and firefighter negotiators have high regard for the chief negotiators on the other side. Municipal officials rated firefighter negotiators consistently higher than their police counterparts in such factors as negotiating skill, bargaining in good faith, and keeping commitments made in negotiations. Interestingly, municipal negotiators were rated lower on these factors by firefighter negotiators than by police negotiators.

Another ingredient influencing the likelihood of a negotiated settlement is the number of organized groups in the jurisdiction that are negotiating simultaneously. The public employer may prefer (1) to have all groups settle at the same time, (2) to settle first with employees other than the public safety forces, or (3) to negotiate an agreement with whichever public safety group is deemed to be weaker. The object in all cases, however, will be to obtain similar agreements in the end. Public safety organizations may object to this employer strategy as well as to the particular terms involved. The greater the number of negotiations involved at the same time, the more complex it will be for agreements to be reached in all cases.

Because mediation is not mandated by Act 111, the Pennsylvania State Bureau of Mediation has no formal role in collective bargaining between public employers and public safety groups. The small size of the mediation staff long made it impossible for the Bureau to render assistance. Doubling the number of state mediators in 1974 enabled the Bureau for the first time to grant requests for mediators' services in public safety disputes. There have been few requests to date. Mediation services are not advertised, and the expressed desire for mediation appears limited at present. Precedent for mediation has not been established, however, and satisfaction with the service may increase mediation on a de facto basis in the future. Earlier opportunities for mediation have occurred and sometimes produced strange mediators. In one case, the president of the police organization found that the municipal bargaining committee and the police bargaining committee (of which he was not a member) were at loggerheads and afraid to moderate their positions. Both sides wished to avoid arbitration but feared that concessions in negotiations might be used against them in arbitration. The president of the police organization met informally and separately with the chairman of each bargaining committee and mediated the dispute.

Once arbitration proceedings have been initiated, it is not uncommon for the parties to settle before an award is reached, or even before an arbitrator is appointed. According to the records of the American Arbitration Association, in the first six years of the act between 15 and 24 percent of the requests for assistance in arbitration were withdrawn because of direct settlement at some point prior to issuance of the award (see Table 2-2). Although the AAA records do not constitute a complete universe of experience in Pennsylvania, the rate of settlement after arbitration has been initiated corresponds to that found in Loewenberg's studies of 1968 and 1969. The proportion of agreements in which arbitration was initiated prior to settlement to the total number of negotiated settlements is probably approximately similar.

Hence, the threat of arbitration does not necessarily terminate negotiations; it may actually provide a catalyst to negotiations. In several cases, employee groups reported that the public employer first began meeting regularly with employee representatives as the deadline for filing for arbitration approached and began making significant counteroffers after the request for arbitration had been filed. In such cases, the employer presumably believed he could make at least as reasonable a settlement with the employee group as was likely to be rendered in an arbitration award. The time and cost of arbitration can provide additional inducements to some parties to avoid a request for arbitration from reaching fruition.

When the request for arbitration places pressure on the parties to negotiate to a settlement, the arbitration procedure can be viewed as a quasi-strike tactic. The procedure does not work in this way for many parties, however. Sophisticated parties know that the time schedule of Act 111 may be flexible; larger groups may be less concerned with expenses; and politically sophisticated groups on both sides of the negotiating table may even be able to gauge quite accurately the outcome of arbitration, yet not wish to bargain to that outcome.

Extent of Arbitration

As mentioned previously, there is no central source for data on police and firefighter collective bargaining in Pennsylvania. Ideally, one would want to know the amount of arbitration in each round of bargaining, the number of justifications involved in arbitration, and the frequency with which any relationship resorts to arbitration to settle impasses.

Respondents to the questionnaire provided answers to these questions, though the number of usable responses limits the reliability of the answers. Altogether, 73 municipal respondents provided sufficient information on the method of achieving bargaining settlements and on the length of the agreed-upon settlements to derive data on negotiations and arbitration for labor agreements effective from 1969 through 1974 (see Table 2-1). The actual number of negotiations varies from year to year, depending on the

Table 2-1

Negotiations and Method of Resolving Negotiations between Pennsylvania Municipalities and Public Safety Organizations, 1969-1974

	Negotiations for the Labor Agreement Effective in Year						
	1969	*1970*	*1971*	*1972*	*1973*	*1974*	*Total*
Police							
Negotiations without resort to arbitration	22	21	25	24	20	19	131
Negotiations after arbitration began but before award issued	1	2	2	2	3	4	14
Arbitration award	9	9	11	11	12	12	64
Negotiations but method of resolution not reported	4	2	1	4	3	7	21
TOTAL	36	34	39	41	38	42	230
Firefighters							
Negotiations without resort to arbitration	3	1	4	6	4	2	20
Arbitration award	4	2	3	4	1	5	19
Negotiations but method of resolution not reported	1	2	1	1	1	1	7
TOTAL	8	5	8	11	6	8	46

Source: Responses to questionnaire mailed to Pennsylvania municipalities that indicated collective bargaining experience with public safety organizations.

number of units with expiring agreements and the number embarking on collective bargaining. The proportion of arbitration awards to the negotiations whose method of resolution is known has inched slightly upward for police, from 28 percent of negotiations for contracts effective in 1969 to 34 percent of negotiations for contracts effective in 1974. The comparable proportion of firefighter negotiations is substantially higher, with the exception of agreements effective in 1973. It should be reemphasized, however, that these findings are partial. They provide an indication of extent of negotiations and arbitration, but do not provide definitive statistical measures.

Another measure of arbitration activity is provided by the American Arbitration Association, which processes arbitration cases through its Pennsylvania offices each year (see Table 2-2). Again, these numbers should be regarded as an index of arbitration rather than an accurate portrayal of the extent of arbitration. First, a few cases involve a grievance rather than an interest dispute. Second, parties implementing the arbitration procedure may select a neutral arbitrator without utilizing AAA services, so that these numbers understate the actual amount of arbitration occurring each year. Loewenberg's studies of the experience of major Pennsylvania municipalities in 1968-69 found that approximately onefourth of the parties involved in interest arbitration did not use the facilities of the American Arbitration Association. Although instances in which parties choose a neutral arbitrator without assistance continue to come to light, it appears that the proportion doing so has decreased.

Since 1968, when compulsory interest arbitration first became available, many communities and their police and firefighter forces have

Table 2-2

Arbitration Requests and Awards under Act 111 as Recorded by the American Arbitration Association, 1968-1973

	Police		Firefighters		Totals	
	Requests	Awards	Requests	Awards	Requests	Awards
1968	48	37	10	8	58	45
1969	69 [a,b]	54 [b]	13 [a,b]	11 [a]	80 [a,b]	64 [b]
1970	85 [b]	64 [b]	19 [b]	18 [b]	103 [b]	81 [b]
1971	83 [b]	65 [b]	27 [b]	22 [b]	109 [b]	86 [b]
1972	57	47	16	12	73	59
1973	83	71	17	14	99	82

[a] One request was submitted jointly by police and firefighters but settled prior to issuance of an arbitration award.
[b] One request was submitted jointly by police and firefighters and resulted in an arbitration award.
Source: Records of the Philadelphia and Pittsburgh offices of the American Arbitration Association. Cases marked as "pending" have been deleted from tabulations.

utilized the arbitration mechanism. Of the responses received from employee groups to the 1974 questionnaire, 70 percent of the police and 80 percent of the firefighters claimed to have been involved at least one time in an arbitration proceeding in which an award was issued. Only 57 percent of municipalities reported similar experience with interest arbitration. The difference between municipal and employee responses may be accounted for by the more numerous employee responses in larger communities. The Allegheny County police and firefighters as well as the Pennsylvania state police have also made use of arbitration under Act 111. All these figures suggest extensive use of arbitration.

While the overall proportion of arbitration to negotiations does not seem to have fluctuated widely, dramatic changes have occurred in some areas. In a suburban Philadelphia county where the likelihood of arbitration was approximately 50 percent of all negotiations in the early days of Act 111, the proportion of arbitrations to total negotiations dropped to 15 percent in 1973. A negotiator familiar with the history of negotiations in the county attributed the decline to the greater sophistication of negotiators who accept the idea of settlement, longer-term agreements that permit accommodation of more items, lack of political elections that enable the political powers to accept responsibility for settlements, and recognition that the public is not opposed to paying for public safety services. Some of these factors can easily change. Police and firefighters may become unwilling to accept long-term agreements except with cost-of-living provisions, which are still novel for public jurisdictions. Political elections and taxpayer resistance to higher taxes occur with almost the same regularity. Thus, changing conditions may affect arbitration experience even for the same parties.

Only a very few communities in Pennsylvania report an unbroken dependence on arbitration to determine conditions of employment for public safety employees. A substantially larger group reports that it has never received an arbitration award. In the majority of cases, however, there has been a combination of settlements and arbitration awards. Even the state's two largest cities, Philadelphia and Pittsburgh, which have a reputation for bringing all public safety disputes to arbitration, have negotiated settlements in some years since 1968. Among those municipalities indicating involvement with interest arbitration, more reported that terms and conditions of employment were determined by negotiations rather than by arbitration in the six years of Act 111.

Insight into the frequency of arbitration awards may be gained from the experience of 20 municipalities that utilized arbitration to resolve impasses in police negotiations. Only 2 of the 20 reported that arbitration was utilized in every negotiation. Another 6 indicated that the majority of their negotiations with police end in arbitration. The others answered that less than half of their negotiations were resolved by an arbitration award. In these cases, arbitration occurred at various times during the years in which negotiations were conducted. The total number of municipalities is too small to permit analysis by population size.

Conduct of Arbitration Proceedings

Once the parties are bent on arbitration, they must deal with several important matters. Parties have learned through experience that the choice of the partisan arbitrators and the neutral chairman of the panel can affect the outcome of the process. In general, they have moved away from using negotiators as representative arbitrators in the same round to increase the appearance and the reality of impartiality and experience. However, there are important exceptions to this generalization, such as in Pittsburgh where the city and public safety negotiators regularly are appointed as arbitration panel members. Here and in similar cases, the negotiators expect to continue negotiations in executive sessions of the arbitration panel. More common is the appointment of a person who is professionally related to the chief negotiator but not a direct party to the negotiations— for instance, the law partner of the spokesman for either side.

A major trend has been the emergence of a group of specialists as partisan arbitrators. For public safety employees, the choice is often a current or former leader of the state or national organization, a person who has worked on public safety credit union or pension affairs, an attorney who has specialized in public safety bargaining, or leaders of local private sector unions. On the public employer side, the selection is frequently a person from state municipal leagues, a management consultant specializing in the public sector, or a local citizen with an extensive background in public sector administration. A review of arbitration panels reveals the frequent appearance of the same names as partisan arbitrators. The degree of sophistication among partisan arbitrators still varies widely, but the overall professional quality has improved.

The choice of the neutral arbitrator can also make a difference to the proceedings and the award. In one case, a city and its police selected a local priest to be their neutral arbitrator. The priest held numerous sessions with the parties individually and jointly and mediated all but two or three of the outstanding issues. On the other hand, one city invariably chooses an outside consultant as its partisan arbitrator because of his knowledge and care in selecting from the AAA lists a neutral chairman who is likely to be sympathetic to the city's main demands. The city prefers an impartial arbitrator who has a record of considering the city's financial position or who is willing to recommend long-term awards.

The names of the same neutral arbitrators also tend to show up frequently on awards. Eight neutrals handled 55 percent of all AAA cases in 1973. Part of the explanation for the repetition is that the AAA is limited by statutory language to include only Pennsylvania residents on its panels for Act 111 cases. Parties also seem to prefer selecting neutrals whose reputation is clearly known. It is reasonable to infer that knowledge of individual qualifications and positions are shared by parties of similar persuasion. In some instances, where both police and firefighters have arbitrated terms or conditions in the same municipality in the same year, the same neutral has been chosen for both cases. Parties have also selected the same neutral arbitrator to determine conditions of employment in two successive years.

The choice of spokesmen presenting the case for each side in the arbitration hearing depends on the selection of the partisan arbitrator representing the respective parties and the atmosphere each side wishes to create. If the chief negotiator is nominated as representative arbitrator, either some other member of the negotiating team or an attorney/consultant is likely to present the case. Often parties who feel competent to negotiate without assistance believe it wiser to let an attorney be the spokesman in the quasi-legal proceedings. Especially if one side uses an attorney, the other may feel deprived of adequate representation without a similarly qualified person. On the other hand, some negotiators familiar with arbitration have come to the conclusion that no outsider can know or present the case more ably than those who have lived with the issues. The ultimate in this direction is the situation where the partisan arbitrator turns out to be the chief spokesman and sometimes the principal witness as well.

Usually the parties bring all items involved in the negotiations to arbitration. In some cases, new issues are introduced. Sometimes the parties try to impress the neutral with their reasonableness by offering to drop or concede to minor items. The neutral may try to whittle the list further by attempting mediation, but such efforts meet with mixed success because one or both parties are unwilling to accept mediation or because the number of issues that can be mediated is limited.

One hearing is all that is now needed in most cases for the parties to present their evidence to the panel. Parties have cut down notably on the amount of time required to present cases over the years, perhaps largely because of the costs involved and the experience of arbitrators who are exposed to similar arguments and evidence in public safety interest cases. Outside expert witnesses and elaborate visual presentations are likely only in larger jurisdictions, if the parties are embarking on their first arbitration or if an attorney or consultant is attempting to impress his client. Of course, in some cases the shortness of the formal hearing is the result of inadequate preparation of testimony.

The reduction in the number of hearings also reflects the growing realization that the real decision-making process usually occurs during the executive sessions of the arbitration panel. The point was given unusual emphasis in one instance where instead of a formal arbitration hearing, the panel held 12 days of executive sessions. It is in the executive session where the neutral chairman's style comes to the fore and the partisan arbitrators have an opportunity to display their powers of persuasion and negotiation. However, some neutral arbitrators utilize the executive session, if they schedule any at all, only to review the main arguments on each issue and/or to present their award to other members of the panel. Professional partisan arbitrators resent such conduct, which they regard as high-handed and ignoring their expertise, but they generally recognize they can do little about it in the immediate case if a majority of the panel is willing to sign the award. Recently, a municipality refused to implement an award because its partisan arbitrator, the municipal solicitor, felt the award was unilaterally determined. He believed there was legal requirement for full discussion and negotiation of the issues in the executive sessions of the arbitration panel. The case has not yet been heard in the courts.

If neutral arbitrators have limited success in mediating between the parties during the arbitration hearing, they appear to be substantially more successful in mediating during the executive sessions where the partisan arbitrators enjoy the opportunity to participate fully in determining the award. One municipal arbitrator recounted:

> As it turned out, the arbitrators ended up doing what the city and the police should have done—we bargained out each issue. . . . After I went over the cost analysis, the police arbitrator and I saw eye-to-eye on most of the issues. The neutral knew very little about our city and showed what I feel was good leadership in directing the executive session to facilitate bargaining between the police arbitrator and myself.

Such active negotiations occur more frequently than does mere confirmation of a previously negotiated award. The acceptability of the final award resulting from such negotiations depends on the relationship between the partisan arbitrator and the represented party as well as the relative negotiating skill and knowledge of the partisan arbitrators. The mediating skill of the impartial arbitrator may influence the outcome of negotiations, but he may still have to make the decision on hard-core issues.[8]

Arbitration Awards

Arbitration awards in Pennsylvania tend to be brief. Justification for the determination of particular issues is rare, and any overall rationale for the entire award is only slightly more common. In some cases, the award makes mention of only those items that the panel has agreed to give in whole or in part; all demands denied in their entirety are then dismissed in a single catch-all sentence. The reason for the Pennsylvania tradition may be the absence of any statutory criteria that must be applied to the award. Since an award cannot be appealed in the courts on grounds of insufficient consideration of criteria, explaining an award on the basis of criteria could be deemed superfluous. Tripartite determination of awards also could make the application of criteria an artificial exercise and per-haps an unnecessary one since the parties could gain insight on the bases of the determination from their representative arbitrators on the panel. Finally, the time constraints of the arbitration procedure and the multiple use of a small band of neutrals in a short time period encourages issuing awards speedily—and in short form.

Wage matters in their many forms—such as rank and shift differentials, longevity pay, and the number of steps and length of time to reach the maximum step in the wage scale—are invariably included in arbitration awards. Also common are other items that may affect pay, such as court pay, pay for temporary assignment to higher rank, and overtime pay. Time off from work is another popular category and includes vacations, holidays (or holiday reimbursement), emergency leave, and sick leave. Fringe benefits center largely on health insurance, life insurance, and clothing allowance. The length of the work week is of critical importance, especially to firefighters who are trying to reduce the work week to 40 hours, much to the dismay of public employers who fear the cost implication of such a demand. Police have been interested in false arrest insurance. Both police and firefighters have requested a reduction in the retirement age in arbitration as well as through the legislative route. Departmental rules —such as residence requirements, promotion policies, and suspension policies—are less common subjects but are not unknown. The utilization of manpower—shift assignments, duties of public safety employees, num-ber of men in a patrol car, and use of part-time personnel—has been raised in arbitration, but is usually not ruled on by arbitration panels. Awards also have generally avoided questions of equipment and facilities (locker rooms and call boxes); however, awards often specify which equipment carried and clothing worn by the public safety officer will be paid for by the employer. Issues raised for the first time because of a new collective bargaining relationship are often among the thorniest and most bitterly fought. The significance of the final step in the grievance procedure, the composition of the bargaining unit, and time off for union business has not been lost on the parties, but these matters have been raised less fre-quently than have economic "bread-and-butter" issues.

From the beginning, the effective length of some awards under Act 111 has exceeded one year. In the early years, however, parties and arbitrators alike were sometimes hesitant to determine conditions of employment for more than one year at a time, but in recent years, the proportion of longer-term awards has increased markedly. Public employers have found advantages to long-term agreements, not unlike those discovered previously by private sector employers. Employee organizations have not been unwilling to agree to longer awards if they could obtain wage reopeners and/or conditions that arbitration panels would not be likely to grant in a one-year award. In a randomly selected group of 25 awards issued in 1972 and 1973, 14 awards were binding for one year, 10 for two years, and 1 for four years.

The incidence of unanimous awards under the act has been high. A random survey of recent public safety arbitration awards in the files of the American Arbitration Association yielded the fact that two-thirds of all awards were unanimous. Of the same 25 randomly selected awards reviewed above, 18 were signed by all three members of the arbitration panel, without dissent. Where the award is issued by a majority of the panel, the dissenter is likely to be the public employer. Of the 7 majority awards in the above survey, the employer representative dissented four times, the employee representative twice, and both representatives dissented to separate parts of the award in the remaining case. The fact of a dissent to an award does not necessarily mean that there was not unanimity in determining the award in the executive session.[9] A partisan arbitrator may be unable to sign the award for political reasons.

The frequency of unanimous awards raises questions about the negotiation and arbitration procedures under Act 111. Are the parties so lacking in negotiating skills or perspective that they cannot negotiate an agreement while the panel of arbitrators can do so? Are representative arbitrators close enough to their constituents to carry the major thrust of their side's position in the executive session? Do partisan arbitrators differ in negotiating skill so that one dominates the other, with the neutral being loath to cast the dissenting vote? All of these situations have occurred. Interestingly enough, however, unanimous decisions have been rendered even in cases where presumably sophisticated negotiators have appointed themselves to the arbitration panel. In one such case, the employee arbitrator protected against any potential political repercussions to the award by asking his constituents to ratify the main points of the award during the arbitration hearings.

It is expected that an arbitration award, once issued, will be implemented, although occasionally one party or both may be deeply upset by it. The public employer may delay implementation, thereby provoking frustration but doing little to change the terms of the award. If he refuses to implement an award, he knows full well that the employee organization will soon file for a writ of mandamus in the courts. (This and other legal challenges will be treated separately below.) Most employers therefore choose to comply with an award and to seek their remedy in other ways and at another time. Public employees have fewer options open if they are disturbed with the terms of an award. Recourse to job actions because of an award is unknown. Employees may always choose to obtain better conditions from the legislature or to improve their performance in the next negotiations. Fortunately, both employer and employee leaders can rationalize an unsatisfactory arbitration award by faulting the neutral arbitrator, the partisan arbitrator, the language of Act 111, or anyone but themselves. Rank-and-file employees may not be as charitable and may choose to vent their disappointment on their leaders.

In a very few cases, awards have been overturned in ways other than through the courts. In one case, a municipality announced that it could not financially afford the award so it would have to lay off half of the police force. No one questioned the employer's right to lay off, but the police aroused the community to question capable police protection from a diminished force. The local Chamber of Commerce and the county commissioner brought the parties together, and the commissioner acted as mediator to extend the two-year award to a third year, with the same amount of wage increases given in the award added on to the third year of the package. In another case, where the municipality and police and firefighters (who had arbitrated together) were dissatisfied with the award, they ignored it and negotiated a new agreement, thereby turning the arbitration procedure into a factfinding process. These cases are exceptions to the rule. Usually, a party that is unhappy with an award accepts it nevertheless and reacts negatively to the arbitration procedure.

Legal Challenges to Act 111

Various aspects of Act 111 have been tested in the courts and continue to be challenged. Since the act first went into effect, the courts have ruled on its constitutionality, its procedural requirements, and awards issued under it.

In the first round of negotiations following the passage of Act 111, the Borough of East Lansdowne refused to carry out an award issued in an arbitration between borough council and the borough police on the grounds that the statute lacked specific criteria and violated the "one man, one vote" principle of the Fourteenth Amendment of the Constitution. The Supreme Court of Pennsylvania recognized that "this case presents a head-on attack . . . upon the validity of the Act of June 24, 1968." It dismissed the borough's arguments and upheld the legality of the act.[10]

Subsequent court tests have been directed primarily at the process and scope of arbitration awards rather than at the overall concept of compulsory binding arbitration. Courts have ruled that public employees forfeit access to arbitration if they fail to observe the filing deadlines specified in the act,[11] or if a majority of the employees in a poll accepted a proposal of the public employer.[12] Arbitration proceedings may not be initiated without prior negotiations, but neither party may refuse to negotiate.[13] In this case the court directed the public employer to negotiate with the police.

In a major test of the scope of an arbitration award, the Supreme Court of Pennsylvania ruled: "An arbitration award may only require a public employer to do that which it would do voluntarily." [14] In this case, the court vacated part of an award that directed the city to pay for insurance premiums for policemen's families because the state legislature had not explicitly authorized third-class cities to pay premiums to anyone but city employees and officials. The same principle was used to remove false arrest insurance for police from an arbitration award.[15] An arbitration award requiring union membership or good dues-standing as a condition of continued employment violated civil service codes and was therefore vacated.[16] In the same case, the court upheld a public employer's right not to implement that portion of an award mandating a grievance procedure with binding arbitration as a final step because Act 111 "cannot be construed to include a grievance procedure for settlement of currently unidentifiable disputes as a proper subject for collective bargaining concerning terms and conditions of employment." The court reiterated its position on arbitration as a terminal step in a grievance procedure in another case that tested the scope of authority of the arbitration board on three other issues as well.[17] The court here also determined that the board could rule on matters of retirement and pension as long as express statutory requirements were not contravened, as had been done. The arbitration award could alter residency requirements of employees because the public employer could do so on its own volition. The court further refused to vacate that portion of the award that exceeded the Economic Stabilization Act of 1970 because the public employer had other channels by which to appeal this action. The courts also have upheld the right of arbitration boards to render retroactive awards and refused jurisdiction to determine the propriety of such awards.[18] At the same time, the courts have removed from the scope of bargaining under Act 111 (and hence arbitration) a city's requirement that police pass a physical examination as a condition of continued employment.[19] The court determined that the requirement fell within the city's managerial rights. Using police cars to pick up for duty and return police to their homes is beyond the scope of terms and conditions of employment as intended by the act and hence is not negotiable; [20] in this case, the court removed such a provision from the arbitration award.

A public employer could be willing to accept an award but plead that he could not implement it fully because of lack of funds. In *Harney v. Russo,* the Supreme Court included the following dicta in its opinion:

> Furthermore, if we do hear a case in which the tax millage, as a matter of record, cannot permissibly be raised so as to provide sufficient funds to pay the required benefits to the employees, it will still be open to this court to rule that the Act of June 24, 1968 impliedly authorizes a court-approved millage ceiling increase to pay the arbitration award where necessary, or to hold that the municipal budget must be adjusted in other places in order to provide resources for policemen's and firemen's salaries.

The issue was raised directly by the City of Philadelphia when it unilaterally stopped disability benefit payments because budgeted funds had been fully expended.[21] The court ruled that the benefit was part of the labor agreement: "Simply because City Council refuses to appropriate funds to effectuate payment, the City as public employer is not relieved of its duty to follow the mandate of the arbitration panel."

The drafters of Act 111 believed that they had limited court intervention by including the stipulation that an award could not be appealed to the courts. Despite the stipulation, the courts have taken a more active role in reviewing and limiting awards than was envisioned. The Supreme Court of Pennsylvania has held that it will accept appeals of arbitration awards only if the matter involves the following subjects: (1) the question of jurisdiction; (2) the regularity of the proceedings before the panel; (3) questions of excess in exercise of powers; and (4) constitutional questions.[22] The appeals to date indicate that the limits of these subjects remain to be tested.

Reactions to Act 111

The legal challenges to Act 111 and to the individual awards reviewed above, represent one form of reaction to the statute. Two other forms will be discussed in this section: legislative proposals to change the law, which reflect some of the chief complaints about the system; and attitudes of the parties as garnered in questionnaire responses and interviews.

Legislative Proposals to Change Act 111

In addition to legal suits, Act 111 has also faced repeated challenges in the state legislature. Ever since the act was passed and signed into law in

1968, individuals and organizations have complained about it and sought to have it changed. The principal complaints about the act at the present time are offered by employers:

1. The act contains no criteria for unit determination. The resulting pattern of public safety units is confusing and senseless, with decisions being made on an ad hoc basis.
2. The act lacks definition of "good-faith bargaining." A party should not be able to initiate arbitration without having bargained in good faith.
3. The act does not provide for any intermediate steps between negotiations and arbitration. Mediation and factfinding prior to arbitration might improve bargaining and reduce the need for arbitration.
4. The scope of bargaining is too broad. Management rights are not defined, and the restriction on appeals to the courts is too narrow.
5. Most neutrals have no stake in the award. The neutral arbitrator is usually a person from outside the community who does not know enough about the local situation and who does not give proper consideration to the employer's ability to pay. (There are two complaints here—one concerned with the qualifications of the neutral arbitrator and the other with the criteria used in deciding the award.)
6. The division of costs between the parties is unjust to public employers and hence to the public.
7. The act does not make collective bargaining the exclusive channel for changes in conditions or deciding on grievances. Employees are able to take issues through bargaining and civil service channels and/or political appeals.

It should be noted that all of these complaints concern details of the current procedures or, as in the last complaint, apply to public sector collective bargaining in general. They do not attack the basic idea of arbitration as a method for resolving impasses.

To answer these complaints, a number of amendments to Act 111 have been proposed over time. One would have required mediation prior to arbitration; another would have required the impartial chairman of arbitration panels to be a resident of the political jurisdiction involved in the arbitration proceedings. Other proposals have been directed at repeal.

One attempt to alter the labor relations system for police and firefighters was initiated by the Local Government Conference, a coordinating committee of legislative directors from the Pennsylvania League of Cities, Pennsylvania State Association of Boroughs, Pennsylvania Association of Township Supervisors, and similar organizations. The Conference sponsored House Bill 1977 in the 1974 legislature to repeal Act 111 and place police and firefighters in the same category as prison guards and court employees under Pennsylvania Act 195 of 1970. Such employees do not have the right to strike but have to go through mediation and factfinding before submitting disputes to compulsory arbitration. Act 195 also calls for a tripartite panel, but if the representative arbitrators are unable to agree on a neutral chairman, the Pennsylvania Labor Relations Board submits a panel. In addition to the change in impasse procedures, Act 195 contains criteria for unit determination, representation procedures, and unfair labor practices as well as restrictions on the scope of bargaining. Extending Act 195 to police and firefighters would therefore answer many of the complaints in the above list and would change impasse procedures. House Bill 1977 was not acted upon by the 1974 legislature, and even though it may be reintroduced in subsequent sessions, it is unlikely that it will be adopted.

In fact, none of the efforts to date has posed a serious threat to Act 111. Having initiated, drafted, and succeeded in gaining Act 111, police and firefighters are suspicious of any attempt to amend it. Anyone wishing to change the current system, they believe, must desire to weaken the power of public safety employees in negotiations. The strong lobbies of the public employee organizations have been able to convince legislators that the proposals for change are flawed and/or that Act 111 is working well.

The only legislative change to affect Act 111 thus far has occurred because of circumstances that have little to do with police and firefighters. Senate Act 372 of 1974 altered the Retirement Code for all state employees, including state police. Henceforth, changes in pensions of state employees cannot be negotiated but rather must receive legislative approval. While the legislation was not aimed to reduce the scope of arbitration under Act 111, in effect it did do just that for one group covered under the act.

Attitudes of the Parties

Most parties recognize that Act 111 will regulate public safety collective bargaining in Pennsylvania for the foreseeable future. It is important, therefore, to gauge their reactions to and satisfaction with its operation. The attitudes may be analyzed with regard to costs, awards, the act in general, and other forms of arbitration.

For a majority of parties who have had experience under Act 111, the costs involved in arbitration proceedings are a factor in determining whether or not to pursue arbitration. Less than 20 percent of municipalities and police and firefighter organizations responded that the cost consideration was "very important" in the decision-making process. On the other hand, over 35 percent of municipalities and police organizations reported that administrative costs were "not important at all" in deciding whether or not to move to arbitration, and two-thirds of firefighter organizations answered likewise.

Size is a factor affecting attitudes to cost. Almost 23 percent of respondents from municipalities under 10,000 in population replied that cost considerations were "very important" in going to arbitration, whereas only 10 percent of municipalities with larger populations gave a similar answer. The contrast is even more dramatic among police organizations: 22 percent of organizations with less than 24 members in the bargaining unit felt cost considerations were "very important" in deciding on arbitration, compared to less than 5 percent of organizations with 25 or more members in the bargaining unit.

Costs of arbitration differ widely. The lowest amount found was $156 for one firefighter organization that appointed a member of the group to act as the representative arbitrator on the panel and another member to be spokesman in the arbitration hearing. This figure is atypical, however. Most employee groups hire counsel for the hearing and usually pay for a partisan arbitrator. The costs then range up to $25,000 for a single arbitration, though perhaps $5,000 to $10,000 would be more representative. Smaller groups of employees may attempt to economize by hiring either a solicitor for the hearing or an outside partisan arbitrator. In some cases, a state association may agree to furnish a partisan arbitrator at no cost. Employee organization treasuries often are not able to bear the costs of arbitration and cannot be tapped because the organization encompasses a broader geographical area than the employer jurisdiction. Special assessments of employees must then be levied to cover the costs of arbitration; such assessments have amounted to $150 per man and more. Assessments are never popular and, in some cases, can prove fatal to organization leadership. One leader confessed: "Over half of our men wouldn't pay for arbitration out of their pockets without a fight." Another approach has been to accumulate an arbitration fund by having each employee in the unit contribute one dollar each payday. In one case, police felt it necessary to create such a fund to counter a line-item of $5,000, earmarked for arbitration, in the city's budget. It took several years for the fund to reach a point where the police felt they could push for arbitration if they needed to.

The costs of arbitration can be equally large for public employers, though accumulating the funds may not be as difficult. Where employers have elected to use full-time personnel rather than outsiders for arbitration, the costs are cut accordingly. Where the employer's total costs are high, the proportion accorded to the neutral arbitrator (which the employer pays in toto) is significantly less than the fee charged by counsel.

The cost factor cannot be viewed in isolation. A party's view of cost depends on its relation to results. The representative of one middle-sized city, which had been involved in several arbitrations, maintained that the

$7,000 cost for each arbitration was "a good investment from any viewpoint." Likewise, a police organization representative who admitted that extra assessments for arbitration create grumbling and are sometimes difficult to collect felt that the cost was worthwhile because the municipality realized that bargaining was to be taken seriously.

Perhaps a summary economic view would be that the costs of arbitration are worthwhile if the party paying them feels it will gain a better award than could be achieved through negotiation. But for some parties, the complaint of one employee leader summed it up: "It just costs too much to go to arbitration."

As to the awards themselves, acceptability is measured in relative current terms. The award recipient determines his satisfaction by comparing the award to his position or goals at the start of negotiations and to settlements of other jurisdictions with similar socioeconomic characteristics. There is little attempt to compare individual awards to previous conditions or to speculate on conditions without the availability of compulsory arbitration.

Public employers are sometimes characterized as believing the economic portions of awards are inevitably too high, but this is not always true, for in many instances employers feel they have "won" the panel's award. Even when at first they may experience disappointment, their initial reaction may turn to satisfaction as the award is implemented; during recent inflationary times, employers with long-term agreements reported they gained more through awards than was apparent at first. Employee organizations, too, are far from convinced that they always gain what they hoped to from arbitration panels. One employee group that had been involved in three arbitrations was convinced it had "lost" each one. This record, far from discouraging the organization, made it more determined to "win" the next one. Other employee complaints are that awards remove as well as give benefits and that awards do not reflect a balanced package. One employee leader who consistently adopted a hard-line position on wage negotiations admitted that the tactic inadvertently resulted in arbitration wage awards higher than anticipated but at the expense of supplementary items (vacations, pensions) that the unit members really wanted.

On specific issues, employer and employee representatives agree that arbitration awards tend to favor the employees in such matters as wage increases and overtime provisions and to favor employers on such matters as department rules and time off for union business. In other areas, according to the questionnaire responses, there is disagreement. Employee groups felt strongly that arbitration awards favored them on family health insurance and holidays, while public employers believed the awards on these issues were favorable to them. Even in areas of consensus, however, a marked difference in shading of attitudes was apparent. Whereas fewer than 15 percent of employee respondents felt that arbitration awards on wage increases favored the employer approach, more than 30 percent of employers believed that the result favored them. Similarly, less than 20 percent of employee representatives thought that the employer had gained totally on overtime, compared to 33 percent of employers who so responded. In short, on almost all issues, the consensus of employer and employee representatives was that the award had been in their respective favor or had been split between the parties.

Despite dissatisfaction with individual awards, the overwhelming reaction to Act 111 among those who have had to live with it is satisfaction. Employee organizations were practically unanimous in responding that the bargaining and arbitration processes of the act were beneficial. Their representatives usually cited the advantages of the act by referring to pre-1968 events. Over and over again they said, "Without arbitration, we wouldn't have gotten what we did. Arbitration is the only power we have." A more sophisticated presentation of the same view concluded:

> In the long run, threatening to go to arbitration has helped negotiations because it has brought home the power that Act 111 has given us. We can collect the facts and statistics about our wages, pensions, and working conditions and go to arbitration to bring them up if they are deficient.

Public safety organizations pointed to the delay in negotiations faced by nonuniformed employees. They felt that the time deadlines and arbitration features of Act 111 encouraged the employer to bargain and guaranteed a timely agreement. Even groups that believed they had not made out well in negotiations or arbitration maintained faith in Act 111.

With few exceptions, public safety organizations in Pennsylvania continue to look with disfavor on the strike as a weapon they could use in negotiations. Fewer than 7 percent of the questionnaire respondents listed the right to strike as their first choice for a dispute resolution procedure. In only one situation did an organization leader state, "I'm convinced that if the law provided the right to strike, we would have been able to get a better package than under arbitration." More typical was the view of another leader who considered arbitration a "savior" because his group probably would not strike even if it had the right to do so.

When presented with the hypothetical alternatives of factfinding, right to strike, conventional arbitration, or final-offer arbitration, the overwhelming choice of police and firefighter leaders was conventional arbitration. From the interviews, it would appear that not too much significance can be attached to the remaining answers to this question because employee representatives use terms like "negotiations," "mediation," and "arbitration" interchangeably and have little understanding of the differences between conventional and final-offer arbitration.

In general, employer representatives are reasonably satisfied with the operation of Act 111, though many would prefer some modification of the arbitration procedure and support placing public safety employees under Act 195. A majority view is that the time deadlines and arbitration provisions of the act promote bargaining. A dissenting view is that arbitration can have a negative effect on negotiations because both sides realize that arbitration is available if a settlement cannot be obtained within the authorized limits. Arbitration also sharply reduces political influences in collective bargaining, according to one municipal negotiator:

> Without arbitration, the group with the most political pull would determine the settlement. The police are in the stronger power position. Perhaps they hurt themselves by going to arbitration. City council didn't know what they were doing. They would have lost their shirt and not even know it.

When offered alternative dispute resolution procedures, a majority of public employer representatives selected factfinding as a first choice. Among the remaining four options (right to strike, conventional arbitration, and the two variations of final-offer arbitration), conventional arbitration was chosen most often. When the choices were weighted according to preference, there was no appreciable difference between factfinding and conventional arbitration. Only 4 percent listed the right to strike as their preferred procedure for dispute resolution, while 86 percent listed it last. The responses on final-offer arbitration must be interpreted cautiously because of widespread ignorance about the procedure. It is reasonable to conclude that unless public employers could gain more discretion in a dispute resolution procedure, they are content to live with interest arbitration, especially with conventional arbitration.

Impact of Act 111

Unlike reactions of the parties, which may be deemed subjective, an assessment of the impact of Act 111 should be based on available objective measures. In this section, special attention is first given to the economic impact of arbitration awards because of the intense interest in this aspect among practitioners, policymakers, and students. The section concludes with an overall review of the act's impact.

Economic Impact of Arbitration

Attempts to measure the economic impact of arbitration awards are fraught with difficulties. The level of wages is not a true indicator of the economic effect because it fails to take into account levels of employment. Rising productivity may permit absorption of higher individual compensation without affecting the employer's total costs. Even if interest is confined to salary, a number of problems are apparent. First, the range of salaries is broad, regardless of whether salaries are classified by size of municipality, geographic location, or other factors. Second, it is difficult to be aware of all factors that affect local labor markets. The availability of compulsory arbitration is but one ingredient that can change wages. Third, the threat of arbitration is difficult to assess unless one is actually present at negotiations. To what extent such threats are meaningful and recognized does not usually become apparent to outsiders until the parties move to arbitration, and even then, one cannot be certain if arbitration is the result of a stalemate in negotiations or a convenient cover to announce an agreed-upon package. Fourth, there is undoubtedly a relationship between settlements within local areas. The spillover effect between negotiated and arbitrated settlements depends on the timing of negotiations. A single arbitration award can trip off negotiated settlements if both parties at the table perceive a pattern. On the other hand, arbitrated or negotiated settlements also set a standard that subsequent negotiations will hope to match or surpass and thus may encourage arbitration. One would have to be aware of the timetable of local area negotiations to untangle this skein in each round of negotiations.

A popular theory about compulsory arbitration is that employees who utilize the arbitration mechanism receive higher wages than their counterparts who do not. The supposition is based on the hypothesis that employee organizations that utilize arbitration exhibit maximum force and hence get higher settlements. It also assumes that the basic purpose of arbitration is to achieve economic ends. The motivating factors leading to enactment of the legislation and the content of arbitration would seem to support this assumption to date. Data from responses, though incomplete because they are available only from parties who have engaged in collective bargaining, provide one means to test the hypothesis. They are presented in Table 2-3 and indicate that in two of the three population categories the hypothesis is incorrect. Only in the 10,000-19,999 category did employees who utilized arbitration earn more in 1973 than employees who never were involved in arbitration; the former also received greater increases in salary in the 1969-1973 period. In smaller and larger municipalities, however, the reverse situation occurred. Whether the hypothesis is incorrect because municipalities chose to pay higher wages to avoid arbitration, because of local labor market factors, or because of the spillover effect noted earlier cannot be determined.

Because of the interrelationships in bargaining, regardless of the method of settlement, a more fruitful inquiry may be to determine whether the

Table 2-3

Average Patrolman Maximum Salary in 1969 and 1973 in Municipalities Not Involved in Interest Arbitration and Municipalities Involved in Interest Arbitration, by Population Category, 1968-1973

Population Category	Total Category	Number Reporting	Average Patrolman Maximum Salary 1969	Average Patrolman Maximum Salary 1973	Change in Average Pat. Max. Salary 1969-1973
5,000-9,999					
Not in arbitration	14	5	$580	$882	$302
In arbitration	21	7	577	814	237
10,000-19,999					
Not in arbitration	8	3	556	773	217
In arbitration	11	8	575	820	245
20,000-39,999					
Not in arbitration	5	2	619	956	337
In arbitration	8	7	597	878	281

Source: Responses to questionnaire mailed to Pennsylvania municipalities that indicated collective bargaining experience with public safety organizations.

availability of compulsory arbitration has pushed wages beyond levels in comparable areas. This inquiry would be directed not at finding out what wages would have been without compulsory arbitration—a question impossible to answer—but whether a jurisdiction where compulsory arbitration is available ends up paying higher wages than similar jurisdictions with other means of resolving impasses. In a recent study, Loewenberg and Koziara compared wages in New York, Ohio, and Pennsylvania for police in the years 1966 through 1971.[23] Of the three states, only Pennsylvania authorized arbitration as a means to resolve negotiation impasses during the period of the study. The results of the study indicate that increases in police salaries have been markedly higher since Act 111 was passed in 1968 than the rates of wage changes in the years immediately before the act. Percentage wage increases in 1971-72, however, were smaller than those during the period from 1968 to 1971. Despite the increases, the absolute level of police wages in Pennsylvania several years after the introduction of compulsory arbitration remains generally lower than the salaries of police in municipalities in comparable population categories in neighboring states. It would therefore seem that arbitration does not produce excessively high salaries in comparison to other means of impasse resolution. Differentials in salaries between police in Pennsylvania and those in the other two states decreased, however, so that the hypothesis of arbitration's helping employees to "catch up" in wages is supported.

Summary and Evaluation

Act 111 became law in Pennsylvania for three main purposes: (1) to ensure that police and firefighters would receive fair wages and working conditions; (2) to promote collective bargaining between public employers and public safety employees; and (3) to ensure that strikes would not be used in connection with bargaining. These three objectives are generally being met.

Police and firefighters have made substantial progress in wages and working conditions since 1968, in large part because of the low wages paid previously. Employers concede that Act 111 has forced them "to look outside their own community to see what other towns have given their police and firefighters." There is no evidence that the availability of arbitration has raised wages above those being paid in comparable jurisdictions with different bargaining policies. To employee organizations perhaps the most important measure of "fairness" is their overall satisfaction with agreement results.

A large number of public safety employees in the state are bargaining with their employers. Particularly in larger jurisdictions, bargaining began in the first two years after passage of the act. New bargaining relationships continue to be initiated even today.

The absence of any strikes in Pennsylvania by police and firefighters since 1968 has been a notable achievement. Neither in negotiations nor at any point in the arbitration process has there been a known work stoppage of public safety employees.

Even if viewed in narrower terms of encouraging negotiated settlements as opposed to arbitrated terms, Act 111 has succeeded in many situations. Where there has been extensive use of arbitration involving many parties, relatively few of them have become completely dependent on arbitration. Two incidents illustrate the point. An employee leader claimed that the best part of an arbitration award, which he viewed as higher than could have been negotiated, was that it encouraged the municipality to negotiate in the next round of bargaining. In another situation, where both parties were in their first arbitration, they became alarmed about the costs and resented the intrusion of outsiders; they have successfully negotiated three agreements since then. It should not be inferred that arbitration may not occur again in either of these cases. Rather, the point is that arbitration has had a salutary effect in encouraging the parties to bargain seriously.

Problems have occurred, some of which apply generally to public sector bargaining. The turnover among municipal officials and employee leaders requires reestablishing relationships. To the extent that negotiators, lawyers, or consultants are hired by the leadership, the turnover problem is compounded. Decisions in negotiations or arbitrations that constituents view negatively often lead to political repercussions, especially within employee organizations.

Some parties continue to consider collective bargaining in general and arbitration in particular as a game to be won or lost, an attitude which does little to promote negotiations. They also fear that any compromises suggested in negotiations may weaken their position in arbitration should an impasse occur. The lack of a mediation step in the dispute resolution procedure deprives parties not only of an opportunity to gain assistance but also of a learning experience. In too many cases in Pennsylvania the parties have probably done little meaningful bargaining before going to arbitration. The legal challenges to Act 111 have thus far not affected the procedure significantly, but the possibility of judicial intervention and modification of awards continues.

The experience of public safety employees with Act 111 has not prompted other public employees to clamor for compulsory arbitration, though it may have encouraged passage of Act 195. Many nonuniformed public employees oppose compulsory arbitration and prefer the right to strike. In many jurisdictions, however, the conditions gained by police and firefighters set the pattern for other employees. In part, this pattern is due to the number and pay levels of public safety employees, but it is also due to the fact that public safety employees are the only organized groups in many municipalities. Increases gained in negotiations or arbitration are then passed on to nonunion employees. Even where other public employees are organized, the public safety group tends to set the pattern. Thus, the economic effects of Act 111 extend beyond police and firefighters.

Despite the problems and effects, Act 111 seems firmly embedded in Pennsylvania legislation. Although employers are not altogether happy with the language of the law, they have learned to live with it. Inevitably there is discontent with particular awards, but there is little question that the process of collective bargaining with compulsory arbitration to resolve impasses has been accepted by the parties and the public.

Notes

1. Act of June 30, 1947, P.L. 1183 as amended, 43 P.S. §215.1.
2. Act of April 6, 1956, P.L. (1955) 1414 §13.2.

34

3. H.R. 203 (1959).

4. *Erie Fire Fighters, Local 293, IAFF v. Arthur Gardner et al.,* 406 Pa. 395, 178 A.2d 691 (1962).

5. A good summary of the history of Act 111 may be found in Mollie H. Bowers, "A Study of Legislated Arbitration in the Public Safety Services in Michigan and Pennsylvania," unpublished Ph.D. thesis (Ithaca, N.Y.: Cornell University, 1973), pp. 186-95.

6. Act of June 24, 1968, P.L. 237 (Act No. 111), 43 P.S. §217.1 et seq.

7. Studies on experience under Pennsylvania Act 111 include: Bowers, "A Study of Legislated Arbitration . . ."; J. Joseph Loewenberg, "Compulsory Arbitration for Police and Firefighters: The Pennsylvania Experience in 1968," *Industrial and Labor Relations Review* (April 1970), pp. 367-79; J. Joseph Loewenberg, "Collective Bargaining for Police and Firefighters in Pennsylvania in 1969," unpublished manuscript, 1970; J. Joseph Loewenberg, "Compulsory Binding Arbitration in the Public Sector," paper delivered at the International Symposium on Public Employment Relations, New York City, May 1971, and excerpted in *Proceedings of the International Symposium on Public Employment Labor Relations,* pp. 140-50.

8. For further analysis of the behavior of neutral arbitrators on a tripartite board, see J. Joseph Loewenberg, "Compulsory Arbitration and the Arbitrator," *Arbitration Journal* 25, no. 4 (1970), pp. 248-60.

9. Loewenberg, "Compulsory Binding Arbitration . . . ."

10. *Harney v. Russo,* 435 Pa. 183, 255 A.2d 560 (1969).

11. *Local 736, International Association of Fire Fighters v. City of Williamsport,* 47 D.C.2d 317 (1969).

12. *Borato v. Town Council of the Borough of Midland,* 48 D.C.2d 510 (1969).

13. *John Worrilow v. Lebanon Lodge Fraternal Order of Police No. 42, Pa. Commonwealth,* 288 A.2d 837 (1972).

14. *City of Washington v. Police Department of the City of Washington,* 436 Pa. 168, 259 A.2d 437 (1969).

15. *Garbin v. Brentzel,* 54 D.C.2d 365 (1972).

16. *Allegheny County Fire Fighters, Local 1038, International Association of Fire Fighters v. County of Allegheny, Pa. Commonwealth,* 299 A.2d 60 (1973).

17. *Cheltenham Township v. Cheltenham Police Department, Pa. Commonwealth,* 301 A.2d 430 (1973).

18. *DeCarbo v. Borough of Ellwood City,* 3 Comm. Ct. of Pa. 569 (1971).

19. *City of Sharon v. F.O.P. Lodge No. 3,* 814 Commonwealth Docket, Nov. 8, 1973.

20. *Cheltenham Township v. Cheltenham Police Department,* cited in *Government Employee Relations Report* (GERR) #538, Jan. 21, 1974, pp. 8-10.

21. *Tate v. Antosh,* 3 Commonwealth Court 144 (1971).

22. *Supra,* note 16.

23. J. Joseph Loewenberg and Karen S. Koziara, "Wage Effects of Alternative Bargaining Policies in the Public Sector" (unpublished manuscript, 1975).

3

The Michigan Arbitration Experience

In 1969, a year after the passage of the Pennsylvania statute, Michigan enacted legislation providing for compulsory arbitration of interest disputes in collective bargaining impasses involving its municipalities and counties and their public safety employees—that is, police, firefighters, and deputy sheriffs. The original arbitration statute called for conventional arbitration by a tripartite panel and in this respect was similar to the Pennsylvania law.[1] In 1972, however, when the initial three-year trial period expired, the statute was renewed but amended in one important respect. (See Appendix B for a copy of the amended statute.) The amended law substituted final-offer selection on each economic issue.[2] It, too, is experimental and expires June 30, 1975.

Under this system, the arbitration panel must select the offer of either party on each separate economic issue and, in contrast with conventional arbitration, may not adopt a compromise position. In this chapter, the bargaining and arbitration experience under the conventional system and under the final-offer-by-economic-issue system will be analyzed and compared.

The reader should keep in mind that while the system adopted in Wisconsin, which is analyzed in Chapter 4, is also called final-offer arbitration, it differs from the Michigan system in that the Wisconsin procedure forces the arbitrator to select the entire final-offer package of one or the other of the parties. In a multiple issue case, therefore, the Wisconsin system will differ from the Michigan system; in a single economic issue case, it will not differ on this particular point although, as the reader will discover, there are other significant differences in the procedures.

The format followed in this chapter is to review first the history of the legislation and developments leading up to the present. Next the statute and its administration are described; then the activity under the act is summarized. Finally, the views of the parties about the procedure are considered and the act as a whole is evaluated.

Legislative History of Police-Firefighter Arbitration in Michigan [3]

Police and firefighters were among the relatively few groups of public employees who organized successfully and gained some semblance of collective bargaining under Michigan's Hutchinson Act of 1947.[4] This act provided that public employees of Michigan had the right to "meet and confer" with public employers and therefore, impliedly at least, granted public employees the right of organization and representation. Under the Hutchinson Act, public employers retained ultimate decision-making authority for determining wages and other conditions of work of their employees. The act did provide for mediation and factfinding procedures to encourage peaceful settlement of disputes. Strikes were expressly prohibited, and harsh penalties were provided for violation of the strike ban.

In spite of the fact that the Hutchinson Act provided no more than a skeleton for public employment labor-management relations, joint discussion of wages, hours, and conditions of work resulted in a number of cities. Approximately 35 written collective bargaining agreements were signed, but the more common result of such "meet and confer" relationships was a joint agreement providing a basis for subsequent enactment of a municipal ordinance. These early experiences created some sophistication among public labor and management negotiators, particularly in a number of the larger Michigan cities. Given developments in several other states and the federal sector and the fact that in Michigan private sector labor-management collective bargaining relationships are generally pervasive, further moves for broadening of public sector collective bargaining rights were perhaps inevitable.

The Michigan State Fire Fighters Union (MSFFU), the Fraternal Order of Police (FOP), and the American Federation of State, County, and Municipal Employees (AFSCME) were the principal employee organizations that pressed to revise and expand public employee collective bargaining rights in Michigan in the early 1960s. Their efforts were supported by the Michigan Employment Relations Commission (formerly the Michigan Labor Mediation Board) that had been established in 1939 to promote peaceful collective bargaining in the private sector. A comprehensive public employee labor relations bill, the original version of which had been drafted by legal counsel for the MSFFU, was modified considerably and enacted by the legislature; it was signed by Governor George Romney in 1965. The primary opposition to this bill was led by the Michigan Municipal League. The new law, called the Public Employment Relations Act (PERA),[5] gave public employees in Michigan the explicit right to organize and bargain collectively, provided a system for determination of representation rights through elections, specified employer unfair labor practices, and continued mediation and factfinding as dispute resolution procedures. Public employee strikes remained prohibited, but the severe penalties were removed.

Simultaneous with the enactment of PERA, the Michigan Fire Fighters Union proposed a bill that would have provided for arbitration in all public sector bargaining impasses, but this bill never was reported out of committee. The following year a second effort was mounted by the MSFFU and the FOP to provide for compulsory arbitration, but covering only employees of municipal police and fire departments. It too failed, but momentum for compulsory arbitration in the public sector was growing.

In 1966, Governor Romney appointed an Advisory Committee on Public Employee Relations to analyze experience thus far under PERA and to make recommendations deemed necessary for change. A key recommendation in the committee's report was that for a two-year period compulsory arbitration be experimented with to avert police and firefighter strikes. Two bills embodying this recommendation were submitted in the state legislature in 1968, but both were unsuccessful.

The reason for the committee recommendation was that a number of Michigan communities were encountering various forms of job actions by police and firefighters in collective bargaining impasses. Eight public safety officer strikes occurred over these years—three by police and five by firefighters.[6] During the same period, both police and firefighters in a number of cities conducted other forms of job actions such as "work to rule" strikes, ticket-writing strikes, and, in the case of firefighters, refusal to perform any duties except that of fighting fires.

A decision of the Michigan Supreme Court in 1968 further eroded PERA's no-strike ban. Prior to 1968, public employers had been largely successful in appealing to local courts for injunctive relief in the case of strikes. In *Holland School District v. Holland Education Association,*[7] the court ruled that injunctive relief against even illegal strikes was subject to traditional rules for equitable relief. This decision meant, in effect, that before injunctive relief was available, a public employer had to comply with its statutory duty to bargain in good faith, avail itself of the mediation and factfinding remedies available under the law, and, most importantly, demonstrate that irreparable damage to the public health, safety, and welfare would result unless the strike were enjoined. This decision resulted in the de facto legalization of a large number of strikes by nonessential public employees. Although nonessentiality was not ordinarily considered applicable in strikes involving public safety employees, the decision tended to encourage their resort to various forms of job actions in bargaining impasses.

Enactment of Arbitration

In 1969, the Michigan State Fire Fighters Union intensified its lobbying efforts to gain compulsory arbitration of impasses involving its members. Organizations of police generally favored arbitration but were involved at that time in a number of jurisdictional disputes that weakened their ability to engage in joint lobbying efforts. The Michigan Municipal League opposed compulsory arbitration, claiming that it would inhibit free collective bargaining and destroy the accountability of elected public officials. A spokesman for the League told the House Labor Committee in 1969:

> There is [already] a final step for the resolution of public employee disputes, that is final determination by the local legislative body or the people themselves. The Municipal League favors additional procedures such as show-cause hearings before the local legislating body, in an effort to resolve public employee disputes.[8]

Robert Howlett, the long-time chairman of the Michigan Employment Relations Commission, articulated the view that was eventually to prevail:

> The attitude [of the League] is understandable, as petition to the legislative body, including lobbying, has been the traditional and constitutional method of securing improvements in working conditions. . . . In some instances, public employees may convince the voters that the actions of commission or school board members are not in the public interest, but elections are infrequent, terms of office are staggered, and the education process in lengthy. Lobbying, too, is generally a slow procedure.
>
> Employees will not wait! They will insist on prompt action in resolving a last-ditch confrontation. One way is to strike; the other is to arbitrate.[9]

On August 14, 1969, Public Act 312, the Police and Firefighters Arbitration Act, was signed; it became effective six weeks later. The act provided for conventional binding arbitration by a tripartite arbitration panel. One representative was to be selected by the public employer and one by its employees, and the representatives, in turn, were to select an impartial chairman; if they failed to agree on a neutral, the chairman was to be appointed by the chairman of the Michigan Employment Relations Commission (MERC).

Renewal of the Statute

In 1971, discussion of whether the compulsory arbitration statute should be extended or allowed to expire began in the state legislature. The Michigan Municipal League, which led the opposition to extension, contended that the statute had eroded both collective bargaining and mediation and that there had been more strikes by police and firefighters after the statute was enacted than there had been previously. Joining the active opposition were the mayor of Dearborn, whose city litigated the constitutionality of the statute, and the mayor of Detroit, who urged the state's lawmakers to consider "other alternatives to compulsory arbitration." [10]

The MSFFU, the FOP, the Police Officers Association of Michigan (POAM), and the Michigan AFL-CIO all urged that the statute be extended. They were supported by the director of the Michigan Department of Labor and the chairman of the MERC. Several prominent arbitrators who had served under the statute also supported it by testifying that extension of the law would provide a better basis for assessing the long-term performance of compulsory arbitration. [11]

Even legislative proponents of extension disagreed as to whether the statute required change. One major concern was that it diminished the parties' efforts to resolve their own disagreements in the course of collective bargaining. A proposal to remedy this problem, first introduced in the Senate Labor Committee and later agreed to by the House, provided that the arbitration panel be given authority to remand a dispute to the parties for further negotiations if it was felt that adequate or good-faith bargaining had not already taken place.

The second major area of disagreement arose over whether conventional arbitration resulted in giving arbitration panels too great an opportunity to render excessively high economic awards. It was asserted that unions submitted inflated economic proposals in an effort to accommodate their desires. As a result of these allegations, the chairman of the Senate Labor Committee proposed that arbitration panels be limited to a choice between the last offer of either the employer or the union. The premise was that a forced choice between the last offers would put pressure on the parties to come much closer together in negotiations and would either result in their making their own settlement or, if not, severely circumscribe the ultimate range of arbitral discretion.

In general, members of the House Labor Committee opposed the Senate's proposed amendments because they felt that the original compulsory arbitration statute had worked satisfactorily. House members questioned whether the proposal to allow the panel to remand disputes for further bargaining conflicted with the MERC's authority to rule on allegations of failure to bargain in good faith, and they opposed final-offer selection because it provided neither guidelines as to the kinds of issues to which the procedure would be subject nor standards to guide the arbitration panels in making the choice between final offers. On balance, however, it appeared that no extension would pass the Senate unless the final-offer selection process were incorporated in the revised bill. The chairman of the MERC, recognizing the political reality, helped to persuade the legislators to subject only economic issues to final-offer selection and to make final-offer selection applicable on an issue-by-issue rather than "whole-package" basis. These changes helped to make the final-offer procedure acceptable to the House.

The final bill passed in both the House and Senate by substantial margins and was signed by Governor William Milliken in June 1972. In order to give negotiating parties time to become familiar with the new procedure, the act provided that conventional arbitration would be continued for six months and that the final-offer-by-economic-issue procedure would take effect on January 1, 1973. Again, the legislation is experimental and expires under its own terms on June 30, 1975.

Constitutionality of the Statute

The constitutionality of binding arbitration, either under the original statute or as amended, has not been ruled upon by the Michigan Supreme Court. The City of Dearborn refused to appoint a panel member or to participate in two early arbitration proceedings involving negotiating impasses with its firefighters and police. Two-member arbitration panels proceeded in each case to hold ex parte hearings and render awards. The city then refused to put the awards into effect, claiming that the compulsory arbitration statute violated the Michigan constitution. The city contended that binding arbitration divested home rule cities of their powers, delegated legislative authority to private individuals, and forced cities' elected officials to surrender their powers of taxation.

The Dearborn Firefighters Union and the Police Officers Association of Dearborn challenged the city's refusal to implement the awards in a direct appeal to the Michigan Supreme Court. The court gave summary judgment that the challenged arbitration awards should be given immediate effect, but the constitutional issue was sent back for hearing in the lower courts. The district court judge ruled against the city on all three bases of its challenge. This decision was appealed to the Michigan Court of Appeals which unanimously concluded that the statute is constitutional.[12] The court found that (1) the powers of home rule cities are subject to the constitution and the law; (2) the power delegated to the arbitration panel by the statute "of itself renders it a public body"; and (3) an arbitration panel's award neither imposes a tax nor diminishes a city's taxing authority, and thus no surrender of the city's power to impose taxes is involved.

The City of Dearborn appealed this adverse decision to the Michigan Supreme Court. The case was argued and final briefs were filed during the summer of 1973. The decision of the court is still pending as of April 1975.

The Statute and Its Administration

It is suggestive that while all public employees in Michigan are forbidden to strike by PERA,[13] only in the case of police and fire services is a binding procedure mandated to end bargaining impasses. The state's policy is stated in Section 1 of PFFA: ". . . it is requisite of the high morale of such employees and the efficient operation of such departments to afford an alternate, expeditious, effective and binding procedure for the resolution of disputes. . . ." Stated colloquially, Michigan's public policy is that "No public employees may strike, but for police and firefighters we really mean it."

Despite the low number of public safety strikes that had occurred—eight in total—the legislators felt compulsory arbitration was necessary to avoid more in the future. They nevertheless recognized not only the dangers in imposing binding, third-party decision making on the state's subunits of government but also their own lack of experience with precisely how such a statute should be framed. For this reason, the legislature formulated a statute that was to be both flexible in operation and "liberally construed."

Scope of Coverage

The statute covers "any department of a city, county, village or township having employees engaged as policemen or in firefighting or subject to the hazards thereof." Thus, in addition to municipal police and firefighters, county deputy sheriffs and public airport fire departments are also included.[a]

Under court rulings and MERC administration of PERA, supervisors enjoy the right of organization and negotiation.[14] Thus, by extension, supervisory police and fire units are covered by PFFA. It has been MERC's policy, also affirmed by the courts, that public employee supervisors exercise their right only through bargaining units and organizations separate from their nonsupervisory employees.[15] PERA, however, imposes a significant exception to this policy: ". . . in any fire department . . . no person subordinate to a fire commission, fire commissioner, safety director or other similar administrator shall be deemed to be a supervisor." Thus in contrast with police, in organized fire departments, all personnel

---

[a] According to a memorandum to the authors dated July 30, 1974, from Robert G. Howlett, Chairman, Michigan Employment Relations Commission, the chairman of MERC has refused to appoint interest arbitrators in disputes involving state university police forces and park rangers.

up to and in some few cases including the chief are represented in the same bargaining unit. Police and deputy sheriffs are subject to the same rule as nonuniformed employees. Supervisors and nonsupervisors must be in different units with division coming at about the rank of sergeant, depending on the facts in the particular care. Police department clerical employees may be joined in nonsupervisory units with uniformed employees. When clerical personnel are represented within units of public safety officers, their wages and fringes and conditions of employment may be processed to compulsory arbitration along with those of the public safety officers.

Initiation of Mediation and Arbitration

Under the most recent amendments to PERA (June 14, 1973), the parties to negotiation are required to notify MERC of the status of their negotiation 60 days prior to the expiration of the existing collective agreement. If, after 30 days of such notification, the dispute remains unresolved, the parties may request or MERC may unilaterally appoint a mediator. In the majority of cases, the 60-day report is made; failure to report has no sanction and is never a basis for denial of mediation.

The statute requires the parties to petition for mediation 30 calendar days prior to requesting arbitration. While mediation ordinarily begins within 30 days, the number of mediation sessions held is usually fewer than 10; often only one mediation session takes place.[b]

Within 10 days after requesting arbitration, the employer and the employees' representative each select a delegate to the arbitration panel and notify the other party and MERC of their selection. Within five days, "or within such further additional periods to which they may agree," the delegates are to select a third impartial panel member, the neutral arbitrator or chairman, under the statute. The statute directs: "Upon their failure to agree upon and appoint the arbitrator . . . either of them may request the chairman of the state labor mediation board to appoint the arbitrator." In

---

[b] Through an oversight resulting from the rush to pass the statute before the close of the legislative session, reference to factfinding is made in both Sections 3 and 4 of the statute, which would infer that police and fire disputes may be processed through factfinding prior to arbitration. Factfinding was never intended, in Michigan at least, as a required or preliminary step to the arbitration process because it was thought to be a duplication of effort. Any doubt is removed by Section 14 of PFFA which states, ". . . any provision [of PERA] requiring factfinding procedures shall be inapplicable to disputes subject to arbitration under this act." Thus factfinding is not and has never been part of the police and fire compulsory arbitration process.

practice, the delegates (or the parties' representatives or attorneys) agree upon the neutral about a quarter of the time—58 times out of 212 appointments through June 30, 1974. All appointments are made by the MERC chairman upon failure to agree.

The only qualification stipulated for the neutral is that he or she be "an impartial, competent and reputable citizen." However, under MERC's administration, only the most experienced arbitrators are used for contract arbitration. A question regarding the intent of the word "citizen" came up only once, upon the appointment of a non-Michigan resident as the neutral. MERC's chairman ruled that the term "citizen" should be interpreted broadly to mean "of the U.S." and rejected the challenge to the appointment.

Responsibilities and Authority of the Arbitrator

The statute requires the arbitrator to preside at the hearings, to arrange for a verbatim record, and to begin hearings within 15 days of his appointment. In practice, the hearings do not usually begin within 15 days, but are scheduled during that period to take place at the earliest convenience of all involved. Arrangements for the recording service may be made by the arbitrator, but ordinarily a MERC court reporter is made available. The requirement that verbatim records be kept, although criticized as adding unnecessary costs to already expensive proceedings, perhaps was formulated with the provisions of Section 12 in mind, which state that the arbitration panel's award is reviewable by a circuit court, which in turn would require "competent, material and substantial evidence on the whole record." This requirement is not always costly; it can be, and sometimes is, met by use of a cassette recorder. Moreover, even where a stenographic record is made, it is often not transcribed.

The neutral's fee is set by MERC at $150 per day, which is less than the usual fee of experienced arbitrators. The arbitrator's fee and other expenses incurred by the proceedings, such as transportation for the neutral and hearing room rental, are paid one-third by each party and one-third by the state.

At the discretion of the arbitration panel, and "upon application and for a good cause shown, and upon such terms as are just, a person, labor organization, or governmental unit having a substantial interest therein may be granted leave to intervene by the arbitration panel." If broadly interpreted, this provision would allow literally any individual citizen or group to intervene. In practice, however, requests for intervention have been few, and arbitration panels have been cautious in allowing excessive intervention even when requested. At the request of one city, the courts ordered a single hearing involving both police and firefighters before a single arbitration panel, but this situation was unique.[16]

The arbitration panel has authorization to issue oaths and require pertinent testimony and evidence by issuing subpoenas if necessary, even to the extent of invoking the aid of a circuit court. In an early case under the original statute, the arbitration panel did utilize court-issued subpoenas to compel the participation of a reluctant governmental unit; six months elapsed before the hearing could be held. Finally, the chairman of the arbitration panel, "If he is of the opinion that it would be useful or beneficial to do so," may remand the dispute to the parties for further collective bargaining for a period not to exceed three weeks.

Final-Offer Selection

In essence, the basic final-offer selection procedure is (1) the panel makes the final determination of issues in dispute and whether they are economic or noneconomic; (2) the last, best-offer determination applies only to economic issues; (3) noneconomic issues are subject to conventional arbitration; and (4) the opinion and award are to be written. This procedure should be contrasted with that of the earlier arbitration statute. Formerly, all issues presented to arbitration panels, economic and noneconomic alike, could result in awards of the position of either party or any compromise deemed appropriate.

The provision of the amended statute—that the arbitration panel may decide which issues are economic and thus subject to final-offer and which are noneconomic and subject to conventional arbitration—has led to some unusual results. Insurance, holidays, and sick-leave accumulation have at various times been determined to be noneconomic issues and subject to compromise. Several panels have concluded that duration of the agreement is a noneconomic issue, which thus allows them to compromise on a two-year award when the parties' final offers were on one and three years, respectively. In one peculiar award, where duration of the agreement was an issue but where one party refused to make an economic offer on the second year, that party's first-year proposal was made the basis for the economic award on a two-year agreement, with the panel stating that the one-year offer was the only offer available! Such aberrant awards are uncommon, however.

Of considerable, and perhaps largely unforeseen, significance is the provision's nonspecificity as to when the parties' final offers on each economic issue shall be given to the panel. "At or before the end of the hearing," and "within such time limits as the panel shall prescribe," permit great latitude. In practice, final offers have been made in writing before or at the hearing, orally in the presence of the other party, or in written form after the actual hearing has taken place but before formal closure. The impact upon the arbitration process of this latitude granted to the panel will be discussed in subsequent sections of this chapter.

Nine criteria upon which the arbitration panel is directed to base its findings are listed in the statute. These guidelines are broad and give the panel much leeway on which to base a decision. No priorities are assigned among the various criteria, although in awards generally it appears that wages paid in public employment in comparable communities (with the basis of appropriate comparisons left to the panel), cost of living changes, and ability to pay receive the greatest attention. The final criterion, any factors "normally or traditionally taken into consideration in setting wages, hours and working conditions" leaves the whole matter fully open. Some panels, for example, have used this final clause to consider past practices of the parties.

As arbitration panels under the PFFA are tripartite, some parties select "outsiders," such as attorneys, to represent them. Others simply select an official out of their constituency. In either event, their degrees of partisanship vary individually. In general, however, because they are not "brothers" in the work force, unanimous awards have been more common when "outsiders" are the partisan panel members. The main benefit of a tripartite panel is the input and insight the neutral receives from some partisans' expertise and point of view throughout the decision-making process. The majority vote ensures that the neutral consider carefully the position of each party and, in theory, prevents the neutral from making an unrealistic award or one that is unacceptable to both parties. If, however, subsequent to the award both parties consider a ruling unreasonable or unworkable, the parties may mutually agree to "amend or modify an award of arbitration."

The majority decision of the arbitration panel is final and binding upon the parties and enforceable at the request of either party in circuit court. The matter of giving partisan members a vote has been the subject of much discussion. Some contend that the neutral must often compromise too greatly in order to obtain the vote of one other panel member. Hence, he becomes a mediator rather than an honest adjudicator. Others believe that the neutral member can and should maintain what he believes to be the "equitable" solution, thereby forcing one of the partisans to move to him in order that there be a majority decision. This latter tactic is obviously most practical if the panel votes on an issue-by-issue rather than a whole-award basis. The statute is silent on the appropriate practice. Clearly, if the vote is to be on the whole award in a multiple issue dispute, and particularly if the neutral seeks a unanimous award, some negotiation and some compromise by all panel members, including the neutral, is necessary. Unanimity is not required by the statute, of course, and in practice, one or both partisan members often dissent to some parts of an award. During the conventional arbitration period and the period through June 30, 1974, 35 of 135 awards have been unanimous. Even if this degree of unanimity has been reached by negotiation and compromise within the panel, such action is no more imprecise or improper than the process of collective bargaining. The listing in the statute of many criteria as appropriate for consideration by the panel suggests that a kind of "bargain" is both necessary and appropriate.

Increases in rates of compensation awarded by an arbitration panel may be put into effect "only at the start of the fiscal year next commencing after the date of the arbitration award" unless the arbitration proceedings were initiated prior to the commencement of a fiscal year. In the latter event, the award, whenever finally issued, may be retroactive to the start of the fiscal year in which the proceedings began, "any other statute or charter provision to the contrary notwithstanding."

In other words, in cases where the union contract and the fiscal year end simultaneously, the union must file for arbitration prior to the expiration of its current contract so that the award on economic items may be effective for the entire coming fiscal year. Otherwise, the award would not take effect until the following fiscal year, and an existing salary rate might continue for an additional 12 months or even longer. But, as previously noted, the parties must be in mediation 30 days before filing for arbitration. The union must therefore file for mediation more than 30 days prior to the contract and fiscal year expiration in order to be within the fiscal-year time limits for filing for arbitration, should it become necessary. These time limits were imposed to prevent endless negotiations culminating in awards retroactive for several years prior to their issuance, which on the one hand would be unduly burdensome on the employer. On the other hand, they protect employees from losing a year's economic increase as a result of lengthy arbitration proceedings beyond their control. But at times, the time limits force the unions to file prematurely for mediation and arbitration, with occasional adverse effects upon their continuing negotiations. In other cases, unions have been dilatory or ignorant of the need to request mediation 30 days before the end of the fiscal year, and have requested mediation from MERC while simultaneously filing for arbitration, which often does not permit effective mediation before the end of the fiscal year.

The award of the arbitration panel is subject to review by a circuit court "but only for reasons that the panel was without or exceeded its jurisdiction; the order is unsupported by competent, material and substantial evidence on the whole record; or the order was procured by fraud, collusion or other similar and unlawful means. The pendency of such proceedings for review shall not automatically stay the order of the arbitration panel." The major challenge to an arbitration award under this section of the statute is that of the City of Dearborn, now pending before the Michigan Supreme Court along with the city's challenge to the constitutionality of the statute. The city repeatedly refused to appoint a panel member or to participate in the proceedings that led to the award in issue, and the two duly appointed members of the panel elected to proceed with hearings on an ex parte basis rather than to go through the process of requiring attendance of the city by subpoenas that had so delayed the beginning of arbitration in the situation noted earlier. Dearborn protested the award it received on the basis that a two-member panel was "without jurisdiction." On this issue, a majority of the Michigan Court of Appeals held, "Jurisdiction stems from the legislative grant over the subject matter," rather than referring to the composition of the panel. The majority held further that the panel composed of an impartial and one partisan had proper jurisdiction, adding that "it would be quixotic" to allow the city to sabotage the arbitration process by its own inaction.[17]

The statute specifies punishment against an employee organization or an employer who "willfully disobeys a lawful order of enforcement by a circuit court . . . or willfully encourages or offers resistance to such order whether by strike or otherwise." The punishment for each day of such "contempt" is to be fixed by the court in amount not to exceed $250.00 per day. There have been no instances of contempt or punishment under this clause even though the daily fine is unrealistic, at least with respect to large cities and unions. Finally, it should be noted that imprisonment for violation of the act or refusal to implement an arbitration award is prohibited by the act.

Scope of Arbitrability

The statute does not define issues subject to arbitration; rather, as the statute is "deemed supplementary to Act No. 336 [PERA]," all issues subject to collective bargaining are likewise subject to arbitration. The scope of bargainable issues under PERA is identical to the subjects specified in the National Labor Relations Act, namely, "wages, hours and other terms and conditions of employment." It is nevertheless true that public employers can bargain only with regard to those powers vested in them by the legislature. Hence, there are subjects that are bargainable in the private sector that are not bargainable or subject to arbitration in the public sector.

The issues of pensions and residence requirements have generated much controversy and litigation. Both have recently been held by the Michigan Supreme Court to be mandatory subjects of bargaining,[18] and therefore may be brought to arbitration if necessary. An agency shop union security agreement, typical of those commonly negotiated and awarded by some arbitration panels, was voided by the Supreme Court in 1972 as being impermissible under PERA.[19] That statute was amended in 1973 to permit the negotiation, and thus the arbitrability, of such agreements.

Statistical Summary of Activity under the Police-Firefighter Arbitration Act

Michigan's population was 8,900,000 as of the 1970 Census. The state is divided into 83 counties, and it contains 127 municipalities with populations greater than 5,000, which is the minimum population size for cities selected for inclusion in the present study. (Cities under 5,000 were excluded from the sample.)

Michigan's population is far from evenly distributed throughout its geographic area. Approximately 90 percent of Michigan residents live in one-third of the state's total geographic area—the lower half of the lower peninsula. Within this area, population is concentrated even further. Almost half of the citizens of the whole state, 48 percent, live in the Detroit Metropolitan Area—that is, the three counties of Oakland, Macomb, and Wayne that include and immediately surround the City of Detroit.

Extent of Collective Bargaining

As might be anticipated, collective bargaining among police, firefighters, and deputy sheriffs tends strongly to occur in areas of population concentration. So far as counties are concerned, 63 of 83 Michigan counties had by 1974 established collective bargaining relationships and negotiated agreements with deputy sheriffs. Of the 20 counties that do not yet bargain, 16 are in the lightly populated areas of the upper peninsula or the upper half of the lower peninsula and most commonly are counties that have no major cities.

The prevalence of collective bargaining among police and firefighters correlates with city size. Bargaining with police and/or firefighters takes place in 116 of 127 Michigan cities over 5,000 in population, but only in cities under 10,000 is there any great likelihood that collective bargaining for public safety employees is not already established. Of the collective bargaining relationships in these cities, 108 are with police and six are with combined public safety bargaining units. Eighty-seven of the 116 cities also have collective bargaining agreements with firefighters. Only two Michigan cities in our sample have a collective bargaining relationship with firefighters and not with police.

Use of Mediation

Michigan's original Public Employment Relations Act made mediation available in all public negotiations and encouraged its use; under the 1969 arbitration statute, it was made a prerequisite to arbitration. Our information on the use of mediation in public safety bargaining is incomplete, but of the 102 out of 116 cities on which we have data, only 22 have never used mediation in negotiations with police or firefighters. Twenty-four of these 102 cities have used mediation only once since 1969, 19 have used mediation twice, and 37 have used mediation three or more times. Of the 57 out of 63 counties that negotiate with deputy sheriffs and on which we have data, 10 have never used mediation in these negotiations. Twenty-four counties have used mediation once in threatened impasses with deputy sheriffs, 16 twice, and only 7 three times or more. It would appear from these figures that mediation is at present not quite as commonly resorted to in county deputy sheriff negotiations as in municipal bargaining with police and firefighters. Its effectiveness as a dispute resolution technique, particularly where arbitration is available, will be discussed later.

Use of Arbitration

The Michigan Department of Labor issues an annual summary of activity under PFFA. This summary, as published for the years 1970 through 1974, is not precisely comparable to our sample of cities and counties, as it includes cities that are smaller than 5,000 population, villages, and townships, as well as public safety command officer bargaining units. It does depict the total volume of activity during the first three years of the conventional arbitration statute as compared to the first complete fiscal year (1973-74) of final-offer arbitration.

According to the data in Table 3-1, arbitration shows no signs of withering away. The number of cases submitted to arbitration in 1973-74 was almost identical with that of 1972-73. Also, the parties are able to select their own neutral third panel member about one time in four; three-quarters of the neutrals are appointed by the chairman of MERC. The

Table 3-1

Police-Firefighter Arbitration Act Activity, Four-Year Summary, 1970-74

	1970-71	1971-72	1972-73	1973-74	Total
Cases submitted	47	61	106	104	318
Cases settled	9	26	24	89	148
Arbitrators appointed:					
By MERC chairman	32	24	56	42	154
By parties	10	14	16	18	58
Ineligible for arbitra-					
tion under PFFA	0	1	5	0	6
Cases pending	9	25	50	59	—
Reports issued	36	29	30	40	135

most interesting figure in the table, the large upswing in 1973-74 in cases settled by the parties after petition for arbitration, will be highlighted subsequently.

The Users of Arbitration

One striking similarity is apparent among the 114 police bargaining units, 87 firefighter units, and 63 deputy sheriff units in our sample. In slightly more than half (52-55 percent) of all of these bargaining relationships, public safety employees have never felt the need to petition for binding arbitration to resolve impasses in negotiations. About one-quarter (22-27 percent) of the units have petitioned for arbitration only once, and slightly less than one-quarter (19-23 percent) more than once.

As is apparent from Table 3-1, not every petition for arbitration results in an award. Frequently the parties settle their dispute after a petition is filed—either before the hearing begins, during the hearing itself, or subsequent to the hearing but before the award is rendered. Hence, although at least one petition for arbitration has been filed in nearly half of all bargaining relationships, awards have been issued in less than one-third of them. The actual numbers in which there were awards are 33 of 114 police relationships (29 percent), 24 of the 87 firefighter relationships (28 percent), and 20 of the 63 deputy sheriff relationships (32 percent). Overall, awards have been rendered in 77, or 29 percent, of the 264 bargaining relationships in our sample.

Arbitration is petitioned for and awards are rendered far more commonly in large than in small cities. Cities under 10,000 make up 28 percent of the cities that negotiate but have received only 13 percent of the awards. Cities over 100,000 represent only 7 percent of the negotiating cities but have received 23 percent of all arbitration awards. This disparity undoubtedly results in large part from the severe impact of the cost of arbitration on small bargaining units in small cities. It may also reflect a difference in levels of tensions and difficulties in bargaining relationships in small compared to large cities. Certainly, several of the largest cities in Michigan have severe financial problems. Satisfaction of public safety employee demands, and the consequent reductions in other services that they would necessitate, cannot in light of political considerations be negotiated voluntarily and must be compelled by an arbitration award.

Because we were interested in seeing if any of the three groups of public safety employees involved in our study showed differing tendencies to use arbitration to resolve bargaining impasses, we compared the numbers of petitions for arbitration by each group with the approximate numbers of negotiations by each group in our sample of cities and counties over a four-year period. The result is shown in Table 3-2 in percentage terms, since we cannot identify the precise number of negotiations that took place in the sample cities and counties during these years. The approximation used, if in error, is slightly low.

As can be seen in Table 3-2, deputy sheriffs show a slightly higher tendency than do police or firefighters to request and use arbitration, but the difference is not large. Why they show this slightly higher tendency to use arbitration than the other two groups but, as shown previously, a slightly lower tendency to use mediation is not readily apparent. It probably reflects a wide divergence between highly sophisticated negotiators and the quite inexperienced ones among deputy sheriffs.

Overall, the three groups of public safety employees request arbitration at about the same frequency—that is, in one of every three or four negotiations. They ultimately need an award in only one negotiation in six. This latter ratio, while presumably larger than the ratio of strikes to negotiations that one would find if strikes were legally permissible, nevertheless does not show that the availability of arbitration has substantially eroded

Table 3-2

Arbitration Petitions and Awards, by Public Safety Group, 1970-1973

	Police	Firefighter	Deputy Sheriff	Total
Contract negotiations (approximate)	305	235	110	650
Petitions for arbitration	26%	29%	37%	30%
Arbitration awards	15%	15%	20%	16%

the possibilities of settlement through the parties' own collective bargaining efforts.

Settlement After Petitions for Arbitration

As was noted in connection with Table 3-1, subsequent to the passage of the amendments that became effective on January 1, 1973, the overall number of settlements reached subsequent to a petition for arbitration increased markedly. As is shown in Table 3-3, this tendency is equally

Table 3-3

Petitions, Settlements, and Awards, by Public Safety Group, 1969-1972 and 1973-1974

	Police	Firefighter	Deputy Sheriff	Total
	October 1, 1969–December 31, 1972			
Petitions	56	53	32	141
Closed by settlement	17 (30%)	23 (43%)	15 (47%)	55 (39%)
Closed by award	39 (70%)	30 (57%)	17 (53%)	86 (61%)
	January 1, 1973–June 30, 1974			
Petitions	28	16	20	64
Cases pending	3	1	10	14
Closed by settlement	18 (72%)	9 (60%)	5 (50%)	32 (64%)
Closed by award	7 (28%)	6 (40%)	5 (50%)	18 (36%)

noticeable in our sample of cities and counties and holds true for all groups of public safety employees.

The basis for closing arbitration cases has shifted from 61 percent by award under the original statute to 64 percent by settlement under the amended statute. This shift from settlement by award to settlement by the parties after a petition for arbitration has been filed is the only striking change in the statistics when final-offer arbitration is compared to the conventional arbitration phase of the Michigan statutory experiment. The reasons for this shift will be discussed subsequently.

Perspectives on Final-Offer Arbitration

Bargaining units of police in our sample range from 3 patrolmen to nearly 4,000 members in the unit, the latter number being in the City of Detroit. If Detroit is excluded, the average police patrolmen's bargaining unit in Michigan has 45 members. Deputy sheriff units range from 3 to 470 unit members (in Wayne county) and average about 33. Firefighter units range in membership from 4 to 1,733. If the largest, Detroit, is excluded, the average size is less than 50. Ninety-eight percent of public safety bargaining unit members pay dues to the organization representing them.

Sixty percent of police units and 70 percent of firefighter units have been organized for more than five years. Deputy sheriff bargaining units are somewhat younger, over two-thirds having been organized within the last five years. Only 13 percent of the cities and 24 percent of the counties have negotiated public safety collective bargaining agreements annually since the inception of their collective bargaining relationships. In other words, most cities and counties tend sooner or later to negotiate longer than one-year agreements.

So far as the final-offer amendment to the public safety arbitration law is concerned, most of the parties who responded to questionnaires or who were interviewed had some familiarity with it.[c] However, there were a few individuals who led local unaffiliated organizations in small cities who seemed to be wholly unaware of this amendment to the arbitration law. About one-third of those whom we interviewed had seriously considered petitioning for arbitration, had actually petitioned for arbitration, or had participated in final-offer arbitration. The remaining two-thirds ranged from some who had a vague awareness of the final-offer statute to those who had well-thought-out perceptions of the procedure's potential impact both on their own bargaining relationship and on possible future arbitrations.[d]

The Impact of Final-Offer Arbitration on the Collective Bargaining Process

Here we will summarize generally the attitudes of negotiating parties in Michigan with regard to various significant aspects of the impact of final-offer arbitration. The indented material is intended to give a general flavor of characteristic responses from labor or management negotiators or to

---

[c] Our sample of 210 bargaining units in the 127 Michigan cities over 5,000 and 83 counties includes over 80 percent of the legislated arbitration experience that has thus far occurred under PFFA. Our questionnaire return rate from representatives of all parties involved in public safety negotiations was 60 percent. We interviewed 80 representatives of the parties involved in 27 of these negotiating relationships, as well as statewide union officials and attorneys representing the parties in a number of public safety negotiations.

[d] On the questionnaire asking for opinions on various aspects of the final-offer procedure, the number responding "don't know" ranged from 10 to 40 percent, depending on the issue.

highlight interesting comments and perceptions of specific individuals as they bear on the final-offer process.

Circumvention of the Bargaining Process. It appears that police and firefighter negotiations in some cases are at least in part a facade, and wages and working conditions are still basically determined by various forms of political pressure, including by-passing the negotiator and establishing direct relationships with mayors or city or county council members or appealing to the public at large to support the equity of bargaining demands. Resort to these kinds of pressures appears to have diminished considerably since arbitration was first legislated to resolve impasses in 1969, and was not affected one way or the other by the shift from conventional to final-offer arbitration.

The majority of management spokesmen whom we surveyed responded that their public safety employees "seldom" or "never" engage in such tactics. This response presumably reflects a managerial evaluation of the effectiveness of such strategies, as nearly all of the public safety organizations reported having engaged in pressure tactics simultaneously with their collective bargaining at one time or another. Fifty percent of the firefighters' units had engaged in door-to-door public campaigns or petitioning activity to obtain public support for their bargaining position. Among police and deputy sheriffs, a more common tactic was to have large numbers of their members appear at city or county council meetings. Half of the deputy sheriff organizations, two-thirds of the police organizations, and fully three-quarters of the firefighters reported that they had made immediate contact with city or county council members privately to urge the validity of the views they simultaneously expressed at the bargaining table. The following summary of and excerpts from typical survey responses illustrate this point:

> *In one city it appears that collective bargaining decisions are not made at the table but fundamentally through the interworking of an "old boy" network. Relationships based on blood, marriage, money, and even sex interweave the city administration, the city council, and public safety organization leaders. This informal but tight political network is readily used to arrive at a collective bargaining result satisfactory to the organization.*

. . . Ultimately I always have to deal with several friendly city commissioners because I consider the management spokesman both powerless and personally hostile to me. (*Union Spokesman*)

. . . I deal directly with council members because collective bargaining is frustrating. I have had good success with personal contacts in the past, and "besides, it's cheaper than arbitration." (*Union Spokesman*)

While a majority of public safety employees' organizations had engaged in political pressure tactics, obviously with varying degrees of success, only a small number of units reported having engaged in forms of "job action" to augment their bargaining power. Only 15 percent of firefighter units, 10 percent of police units, and 6 percent of deputy sheriff units acknowledged ever engaging in slowdowns, sick-outs, or other forms of job actions.

A number of public safety representatives reported, as illustrated by the summarized and excerpted responses below, that they had long engaged in political pressure tactics but had discontinued them because arbitration is more acceptable than the "begging" they traditionally had engaged in. There does not appear to be any common characteristic among parties who have either continued to use or discontinued their use of outside channels of persuasion, nor has the transition from conventional to final-offer arbitration had any impact on such changes.

One firefighter unit learned that petitioning the public simultaneously with arbitration can backfire. The firefighters went to arbitration to retain parity with police. They became concerned that they would lose the issue in arbitration and embarked simultaneously on a petition drive and voter referendum on parity. The arbitrator awarded the maintenance of parity, but the public voted against them. As a consequence, they lost parity.

. . . No matter how high the cost of arbitration, it is worth it because it allows us to attain our goals with "our heads held high." (*Union Spokesman*)

. . . We gave up informal appeals because they were no longer fruitful. Management's negotiating team has become too sophisticated to make such actions effective, and they have persuaded the city council not to undercut them. (*Police Negotiator*)

. . . It is unreasonable and inequitable for us to receive benefits of collective bargaining and then put political pressure on city councilmen to obtain benefits that we traded away or could not justify at the table. (*Firefighter Representative*)

Preparation for Negotiations. A majority of both management and union spokesmen said they do not prepare for negotiations any differently under final-offer than they had under a conventional arbitration impasse system. Arbitration itself, however, has required both sides to prepare more intensely and carefully than they had prior to arbitration. On the management side, approximately half of the negotiators reported that in recent years they had taken an offensive rather than a purely reactive posture in negotiations. About one-third of management negotiators stated that they are now taking "very aggressive stands" in collective bargaining. In no case, however, was this change in management's posture attributed to the change from conventional to final-offer arbitration.

Several cities report that in addition to traditional statistical research for negotiations, they also engage in an intensive survey among administrators and council officials to obtain managerial collective bargaining demands. They believe this enables them in negotiations to discuss trade-offs between union and management demands rather than simply bartering over the size of the package to be given their unions.

. . . I put numerous demands on the collective bargaining table not because I seriously think I can achieve them but simply to have the table "laden with goodies for the arbitrator to use in stuffing the union stocking." (*Management Negotiator*)

. . . Management's aggressive stance in collective bargaining can be used to their disadvantage. They put all sorts of "demands" on the table that they could have implemented unilaterally under the management rights clause. We quickly accepted them, thus putting them within the contract where they can be negotiated and perhaps even taken to arbitration in the future if we desire. (*Firefighter Spokesman*)

On the union side, the major general impact of arbitration on preparation for bargaining has been an increasing reliance on attorneys, both to counsel the union in negotiations and as spokesmen in arbitration proceedings. A number of union representatives believe that the trend toward increasing reliance on attorneys has been intensified by the institution of final-offer arbitration simply because inexperienced and small locals need expert guidance as to a reasonable final offer that is likely to receive neutral acceptance in arbitration. Nevertheless, many union spokesmen decried this development, as illustrated by these summarized and excerpted responses:

The use of attorneys in arbitration proceedings has increased their formality and contributed both to the length and cost of proceedings. Moreover, this causes local union representatives and the rank and file to feel powerless in the determination of their wages and working conditions.

. . . We use attorneys in arbitration because most of the arbitrators are lawyers and "it takes one to talk to one." (*Union Spokesman*)

Labor lawyers themselves and bargaining representatives in large cities appear more resigned than enthusiastic about the increasing use of attorneys to represent unions in bargaining and arbitration. They nevertheless believe that the complexity of municipal law makes attorneys essential. Moreover, while using attorneys is expensive, the quality of the contracts obtained and awards received "makes the costs worth it."

. . . Our negotiating relationship has improved considerably since the union hired an attorney for negotiations. Objectivity and reason have replaced acrimony. (*Management Spokesman*)

. . . Both we and the union agreed later that the hostility between our respective attorneys had worsened the negotiating relationship. In one case, the hostility of attorneys resulted in an unnecessary arbitration proceeding. (*Management Spokesman*)

In general, it appears that reliance on outside counsel is increasing but is viewed by many parties as a necessary evil.

The Parties' Willingness to Make Concessions. An underlying premise of final-offer arbitration lies in its hoped-for beneficial impact on negotiations. The hypothesis is that given the strictures of a zero-sum game—that is, I win, you lose, or vice versa—each party will be inclined to minimize its likelihood of losing. Thus, each will tend to make new offers narrowing the difference between them and ultimately coming so close together that they will settle without recourse to arbitration at all. This hoped-for benefit of final-offer arbitration has not occurred thus far in Michigan.

During the last 18 months of the conventional arbitration statute as well as during the first 18 months of final-offer, the number of arbitration petitions received by MERC remained almost constant—about 7 per month. These statistical results are explained in our questionnaire responses and interviews. At least half, and often far more, of the respective representatives of cities, counties, and the three public safety organizations felt that final-offer arbitration had not increased their likelihood to compromise or to make concessions in negotiations.

Among negotiators with experience in conventional arbitration but who have yet to negotiate under the final-offer statute, the preponderance of opinion was that while the theory of final-offer might appear sound, they did not think it at all likely that the other party to their negotiations would become more realistic. So far as their own bargaining positions were concerned, they generally felt they were already realistic and therefore final-offer could have no impact upon them. No consensus is apparent among negotiators who have actually negotiated since the final-offer amendment became effective. Some felt that the statute had had no impact. Two who felt the statute had had a beneficial impact nevertheless reported that they still went to arbitration.

> . . . Final-offer had no impact. We went to arbitration as before. The arbitrator remanded the issues to us for further negotiations, however, and because we were both apprehensive about what he would do, we settled. (*City Spokesman*)

> . . . Management gave our proposals more serious consideration than they would have without final-offer arbitration and was more willing to discuss certain areas which they had refused to negotiate in previous years. We decreased our demands as well. We nevertheless wound up in arbitration. (*Union Spokesman*)

> . . . Final-offer by issue does not put any real pressure on unions. They can still take unreasonable fringe benefit demands to arbitration knowing that even if they lose them their wage position will not be in jeopardy. (*Management Spokesman*)

> . . . Firefighters are more difficult negotiating adversaries than police. They have a strong international organization, they live together in the fire station and plan negotiating strategy, and they have more free time to prepare for negotiations. Moreover, firefighters' insistence upon obtaining or maintaining parity with police is an issue which almost inevitably leads to arbitration. (*Management Spokesman*)

Many management representatives, some with and some without arbitration experience, praised the unions with whom they dealt for their willingness to bargain in a serious and conciliatory fashion. We cannot be sure that this reflects a favorable influence of final-offer arbitration since we have no comparable attitudes from the earlier period. It may be, however, that this management judgment does reflect a beneficial impact of the new procedure. Finally, as will be discussed in greater detail subsequently, the flexibility of the Michigan statute permits the parties to anticipate the possibility of continued negotiations during the arbitration proceeding. As a result, the parties are under less pressure to make their final concessions before their hearing begins than they would be under a more rigid procedure.

The Parties' Ability to Innovate. There was complete lack of consensus among parties as to whether final-offer affects their ability to innovate. Moreover, on this issue there was a somewhat higher than normal tendency toward "no opinion." This lack of consensus or opinion is present whether or not a party had had experience with final-offer arbitration. Some experienced union negotiators believed that final-offer severely limits their ability to innovate because of the conservatism of arbitrators. Others with equal experience with final-offer could not see that the process had had any impact upon their ability to introduce new patterns and settlements.

Both experienced and inexperienced negotiators stated, in effect, "We'll try anything reasonable, and up to now, we have no reason to believe that it won't work."

. . . How can one innovate when the name of the game is comparability? (*Union Spokesman*)

. . . Final-offer will make it easier for us to win and set new patterns in economics. Management always takes "ridiculous positions" on wages. I think, as a result, that under final-offer we can win an economic award which the arbitrator would undoubtedly reduce or compromise if we were in conventional arbitration. (*Employee Representative*)

Recurrent Arbitration. Virtually none among those whom we interviewed felt that the final-offer statute fundamentally would influence their forthcoming negotiations or increase their likelihood of going to arbitration. Those parties who had generally been successful in settling their differences without third-party intervention in the past anticipated the same for the future. Those who had frequently or regularly gone to arbitration expected that they would do so again. Interestingly, a number of management representatives anticipated that they might have to go to arbitration only because of the difficulty of "selling" a reasonable settlement to the board or council to which they report. These negotiators often feel that they could settle relatively easily with their unions if they had full negotiating authority, but faced with the necessity of obtaining council or board approval, arbitration commonly becomes their alternative.

Several of the larger cities in Michigan go to arbitration with both police and firefighters in almost every round of negotiations. In one city, a strong mayor's hostility to public employee unions generally and to their recurrent opposition to him at the polls appears to be the major reason for repeated arbitration. In the remainder of these recurrent-user situations, the problem is both political and financial. These cities' tax bases are eroded, their costs are skyrocketing, their budgets are already deeply pared, and their reserves are gone. Hence, increased labor costs for public safety employees almost inevitably entail layoffs of other city employees and/or a reduction in public services. The political costs of a voluntary negotiated agreement with such consequences are too high. City management is thus forced to go to arbitration in order to be able to defend its settlement as having been forced upon it. Given such parameters, it appears likely that any procedure of statutory arbitration would be used, no matter how risky or unpalatable the procedure might appear.

The Impact of Final-Offer Arbitration on Mediation and Arbitration Procedures

In theory, final-offer arbitration should stimulate mediated settlements. If the parties in mediation realize that their next step is third-party selection of their final offers, one might assume that each would be intent on framing a final offer in the most realistic and attractive terms. It would seem that a mediator would be particularly helpful and persuasive in moving them toward settlement in such an atmosphere. Some mediators have reported to us that this is the case. Our interviews, however, are remarkably unanimous: Mediation as the parties have evaluated it since the final-offer amendment has been largely a waste of time.

It should be noted, however, that MERC statistics contradict this point of view. The MERC chairman stated, "Since January 1, 1973, when last offer arbitration began, there have been an estimated 285 cases submitted to mediation. During that same period, 120 cases were submitted to arbitration. There have been 14 awards. The mediation-arbitration concept has not eroded the effectiveness of [state] mediation." [20]

We were often told, however, that mediators now hold only one or two fruitless and pro forma meetings and then give up, which leaves the parties no closer to settlement than before. In part, this management and union response regarding a general futility of mediation may be due to the fact that our interview sample was designedly weighted toward bargaining relationships in which arbitration, or at least a petition for arbitration, had taken place. The sample even included a few relationships "addicted" to arbitration. It is likely that there are many negotiating relationships in Michigan in which mediation is making a significant contribution to negotiated settlements even in the presence of statutory final-offer arbitration. Our respondents told us of very few such situations, however, even in those relationships in which no petition for arbitration had ever been filed. Each of the views excerpted below was expressed by several respondents in similar positions.

. . . Mediator effectiveness declined with the beginning of the enactment of the compulsory arbitration statute in 1969. Prior to arbitration, mediators had been aggressive and persistent. After arbitration their approach has been defeatist—a few perfunctory meetings heading directly toward impasse. (*Management Negotiators*)

. . . Mediation is still useful with very inexperienced parties whose positions are not realistic and who go into mediation a long way from "rock bottom." Where these circumstances are not present, mediators can do little for us when the arbitration alternative is available. (*Management Negotiators*)

. . . We have a good relationship and a very able mediator whom all of us trusted. As a consequence, he was able to reduce the number of issues significantly, and we reached agreement. (Management, Police, and Firefighter Negotiators from the Same City)

. . . Too many mediators are glorified messenger boys, carrying each parties' proposals to the other. Too few mediators come up with their own suggestions for settlement which they push aggressively. (*Management Representatives*)

Several experienced and thoughtful negotiators suggested an improvement in impasse procedures, which they believe would strengthen the mediation process. If the mediators were given some of the authority now given by the existing statute to the arbitrator—either by allowing the mediator to certify an impasse, by allowing the mediator to certify the issues to go to arbitration, or, most importantly, by giving the mediators specific authority to certify the only final offers of the parties to be considered by the arbitration panel—mediation would again become an important part of the settlement process.

There was universal agreement among our respondents that a voluntary negotiated settlement is far superior to any arbitration award. As a consequence, most of our respondents did not oppose the arbitrator's allowing, suggesting, or requiring that negotiations be continued at some point during the arbitration process. Many were perfectly willing to have the arbitrator mediate. This opinion was not universal, however.

The parties were in agreement that arbitrators generally mediate or at least are willing to do so. The possibility was suggested that nonlawyer arbitrators are somewhat more likely to mediate than practicing attorneys. Several negotiators—representatives of both management and unions— discussed favorably arbitration proceedings in which the neutral arbitrator mediated a reduction in the number of issues in dispute and even a total settlement. A minority of those whom we interviewed, but among them some very experienced practitioners, wholly disapproved of an arbitrator's mediating. Some among this latter group distinguished between the arbitrator's mediating personally and his using his partisan panel members as quasi-mediators. They suggested that if he mediated between his panel members and then allowed the panel members to encourage settlement discussions between the parties, this would be perfectly satisfactory.

. . . I have had two completely satisfactory mediation-arbitration experiences. Some issues were mediated to settlement prior to the hearing, and a number of others were settled in mediation in executive sessions subsequent to the hearing. In both cases no awards were necessary. (*Management Negotiator*)

. . . Even though we were in final-offer arbitration over a 1½ percent wage difference, the arbitrator kept prodding us to compromise and settle. We did, and although the settlement was slightly in management's favor, I still approve of any procedure which results in a voluntary settlement. (*Police Negotiator*)

. . . In our final-offer proceeding, the arbitrator drew up a "tentative award" and encouraged us to modify our positions to approximate his formulation. We were able to settle on this basis. (*Management Negotiator*)

. . . Mediation by the arbitrator is "mediation with a hammer." (*County Negotiator*)

. . . During the arbitration proceeding, the panel never seemed willing to decide anything and instead continually prodded us to discuss our positions with each other. Initially, I was very dissatisfied. Ultimately, however, we did reach our own settlement on all issues and "that's the name of the game." (*Police Negotiator*)

. . . We shouldn't kid ourselves. There is nothing voluntary about a settlement reached "under an arbitrator's gun." It forces us either to compromise more than we should, or, if we refuse to compromise as he suggests, we look bad and then he may decide against us. Either way, we lose. (*Experienced Negotiator*)

. . . Arbitrators mediate both because they like unanimous awards and because they don't like to make final-offer awards they consider inequitable. But arbitration was not intended to please the arbitrator and make him popular. "If he's unhappy, that's just too bad." (*Several Negotiators*)

A majority of those whom we interviewed felt the present statutory imprecision as to when the final offer must be made is perfectly satisfactory in that it leaves open the possibility of settlement during the arbitration proceeding. A decided minority, but one that includes a number of experienced negotiators who have been involved in final-offer arbitration, were insistent that the final offer should be made in writing at the outset of the arbitration hearing if not before. The difference between the two views is fundamentally the same as the differing views of mediation by the arbitrator expressed in the preceding section.

. . . I approve of allowing the arbitrator to decide when the final offers must be made. In one situation the hearing was held, the arbitrator made comments on the issues before him, and then remanded the issues to us for negotiations. He told us that our final offers should be made in writing at the end of three weeks if we were not able to settle. We settled. (*Management Spokesman*)

. . . It is outrageous to allow the arbitrators to accept "new final offers" throughout the proceeding. If we had gone to arbitration on our final offers as they stood at the outset of the proceeding, we clearly would have won; but since he allowed the union to keep making new and lower offers, we had to keep coming up, and thus we spent far more than we should have had to under what should be the rules of the final-offer game. (*Management Negotiator*)

The Impact of Final-Offer Arbitration on Awards

Management representatives generally anticipated that final-offer arbitration would increase the size of economic awards. Union negotiators were split on this issue: One-third of them believed that final-offer would increase the size of the awards, one-third believed it would decrease them, and one-third anticipated no change.

. . . Settlements will be smaller under final-offer because arbitrators are generally extremely conservative and will go with management if their final offer is anywhere near the ballpark. (*Several Union Spokesmen*)

. . . Arbitrators want to please the greatest number. Because they deal with affiliates of statewide union organizations repeatedly and the same governmental units rarely more than once, they will tend to go with the unions more often than not. (*Several Management Representatives*)

. . . We will see what appear to be excessively high awards under the new final-offer procedure. This is not a fair evaluation of the final-offer procedure itself, however, but simply a reflection of spiraling inflation and the general tendency of arbitrators to minimize ability to pay arguments in such times. (*Experienced Management Spokesman*)

. . . The awards under final-offer will be lower. This is not due to the procedure itself, however, but rather to the fact that there was a "catch-up" period under conventional arbitration which is now generally over. (*Experienced Police Negotiator*)

. . . Settlement under final-offer will be higher than under conventional arbitration. Under conventional, management would retreat to an unreasonably low position, at worst risking a compromise. As a result, unions sometimes got less than they had been offered at the table. Under final-offer, management must make at least a reasonable offer or risk losing everything, and thus settlements will be higher. (*Several Union and Management Negotiators*)

Among those who anticipated that final-offer would have no impact on the size of economic settlements, the reason most commonly given by both union and management spokesmen was that under the Michigan statute the arbitrator can award wages to one party and fringes to the other, thereby splitting the difference and making the total cost impact stay within the range deemed appropriate by the arbitrator at any given point in time.

Alternative Impasse Procedures

Five groups of respondents—city and county officials, and police, firefighter, and deputy sheriff representatives—were asked to indicate their rank order of preference among five different forms of impasse resolution procedures. The choices were strikes, factfinding, conventional arbitration, final-offer by issue, and final-offer by package.

The only choice on which there was consensus among all five groups was on the issue of legalizing the right to strike: A clear majority of all parties ranked this alternative last. While there was considerable overlap between management and union representatives in their reasons for concluding that strikes were not an acceptable form of impasse resolution among public safety officers, there were also some very different perspectives.

. . . The public is too greatly hurt by public safety employee strikes. (*Consensus*)

. . . Public safety officers are more powerful than other organized groups of public employees. To allow public safety officers to strike would allow them to clean out the till. (*Several Representatives of Both Sides*)

. . . Strikes would not take place even if legalized. If the employees faced losing wages, they would get down to serious negotiations as the strike deadline loomed. (*Several Management Representatives*)

. . . If these men could only strike! Then we could let them sit and rot. (*County Management Representative*)

. . . The legal ability to strike, without the interference of the state, would bring about fair settlements and gain the attention of the public. (*Deputy Sheriff Representative*)

. . . Strikes would take place but would pose no serious problem because we have readied detailed strike plans and have reserve units. (*Several Large-City Management Representatives*)

. . .. Legalization of strikes would not help us because the modern professional and dedicated public safety officer would continue to perform his duty no matter how unfairly dealt with. Besides, the membership was divided as to whether or not our last walkout had been worth the trouble. (*Union Spokesman*)

Factfinding was clearly the preferred impasse resolution technique among management representatives. They supported it due to its voluntary aspect. Unions generally opposed factfinding as of little value and ranked it low on their list of preferences.

Conventional arbitration was the preferred alternative form of dispute resolution among all groups of union respondents; it was the second choice of county managements. They believe that arbitrators should be given the discretion to construct a fair economic package. Negotiators from both union and management sides who prefer conventional arbitration may be somewhat inexperienced and willing to defer to an arbitrator's more experienced and objective point of view. There were, however, a few extremely experienced negotiators who, if forced to go to arbitration, seemed confident of the good sense of the arbitrators with whom they had had experience.

As only to be expected, respondents who were satisfied with conventional arbitration dislike final-offer, and it is therefore the overall third choice among all respondents. Interestingly enough, while neither city management nor city union negotiators make final-offer by issue their first choice, it is the second choice among all city negotiators on either side of the bargaining table. Only county and deputy sheriff representatives, often the least experienced respondents in our sample, put it farther down on the list.

The large majority of our respondents consider final-offer by whole package the next worst choice to strikes. A small group of management representatives listed it first, however. Their overriding theme was that final-offer by package is desirable in that it reduces arbitral discretion. Each of the views excerpted below were expressed by several respondents.

. . . All economic proposals are made contingent upon acceptance of other economic proposals. To allow arbitrators to pick and choose among them is illogical. (*Experienced Negotiators*)

. . . Final-offer by package would force realistic negotiators and the dropping of superfluous proposals. (*City Negotiators*)

. . . Final-offer by package would allow us to make inroads upon management rights. By making our economic package "irresistible," we could slip in a clause reducing management's rights which we could never attain in negotiations or conventional arbitration. (*Union Negotiators*)

. . . Final-offer by package is particularly dangerous for unions. We might be forced for political reasons to leave in a proposal the leadership knew to be a "loser" and thus risk losing everything. (*Union Negotiators*)

The Parties' Suggestions for Improving Impasse
Resolution Techniques

The parties' suggestions for change in the present procedures fall into two general categories: (1) suggestions to toughen the impasse procedures with the intent of discouraging their use, and (2) suggestions to make the present procedure more palatable.

Most of the suggestions to toughen the impasse resolution procedures have already been mentioned. Among these are requiring that final offers be made during mediation or requiring that final offers be made in writing prior to arbitration with no modification permitted. Finally, of course, those who favored this general idea favored a shift from final-offer-by-issue to final-offer-by-package.

Among those who would like to make the present procedure more tolerable, the main complaint was from unions and involved the cost of arbitration. Some management representatives too were concerned about the cost of arbitration, but this was ordinarily a secondary consideration with them. Among the suggestions made to ameliorate the cost impact were to have the state pay the full cost of arbitration, allow the mediators to arbitrate, or to adjust the arbitrator's total fee on some basis related to ability to pay, such as size of city or bargaining unit.

Finally, a number of both union and management representatives contend that arbitrators too often possess insufficient understanding of the local situation. They assert that arbitrators do not fully understand the nature of either police or firefighters' jobs and suggest that arbitrators be required to specialize among public safety employee groups. Management representatives, on the other hand, would require that arbitrators be given special training in municipal finance.

Tentative Conclusions

The Michigan three-year experiment with final-offer arbitration is only half over. At the time this study was completed, fewer than 25 final-offer arbitration awards had been rendered. Many public safety negotiating parties, because they are working under more than one-year contracts, have yet to renegotiate under the final-offer impasse procedure provided for in the amended statute. Under these circumstances, judgment as to the effectiveness of the statute and its impact upon negotiations must necessarily be tentative, and the conclusions that follow may have to be modified in the light of future developments.

The Effectiveness of the Statute

Legislated interest arbitration, whether conventional or final-offer, is a device to resolve impasses in negotiations. This fact tends to obscure the underlying purpose of an arbitration statute—that is, to provide some equality of bargaining power between negotiating parties where there is no right to strike. Viewed in the light of this purpose, the Michigan statute is clearly successful. Collective bargaining relationships, many of considerable maturity, have been established with public safety officers in the vast majority of the larger cities and counties in Michigan. In most of these relationships, the parties are able repeatedly and successfully to negotiate agreements that are deemed by both to be reasonably fair and equitable.

Settlement of negotiations by the parties themselves, with or without mediation, is still the rule rather than the exception. After five years of experience under mandated binding arbitration, in over half of the public safety negotiating relationships in Michigan no petition for arbitration has ever been filed. In over two-thirds of these relationships, no arbitration award has ever been rendered. Under these circumstances, it is clear that a rough equality of bargaining power has been created between most organized public safety officers and their employers. It is equally clear that the possibility of arbitration has not eroded significantly the ability of the large majority of these parties in most of their negotiations to settle amicably upon terms and conditions of employment.

It is equally clear, however, that the substitution of binding final-offer arbitration on each economic issue for conventional arbitration has not significantly discouraged recourse to arbitration. Where parties have traditionally been able to reach their own agreements without third-party intervention other than mediation, they have continued to do so. Where parties, usually for political reasons, have become "addicted" to arbitration, they continue to go to final-offer arbitration as frequently as they went to conventional arbitration. Those parties who normally negotiate their agreements themselves but occasionally go to arbitration continue to do so at only a slightly lower rate than before. On balance, it does not appear that the final-offer variant in Michigan has had any major impact on either the frequency of settlements or the likelihood of impasses requiring arbitration.

Final-offer arbitration of each economic issue does not appear to have reduced significantly the number of issues the parties take to arbitration. In half of the first 14 awards rendered under the final-offer amendment, 15 or more issues were submitted to the arbitration panel. The average number of issues per case in which awards have been rendered is 12,[21] which figure is almost identical with the average number taken to arbitration under the Michigan conventional arbitration statute.[22] To the extent that it was originally theorized that final-offer arbitration would at least reduce the necessity for awards except on the most intractable and toughest issues, the promise of the theory has not been borne out in practice.

One of the major unanswered questions regarding final-offer arbitration is in regard to its impact upon the size of arbitrated settlements. Nothing in our questionnaire or in our interviews casts great light on this issue. A slight preponderance of our respondents and interviewees believed it likely that awards would be higher under final-offer arbitration than under conventional arbitration, but nearly as many believed that settlements under final-offer would be either lower or not appreciably different than under conventional arbitration.

A major complaint about arbitration made by many union representatives, and by some management representatives as a secondary consideration, is that it costs too much. In Michigan, the two parties and the state divide by thirds the costs of the proceedings and of the neutral arbitrator. The average fee for arbitration to each party in the first 14 cases of final-offer arbitration was $664.[23] This kind of arbitration fee to each party does not seem excessive, although it might appear so to small cities and bargaining units of only a half-dozen members. Finally on this subject, we are aware that arbitral fees are not the only costs of arbitration to the parties. We have noted an increasing reliance upon attorneys to present arbitration cases, which probably more than doubles the total cost, at least to parties who do not have staff counsel. Even if allowance for this cost is made, it is our judgment that arbitration is still less costly to units of government or to employees than the strike alternative.

Of course an arbitration statute has the ultimate purpose of providing an acceptable procedure for dispute resolution without disruption of vital services. During the 39 months of conventional arbitration in Michigan, there were no strikes by firefighters and only a few by police. All but one of these were of short duration and only one was against an arbitration award. There have been no strikes, work stoppages, or significant job actions by public safety officers since the final-offer amendment was adopted.[e] By this test of statutory effectiveness, final-offer arbitration by economic issue has fared well—although no claim of causality is advanced.

Arbitration and Continuing Negotiations

The most significant change in the observable data since the final-offer amendment was made to the conventional arbitration statute is that the number of cases settled after a petition for arbitration has been filed has increased substantially. This does not appear to be related to the change in procedure, but is believed to be a consequence of the increased sophistication of the parties who now may be less likely to allow the statutory time limits for filing for arbitration to interfere with their continuing search for agreement. The number of situations in which a settlement has been reached after the arbitrator has been selected or appointed has also increased in the past year.[24]

This high rate of settlement once the arbitration proceeding has begun—56 percent of the final-offer cases according to the most recent data—almost undoubtedly results from the flexibility of the Michigan statute

---

[e] A slowdown and ticket-writing strike of Detroit police reported during June and July 1974 was not related to collective bargaining but to employee dissatisfaction with departmental reorganization.

with regard to the timing of final offers. It is clear that many Michigan parties view the arbitration hearings as a continuation of the negotiating process, and arbitrators therefore mediate during the proceeding, either directly or through the partisan panel members. The statutory amendment, which permits the panel to remand a dispute for up to three weeks of further negotiations after the hearing has begun, has added further flexibility to the procedure and also tends to encourage negotiated settlements.

A few experienced representatives of the parties decry these developments and insist that once an arbitration hearing has begun, an award is the only appropriate outcome. Most parties, however, and the arbitrators themselves prefer settlements to awards. As a consequence, the arbitrators commonly use all of their skills and every available opportunity to bring about settlements.

Flexible versus Rigid Procedures

Some Michigan parties oppose the flexibility of the Michigan procedures and contend that final-offer should be as rigid and harsh as it can possibly be made in order to discourage resort to arbitration. Among the suggestions that have been made to achieve this end are that final offers should be by total package rather than by issue, that both economic and noneconomic issues should be part of the package, that there should be only one final offer from each party, that this final offer should be submitted in writing before the hearing begins, that arbitration should be by a single neutral rather than by a tripartite panel, that the neutral should be precluded from mediating, and that the neutral's decision should consist solely of an award without written or oral reasoning supporting it.[25] To some degree, this is the philosophy and procedure followed in Wisconsin.

The Future of Arbitration

Several commentators have suggested that the flexible Michigan procedures—which permit continued negotiations through change of offers during the arbitration proceeding and the fact that final-offer-by-issue permits the arbitration panel to create a sort of equitable "package"—mean that this final-offer system is not really different from conventional arbitration. They claim that the flexibility permitted in the timing of final offers means that the parties are not forced to a realistic position during direct negotiations since they anticipate the possibility of further changes in position during the arbitration proceeding. No doubt this is sometimes true, but it does not lead to the conclusion that final-offer in Michigan is fundamentally the same procedure as conventional arbitration.

The two procedures differ particularly in the extent to which they facilitate mediation by the neutral arbitrator. Under conventional arbitration, the neutral might attempt mediation, but the parties were free to refuse to move since they knew that the arbitrator would be likely to make an award somewhere in between their respective positions. Under final-offer on each economic issue, if the neutral hints to the parties or suggests to his partisan panel members that if their side does not move he may feel obliged to award the final offer of the other, all but the most recalcitrant or gamblers among negotiators must change position. This general proposition is supported by the data shown in Table 3-3. Negotiated settlements after the arbitration proceeding has been initiated have jumped from 39 percent under conventional arbitration to 64 percent under final-offer.

Once the parties begin to amend their positions during the arbitration proceeding or during the permissible period of remand to the parties, it is very likely that they will reach a negotiated settlement. Moreover, in some very mature and sophisticated relationships, there is a tendency for a party who is convinced that his final offer will "win" to continue bargaining nevertheless and to modify his final offer slightly if a negotiated settlement thereby becomes possible. The rationale for such movement is that settlement by joint agreement rather than award is healthy for the long-run relationship and is worth paying some price to achieve.

Final-offer on each economic issue in Michigan is fundamentally different from conventional arbitration in that mediation-arbitration is not only possible but is far more likely to be effective in leading to a negotiated settlement. The semicoercive nature of mediation-arbitration is not denied, but many parties regard it as a lesser evil than a settlement by an award over which they have no real control.[26]

In general, under the flexible Michigan final-offer procedures, the experience of the public safety negotiating parties has been good. Most negotiators seem to accept the arbitration system grudgingly but without overwhelming hostility. Just as binding arbitration of grievances was frequently strongly resisted in the public sector only a decade ago and now is often taken for granted, binding interest arbitration now appears to be slowly gaining acceptance.

Notes

1. Act 312 of Michigan Public Acts of 1969.
2. Act 127 of Michigan Public Acts of 1972.
3. We are indebted for some of this history to Mollie H. Bowers, "A Study of Legislated Arbitration in the Public Safety Services in Michigan and Pennsylvania," unpublished Ph.D. thesis, (Ithaca, N.Y.: Cornell University, 1973).

4. Act 336 of Michigan Public Acts of 1947.

5. Act 379 of Michigan Public Acts of 1965.

6. See Bowers, "A Study of Legislated Arbitration. . . ." In 1966, Pontiac police withheld their services for 32 hours. In 1967, Detroit police suffered a two-day "blue flu" epidemic. In the same year, the firefighters in Lansing struck for almost three days, and the strike was ended only after personal intervention by the governor and a specially appointed mediator. A year later, Pontiac firefighters again resorted to several job actions, including picket lines around city hall. In Kalamazoo, eight months of unsuccessful negotiations resulted in a one-week strike that led to the discharge of the entire 150-man fire department. In one dispute, firemen engaged in a wildcat strike. When a fire began, they returned to the firehouses only to find themselves locked out by the mayor and displaced by the police.

7. 380 Mich. 314, 157 N.W.2d 206 (1968).

8. *Government Employee Relations Report (GERR)*, May 15, 1969, P. G-1.

9. Robert G. Howlett, "Arbitration in the Public Sector," in *Proceedings of the Southwestern Legal Foundation,* 15th Annual Institute of Labor Law (1969), p. 244.

10. *GERR,* May 22, p. B-9.

11. Unpublished draft of testimony of Russell A. Smith and Meyer S. Ryder before the legislative committees, Ann Arbor, 1971.

12. *Police Officers Association of Dearborn v. City of Dearborn,* 14 Mich. App. 51, 201 N.W.2d 650 (1972).

13. Police-Fire Fighters Arbitration Act (PFFA), Act 312 of Michigan Public Acts of 1969, as amended by Act 127 of Michigan Public Acts of 1972.

14. *Dearborn School District v. Labor Mediation Board,* 22 Mich. App. 22, 177 N.W.2d 196 (1970).

15. *Hillsdale Community Schools v. Labor Mediation Board,* 24 Mich. App. 36, 179 N.W.2d 661 (1970).

16. *City of Manistee v. Manistee Fire Fighters et al.,* Circuit Court for the County of Manistee, File 1323, October 26, 1971.

17. *Police Officers Association of Dearborn v. City of Dearborn,* 14 Mich. App. 51, 201 N.W.2d 650 (1972).

18. *Detroit Police Officers Association v. City of Detroit et al.,* 391 Mich. 44, 214 N.W.2d 803 (1974).

19. *Smigel v. Southgate Community School District,* 388 Mich. 531, 202 N.W.2d 305 (1972).

20. Robert G. Howlett, "Experience with Last Offer Arbitration—Michigan," paper delivered at the Annual Meeting, Association of Labor Mediation Agencies, July 31, 1974, pp. 3-4.

21. Howlett, "Experience with Last Offer . . . ," p. 4.

22. See Bowers, "A Study of Legislated Arbitration. . . ."

23. See Howlett, "Experience with Last Offer . . . ," p. 6.

24. Howlett, "Summary of Last Offer Awards," appended to "Experience with Last Offer . . . ," p. 10.

25. For an excellent summary of the arguments for this type of procedure, see Arnold M. Zack, "Final Offer Selection—Panacea or Pandora's Box," *New York Law Forum* 19 (Summer 1974), pp. 567-85.

26. See Harry Pollard, "Mediation-Arbitration: A Trade Union View," *Monthly Labor Review* 96 (September 1973), pp. 63-65, and Lawrence P. Corbett, "Mediation-Arbitration from the Employer's Standpoint," *Monthly Labor Review* 96 (December 1973), pp. 52-53.

4

The Wisconsin Arbitration Experience

In 1972, after approximately a decade of experience with factfinding recommendations as the final step in the resolution of disputes about the terms of new agreements, Wisconsin turned to final-offer arbitration of those disputes involving public safety officers—that is, firefighters and law enforcement officers, including city police, county deputy sheriffs, and traffic officers. In this chapter, the historical developments leading to the passage of the legislation are reviewed briefly, the statute and administrative regulations are described, and the extent of third-party involvement in bargaining is examined. Then, the impact of the statute upon the process and outcome of bargaining is analyzed by using information obtained from interviews with union and management representatives and arbitrators who participated in the resolution of disputes under this procedure. Finally, the impact of the statute on the outcome of bargaining is analyzed using regression analysis supplemented by the results of interviews with the parties.

From Factfinding to Arbitration: 1962-1972

In the 1962-72 period, factfinding with recommendations was the terminal step of the impasse procedure covering municipal employees and was used extensively by firefighters and law enforcement officers.[1] However, the law enforcement personnel were specifically excluded from the definition of municipal employees in the statute and, therefore, did not have full bargaining rights, such as the right to petition for representation elections and the right to file "prohibited" practice charges (the Wisconsin euphemism for what are called "unfair" labor practices in most other jurisdictions).[2] They were able to gain access to factfinding only because the statute had a special provision stating that when a majority of members of a police, sheriff, or county traffic department petitioned for changes in wages, hours, or working conditions, disputes arising from such petitions were subject to the factfinding procedure.[3]

During the first part of this decade, law enforcement officers and firefighters were relatively pleased with the results of factfinding. Firefighters used the procedure to achieve substantial reductions in hours; law enforcement officers regarded the factfinding procedure as the first step toward full bargaining rights and found the third-party recommendations helpful to them in their quest for higher wages.

By 1970 the situation had changed, and both firefighters and law enforcement officers sought modifications in the bargaining statute. They argued that some city managements had not fully complied with factfinding recommendations and that binding arbitration should be substituted as the procedure for resolving impasses between their organizations and their public employers. The law enforcement officers also were pressing for full bargaining rights. Two-day firefighter strikes in Madison in 1968 and 1969 and a five-day strike in Racine in 1970 occasioned a good deal of discussion in newspapers and gave added impetus to the idea that firefighter strikes could be avoided if the demand of the public safety employees for arbitration were granted.

Development of the New Statute

In 1972, after the election of a new governor who was sympathetic to the views of the police and firefighter organizations as well as to those of other public employee unions seeking changes in the law, the labor relations statute was substantially revised.[4] All unions supported and were successful in achieving the replacement of "meet and confer" language with a duty-to-bargain clause and the replacement of the ban on compulsory union membership with an agency shop provision. In addition, various groups favored, and obtained, other changes in the statute that applied to problems unique to their particular occupations.

Except for the organizations of firefighters and law enforcement officers, the public sector unions would have preferred to have the right to strike. However, since they feared that this objective was not politically attainable, they decided to support instead the retention of factfinding in the statute—not because they thought so highly of it, but because they thought it might prove less restrictive if they decided to engage in industrial action in preference to third-party adjudication. Thus, when the 1972 statute was being drafted, the firefighter and police organizations, as the only ones that would be affected by the arbitration provisions, took the leadership in formulating the type of procedure that they thought should and could be enacted.

Separate Treatment for Milwaukee. Political rivalries within the police and firefighter groups led originally to the adoption of one arbitration statute for the Milwaukee police and another for all other law enforcement personnel in the State of Wisconsin and for all firefighters, including the

Milwaukee unit. The Milwaukee police opted for conventional arbitration in 1972 and continued their preference for it in 1973 when the law was amended in several respects.

The Milwaukee firefighters were successful in obtaining an amendment in 1973 that exempted them from coverage under the final-offer arbitration provision and left them subject to factfinding, along with many non-public safety employees. The ultimate result was the creation of three somewhat different systems for the resolution of interest disputes of Wisconsin public safety employees.

One explanation for the seemingly backward step of the Milwaukee firefighters was that they were contemplating the possibility of striking at the end of 1973 in support of demands for a new agreement, and they believed that continued coverage by the arbitration provision would make it more difficult politically to exercise that option.[a]

The police and firefighter units, other than those in the City of Milwaukee, and the deputy sheriff units throughout the state, including Milwaukee County, followed the leadership of the state organizations of the International Association of Fire Fighters (IAFF) and the independent Wisconsin Professional Policemen's Association (WPPA) in support of the unique form of arbitration adopted by Wisconsin.

Why Final-Offer Arbitration?   The decision to adopt the little known and untried system of final-offer arbitration rather than conventional arbitration is attributable primarily to the preference for it expressed by the Madison-based IAFF vice president, Edward Durkin,[5] who was a leader in the coalition of public employee unions seeking passage of the legislation.[6] He was able to persuade leaders of the WPPA and his fellow firefighter leaders that this variant of arbitration should be given preferred status in the Wisconsin statute they were supporting.[7]

Final-offer arbitration was viewed by Durkin and many other IAFF and WPPA leaders as a means of forcing city management to bargain seriously with them. They believed that its all-or-nothing consequences would bring greater pressure to bear on management to make offers that would provide the basis for settlement through direct negotiation than would conventional arbitration. It should be noted that this presumed effect of final-offer arbitration applies to both sides of the bargaining table and that union bargainers would be subject to the same type of pressures that they wished to place on management.

---

[a] Wisconsin Employment Relations Commission records show that Milwaukee fire-fighters did indeed strike for five days in November 1973 and then, after extensive mediation, agreed that the remaining items in dispute could be referred to binding factfinding for resolution.

Many management and union bargainers were suspicious of what might be characterized as the "gimmick" aspect of final-offer arbitration, but their fear of arbitral discretion seemed even greater than their reservations about the procedure. In the view of both management and union bargainers, final-offer arbitration would deter the parties from going to arbitration and would restrict the role of the third party in the few instances in which he was involved. The firefighters had an additional reason, however, for they believed they had been penalized in situations under the earlier legislation when factfinders had recommended compromise settlements awarding firefighters more than some other municipal employees had received but less than they had demanded and less than was awarded to police. Use of final-offer arbitration would force arbitrators to choose directly between the maintenance or abandonment of parity and would prevent them from devising compromise solutions.

The Final-Offer Arbitration Statute

The final-offer arbitration provision became effective April 20, 1972, as part of the overall revision of the statute. It provides that either party may petition the Wisconsin Employment Relations Commission (WERC) to order arbitration. WERC investigates the dispute to determine whether an impasse has been reached. Certification to arbitration is not pro forma because WERC conducts an intensive mediation effort during the investigation and orders arbitration only after it is convinced that there is a bona fide impasse. The cost of arbitration is borne by the parties.

If both parties desire to use conventional arbitration rather than final-offer arbitration, the statute specifically authorizes this option. In the absence of such an agreement, however, the parties are bound by what is referred to in the Wisconsin statute as Form 2 arbitration under which "the arbitrator shall select the final offer of one of the parties and shall issue an award incorporating that offer without modification."

The statute provides guidelines for the arbitrator in making his decision. These guidelines, which are the same as those specified in the Michigan arbitration statute, state that he shall give weight to the lawful authority of the employer, stipulations of the parties, ability to pay, cost of living, comparisons with other employees in the public and private sectors doing similar work, comparisons with other employees generally in comparable communities, and other such factors that are normally or traditionally taken into consideration in determining the wages, hours, and conditions of employment in the private and public sectors. Although the statute does not provide specifically that arbitrators may mediate issues, several of the more experienced arbitrators have occasionally attempted to do so.

Eligibility for use of arbitration is confined to county and city law enforcement and firefighting personnel. Access to the arbitration procedure is relatively simple but requires that the parties first make a good-faith effort to resolve their differences through direct negotiations and, if unsuccessful, to participate in mediation efforts under the aegis of WERC.

Effective July 18, 1973, the statute was amended in the following respects: (1) the procedure for selecting an arbitrator was simplified; (2) City of Milwaukee firefighters were exempt from coverage under the statute (Milwaukee police were not affected by the 1973 amendments); (3) the legislation was made permanent by deleting the clause terminating the legislation after a one-year trial period; and (4) the minimum size city eligible to use the procedure was reduced from 5000 to 2500 population. The amended statutory provision, Wisconsin Statutes, Section 111.77, is quoted in its entirety in Appendix C.

Administration of the Statute. Historically, the State of Wisconsin has maintained an active and nationally well-regarded agency (WERC) to administer the labor relations statutes. It is headed by 3 full-time experienced commissioners who are assisted by a staff of 12 professionals. WERC emphasizes the role of mediation and interprets the requirement in the statute that the parties must reach an impasse before proceeding to arbitration as much more than a pro forma requirement. A case may be initiated by a request for mediation or by a request for arbitration. In either situation, mediation ensues, and only if it fails is the dispute certified to arbitration.

The parties may, if they wish, select an arbitrator and request that WERC appoint him. This is done occasionally, but in most instances, WERC supplies a panel of five names at the time it certifies the dispute to arbitration, and the parties, by alternately striking one of the five names on the list, select the arbitrator. They notify WERC of their choice, and at that time, each party also furnishes WERC with a written statement of its final offer for resolution of the dispute. WERC sends the parties' final offers to the arbitrator along with its official order appointing him to the case. The arbitrator then gets in touch with the parties and proceeds in the conventional fashion. Because most evidence in the arbitration hearing consists of statistical material, hearings are rarely transcribed. In many situations, post-hearing briefs are submitted, but in some disputes involving smaller units, this is dispensed with in favor of oral arguments.

The roster of arbitrators maintained by WERC includes mainly experienced individuals who have handled grievance arbitrations for WERC, the Federal Mediation and Conciliation Service, and the American Arbitration Association and who also have served as factfinders in interest disputes. In cases filed by the end of the 1974 fiscal year (June 30, 1974),

17 arbitrators had been appointed to hear 55 cases. Forty-two awards had been issued by 16 arbitrators as of March 1, 1975, and one case was still pending. Seven arbitrators have been appointed only once, and 8 arbitrators have been appointed in 4 or more disputes.

During the first two years that the statute has been in existence, various procedural problems that have arisen have been subject to administrative rulings or court decisions. In several instances, unions have filed unfair labor practice charges alleging that the employer has failed to bargain in good faith. Pending action on these charges by WERC, one union has claimed that it would be improper for WERC to honor the employer request for arbitration.[8]

Several employers have blocked or delayed union requests for arbitration by claiming that one or more of the items in dispute falls outside the statutory scope of bargaining and have asked WERC to issue a declaratory ruling to that effect.[9] In one other situation, a city expressed its irritation with the arbitration process by refusing to participate in the striking-of-names procedure. This action resulted in the appointment of the arbitrator by WERC after the city waived its right to strike names—on the grounds that one arbitrator was as bad as the next and that the city would be treated unfairly in any event. On the whole, however, the statute and the administrative rulings of WERC have been accepted without legal challenge, with one important reservation.

Finality of the Final Offer

A significant question that is still unresolved involves the interpretation of that portion of the statute dealing with the time limitations on the filing and amending of final offers. The statute specifies that "Parties shall submit their final offer in effect at the time that the petition for final and binding arbitration was filed. Either party may amend its final offer within 5 days of the hearing." One interpretation of this language will force the parties to make the decision to settle or to be subject to an arbitral award much sooner than an alternative interpretation and could have a substantial effect on the bargaining process.

Essentially, the choice is between a relaxed interpretation, which may reduce the deterrent effect but will give mediators and arbitrators a greater opportunity to resolve the dispute by mediation, and a stricter interpretation, which will reduce the proportion of cases resolved by mediation but which may also protect the deterrent effect more fully—by reducing the number of requests for third-party assistance and thereby reducing the number of instances in which it is necessary to issue awards. Some insight into this problem can be gleaned by a brief review of two situations in which this problem has arisen.

The Court's View of Finality. In the dispute between the Milwaukee County Deputy Sheriff's Association and the County of Milwaukee, the association petitioned WERC to set aside a portion of an award that it believed to be improper. The arbitrator had ruled that the final offer of the county should prevail. This offer included a contract of two years' duration and a wage increase of 4 percent for the second year, but the association argued that the matter of contract duration was not at issue when it filed its petition for arbitration, that the county had no right subsequently to introduce this demand for a two-year agreement, and that the arbitrator had improperly allowed this item to be considered a part of the impasse.

In effect, the association was arguing two points. It contended first that the initial offer filed with WERC at the time the association requested arbitration is the one specified in the statute as the final offer, rather than an offer listing issues still unresolved after mediation takes place. Its second point was that the statute permitted amendment of the final offer by changing of position on issues already in dispute, but not by the introduction of a new issue.

WERC rejected the petition and the association appealed the decision to the Circuit Court of Milwaukee County. The court upheld the appeal, vacating that part of the arbitrator's award relating to the second year of the agreement and ordering the parties to enter into bargaining to negotiate for 1974. The county, in turn, appealed the decision to the Wisconsin Supreme Court, where the circuit court decision was upheld.[10]

The Wisconsin Supreme Court's ruling that the parameters of the dispute are set by the offer filed with the petition for arbitration may change the procedures followed by groups seeking third-party assistance. In the past, when the parties believed that they had reached an impasse, most of them petitioned for arbitration rather than requesting mediation. Practically, this made no difference since the first step that WERC takes in processing a petition for arbitration is to assign a mediator to the case whose role, technically, is to investigate the petition to determine whether an impasse exists. This step is required by statute prior to WERC certification of the dispute to arbitration (although the mediation process is not compulsory). In a small fraction of disputes, the parties now request mediation rather than arbitration. In these instances, if mediation fails and one of the parties petitions for arbitration, WERC will certify the dispute to arbitration without requiring further mediation. This latter procedure, which is followed in a minority of the disputes, may become the prevailing pattern in the future because of the court ruling.

It is not clear just how this change in interpretation of the statute will affect bargaining. It is quite possible that it will have very little practical effect. It is also possible that some parties will continue to petition directly for arbitration and that the scope of mediation will be reduced. One paragraph of the circuit court decision makes clear, however, that the court's intention was to prevent unfair bargaining and the introduction of new issues that expand the scope of conflict rather than to preclude legitimate amendment designed to narrow the gap between the parties.

> While this is admittedly a case of first impression, it is the court's opinion that the legislature, in allowing either side to amend their offer in existence at the time the petition is filed, did not intend that the amended offer contain substantive matter which was not mentioned nor even considered by the parties during negotiation and prior to the filing of the petition. To hold otherwise would create an anomalous situation of allowing a party to collective bargaining to entirely frustrate the requirements of good-faith bargaining before the petition is filed, and then, afterward, come forward, under the guise of an "amended offer," with new and highly controversial subject matter about which the other side never had any opportunity to negotiate. This is fundamentally wrong.[11]

Another aspect of the timing of amended offers under the 5-day rule has arisen in several other cases. The law states that offers may be amended "within 5 days of the hearing." Some arbitrators have permitted the parties to amend their positions *at* the hearing, some have permitted the parties to amend their position up until 5 days *subsequent* to the hearing, and some have maintained that offers may be amended up until 5 days *before* the hearing. There is no legislative history that can be relied upon for guidance on this timing question. If one of the parties to a dispute is holding back a final offer until the last minute, it becomes rather difficult for him to determine when the last chance to amend has arrived.

The WERC View of Finality. As of this writing, WERC has not been forced to make a ruling on this point and has preferred instead to follow an "uncertainty" approach under which arbitrators are encouraged to be flexible in order to maximize settlement possibilities by the parties themselves. In one situation, in which the attorney for a small city was quite certain that he had a winning position because of the "way-out" position of the police, he was quite disappointed that the city council members overruled him and permitted the police association to make last-minute changes in its position that led to a settlement on the courthouse steps.

In some cases, where the parties have reached an impasse on a dozen items, arbitrators have attempted to mediate some of the issues in order to reduce the dispute to a more manageable size. This has involved a series of amended offers being made at the hearing. There is no difficulty with this procedure if both parties are amenable to it; if one is not, arbitrators usually do not press the point and leave the dimensions of the dispute as they were when the parties entered the hearing.

In one instance in early 1973, WERC was asked to give its position about the propriety of making a change in a final offer verbally about five minutes before the arbitration hearing was scheduled to begin. WERC said that such conduct violated the spirit of the statute and that amended offers should be transmitted in writing prior to the date scheduled for the hearing.[12] Presumably, this would eliminate the element of surprise and if there were disagreement about the lateness of the amendment, the arbitrator could postpone the hearing for 5 days and thereby legitimize the offer that otherwise might be deemed inadmissible on the grounds that it was untimely.

An Arbitrator's View of Finality. A development in July 1974 may make it impossible, however, for WERC to continue its relaxed policy. In a case involving Waukesha County and the Teamster-represented deputy sheriff unit, the arbitrator upheld a county contention that the union could not withdraw a demand and accept the offer of the county on that issue.[13]

At the arbitration hearing, the union had offered to accept the county position on one of the three issues in dispute. The county objected strenuously to this attempt by the union to amend its final offer, even though the amendment was offered for the purpose of agreeing with the county and thereby removing the issue from contention. The county argued that the legislative rationale for final-offer arbitration was to induce the parties to reach agreement by direct negotiation and that this inducement to bargain would be undermined if the arbitrator were to permit any amendments subsequent to 5 days prior to the hearing. The arbitrator upheld the county by stating that:

A last best offer . . . is intended to be considered as a "package"—an offer which must be taken as a whole, and which becomes a different offer with a different impact if any part of it is changed.

This concept is important to parties in bargaining under Form 2 for they prepare total offers, packages, in which individual items are balanced in order to get or hold something more favorable for the parties by also offering something less favorable for themselves. If any element is changed after the final offer, the character of the whole offer is changed. . . .

Further the removal of an item after the last best amended offer is submitted may not be conducive to settlement of the remaining positions as one side or the other may perceive its total positions as intolerably compromised as in the instant case, leading to further dispute.[14]

As one reflects on this question of whether to permit amendments that are probably untimely, at least from a strictly technical viewpoint, it becomes evident that the long-run protection of the deterrent effect of the final-offer procedure is strengthened by adoption of this view prohibiting them. On the other hand, in individual cases in which the parties have not had extensive experience or in which there are many unresolved issues, the strict interpretation removes the opportunity to engage in last-minute "med-arb" techniques. The problem is one that concerns the parties and WERC and may eventually lead to further statutory changes.

Extent of Third-Party Usage

In order to estimate the percent of labor agreements that were negotiated annually by the parties without outside assistance, it was necessary first to ascertain the number of cities and counties that negotiated labor agreements with police, firefighters, and deputy sheriffs and then to adjust this number to reflect the situations in which two-year agreements had been negotiated.[15] In 1974, 143 cities met the size limitations for coverage under the final-offer arbitration provisions of the statute. Of this number, 101 bargain with either firefighters or police; 100 have negotiated labor agreements with police, and 51 have negotiated agreements with firefighters.

Of the 72 Wisconsin counties, 41 have negotiated agreements with deputy sheriffs and/or traffic patrol officers. (Counties do not employ firefighters.)[b] Cities that bargained had an average population of about 20,000 and employed an average of about 190 workers in the public sector, including an average of approximately 30 policemen and 45 firefighters. Counties that bargained had an average population of about 90,000 people and employed an average of 900 workers in the public sector, including 50 deputy sheriffs or traffic control officers.[c] The collective bargaining process is relatively new to a majority of these units, as approximately 55 percent of the 192 units that bargain negotiated their first labor agreements in 1969 or later.

The Wisconsin data presented in the following tables and figures indicate that the parties have tended to settle disputes by themselves rather than abdicate this responsibility to arbitrators. The annual experience from 1968 to 1972 under factfinding and from 1972 to 1974 under arbitration of police, firefighter, and deputy sheriffs is examined separately first and then combined (Tables 4-1 and 4-2 and Figures 4-1 and 4-2).

---

[b] These statistics are based on replies from the 143 cities and 72 counties covered by the statute.

[c] These statistics are based on returns from 71 percent of the Wisconsin units that bargain.

Police. Of the 217 settlements reached by police under factfinding from 1968 through 1971—the last four full years of experience under that statutory arrangement—152 (70 percent) were achieved by the parties through direct negotiations without requesting third-party assistance of any kind. Of the remaining 65 settlements (30 percent) that were subject to mediation, 49 (23 percent) were settled by this process and the remaining 16 (7 percent) necessitated the issuance of factfinding decisions. As can be seen by inspection of Section 1a of Table 4-1, the year-to-year variation from these averages is relatively slight.

The 1972 statistics reflect the changeover from factfinding to arbitration. If a unit had not settled its 1972 agreement by the end of January 1972, it may have decided to delay its request for factfinding in the hope that within the next few months the legislative session then in progress would complete its action on the pending labor relations statute and replace factfinding with arbitration. This came about, effective April 20, 1972, and resulted in the filing of 14 petitions for arbitration regarding 1972 agreements. Although the 1972 experience is not too different from that of other years, it is excluded from the comparison of factfinding years to arbitration years because both processes were used in that year and there are not firm grounds for allocating the credit or blame for settlements or third-party involvement in that year to one procedure or the other.

In the first two full years under the new final-offer arbitration procedure, 163 police agreements were negotiated of which 101, or 62 percent, were reached by the parties through direct negotiations. Of the 62 settlements (38 percent) that were subject to mediation, 47 (29 percent) were settled by this process and the remaining 15 (9 percent) were resolved by arbitration awards. Examination of Section 1a of the table shows that the percent of settlements achieved by direct negotiation in 1974 decreased from the 1973 figure. Furthermore, 1974 is the only year in the six-year comparison in which awards as a percent of settlements exceeded 10 percent.

Firefighters. The number of firefighter units engaging in collective bargaining is less than the number of police units doing so because of the use of volunteer fire departments in many small communities. Section 1b of Table 4-1 shows that the overall experience of firefighters with third-party procedures is similar to that of police; although firefighters used factfinding to a lesser degree than did police, they used arbitration to a greater degree. Only 20 (15 percent) of 131 settlements reached between 1968 and 1971—while the factfinding provision was in effect—necessitated mediation, and of these, only 4 (3 percent) resulted in the issuance of a factfinding decision.

Of the 86 settlements reached during the first two full years that arbitration was in effect, 1973-74, 62 (72 percent) were resolved by direct negotiations of the parties. Of the remaining 24 settlements (28 percent)

Table 4-1

Number and Percent of Agreements Negotiated with or without Third-Party Assistance through Mediation, Factfinding Decisions, or Arbitration Awards, 1968-1974

	1968		1969		1970		1971		1972 [b]		1973		1974	
	Number	Percent	Number	Percent	Number	Percent	Number	Percent	Number	Percent	Number	Percent	Number	Percent
Section Ia: Police														
All settlements	43	100	48	100	58	100	68	100	74	100	89	100	74	100
Direct negotiations	35	82	32	67	37	64	48	71	57	77	58	65	43	58
Third-party assistance	8	18	16	33	21	36	20	29	17	23	31	35	31	42
Mediation	4	9	12	25	17	29	16	23	12	16	25	28	22	30
Factfinding [a]	4	9	4	8	4	7	4	6	2	3	—	—	—	—
Arbitration [a]	—	—	—	—	—	—	—	—	3	4	6	7	9 [c]	12
Section Ib: Firefighters														
All settlements	29	100	30	100	34	100	38	100	38	100	47	100	39	100
Direct negotiations	26	90	25	83	26	76	34	89	32	84	37	79	25	64
Third-party assistance	3	10	5	17	8	24	4	11	6	16	10	21	14	36
Mediation	2	7	5	17	7	21	2	5.5	5	13	5	10.5	8	21
Factfinding [a]	1	3	0	0	1	3	2	5.5	1	3	—	—	—	—
Arbitration [a]	—	—	—	—	—	—	—	—	0	0	5	10.5	6	15
Section Ic: Deputy Sheriffs														
All settlements	15	100	19	100	22	100	23	100	31	100	37	100	34	100
Direct negotiations	9	60	10	53	10	45	8	35	14	45	22	59	20	59
Third-party assistance	6	40	9	47	12	55	15	65	17	55	15	41	14	41
Mediation	6	40	9	47	9	41	13	56	12	39	10	27	9	26
Factfinding [a]	0	0	0	0	3	14	2	9	1	3	—	—	—	—
Arbitration [a]	—	—	—	—	—	—	—	—	4	13	5	14	5	15

[a] Prior to 1972, disputes not resolved by mediation were processed to factfinding; subsequent to 1972, disputes not resolved by mediation were subject to arbitration instead of factfinding.

[b] The arbitration statute became effective April 20, 1972. Therefore, some contracts for calendar 1972, which had not been resolved by direct negotiations or mediation or factfinding awards prior to that date, were resolved by arbitration awards under the newly enacted statute.

[c] As of March 1, 1975, only eight awards had been issued. In the ninth case (Wauwatosa), the dispute was still pending at the arbitration step. It is assumed, however, in these calculations, that an award will be issued.

that were subject to mediation, 13 (15 percent) were settled by this process and 11 (13 percent) were resolved by arbitration awards. In the 1973-74 period, 11 firefighter disputes were resolved by arbitration awards, and in both years this meant that the percent of settlements determined by awards exceeded 10 percent.

Deputy Sheriffs. Section 1c of Table 4-1 applies to deputy sheriffs employed by Wisconsin counties. Collective bargaining is of more recent vintage in counties than in cities, and the number of annual bargaining negotiations in the 72 counties is far less than that in the 143 cities. In the 1968-71 factfinding period, 79 settlements were agreed upon by counties and deputy sheriffs. Of these, only 37 (47 percent) were achieved by direct negotiations of the parties, and of the remaining 42 (53 percent) referred to mediation, 37 (47 percent) were settled by this process and 5 (6 percent) resulted in factfinding decisions.

In the 1973-74 period under arbitration, there were 71 settlements between counties and their law enforcement officers. Of these, 42 (59 percent) were achieved by direct negotiations, and of the remaining 29 (41 percent) referred to mediation, 19 (27 percent) were settled by this process and 10 (14 percent) required arbitration awards.

The county record differs from that of the cities. Deputies exhibited a far greater tendency to refer disputes to mediation during the period when factfinding was the terminal step (53 percent) than did police (30 percent) or firefighters (15 percent). So far as the percent of settlements necessitating a factfinding decision is concerned, however, the records are similar; deputy sheriff disputes went to factfinding in 6 percent of the bargaining situations from 1968 through 1971 as compared to 7 percent and 3 percent of the bargaining situations involving police and firefighters. This record of greater dependency on settlement through mediation probably arises because county boards accepted collective bargaining with greater reluctance than did city councils. In many cases, only after being subject to persuasion by mediators did they engage in meaningful collective bargaining.

In the 1973-74 period there was a further change in the county experience as compared to that of cities. The percent of deputy sheriff disputes referred to mediation during those two years was lower than had been the case in the 1968-71 factfinding era—41 percent as compared to 53 percent—and was almost down to the police and firefighter percentages of 38 and 28, respectively. The percent of deputy sheriff disputes resolved by arbitration was also slightly higher—14 percent as compared to 9 percent for police and 12 percent for firefighters. Several reasons for these differences are set forth in a subsequent section of this chapter dealing with the information gained from interviews with county management and union representatives.

Combined Data. Table 4-2 combines the figures for the police, firefighters, and deputy sheriffs and also consolidates the factfinding and arbitration years into one total for each process. These figures show that the percent of arbitration awards in the first two full years under the new

Table 4-2

Number and Percent of Police, Firefighter, and County Law Enforcement Officer Agreements Negotiated with or without Third-Party Assistance through Mediation, Factfinding Awards, or Arbitration Awards, 1968-1974

Method of Settlement	1968-1971	1972 [b]	1973-74
Number of settlements reached by each procedure:			
By direct negotiations without outside assistance	300	103	205
By third-party assistance through:	127	49	115 [c]
Mediation	102	29	79
Factfinding awards [a]	25	4	—
Arbitration awards	—	7	36
Total number of settlements	427	143	320
Percent of settlements reached by each procedure:			
By direct negotiations without outside assistance	70%	72%	64%
By third-party assistance through:			
Mediation	24%	20%	25%
Factfinding awards	6%	3%	n.a.
Arbitration awards	n.a.	5%	11%

Note The number of settlements was calculated from the questionnaires and adjusted to reflect the 71 percent response rate and the number of two-year agreements. The number of mediations, factfinding, and arbitration awards is drawn from state records. Adjustments were made in state figures to convert them from fiscal years to calendar years because municipal agreements run for calendar years.

[a] Prior to 1972, disputes not resolved by mediation were processed to factfinding; subsequent to 1972, disputes not resolved by direct negotiations were subject to arbitration instead of factfinding.

[b] The arbitration statute became effective April 20, 1972. Therefore, some contracts for calendar 1972, which had not been resolved by direct negotiations or mediation or factfinding awards prior to that date, were resolved by arbitration awards under the newly enacted statute.

[c] Of the 115 requests for third-party assistance in negotiating 1973 and 1974 labor agreements, 59 were made in connection with 1974 agreements. Of this number, one case (Wauwatosa police) was pending at the arbitration step as of March 1, 1975. It is assumed that an award will be issued, and this case is included in the number of awards issued.

statute was almost twice as large—11 percent and 6 percent—as the percent of disputes necessitating factfinding decisions during the last four full
years that factfinding was the terminal step. This difference may not be
cause for alarm for a variety of reasons. The increase may in part represent an initial surge to try out a new bargaining tool, which can be expected to diminish as the parties become familiar with its advantages and
limitations, or it may, instead, indicate that referral to third parties for
final awards has risen to a new level, which can be expected to continue
in the future. On the other hand, it is also possible that there is an upward
trend and that in 1975 and thereafter there will be a higher proportion
of collective bargaining disputes resolved by arbitration.

The trend line in Figure 4-1, which shows the percent of settlements

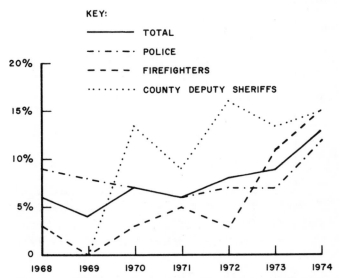

Figure 4-1. Percent of Police, Firefighter, and Deputy
Sheriff Agreements Reached through Factfinding Decisions and Arbitration Awards, 1968-1974.

reached by arbitration for all three groups combined, is clearly an upward
one and is presently rising from the 10 to 15 percent level. The percent of
negotiations in which mediation is invoked has also been rising and in
1974 was between 36 and 41 percent for each of the three groups (see
Figure 4-2). This is a rather high involvement of mediation, as compared
to the private sector. However, the Wisconsin Employment Relations
Commission expects it to level off as the parties gain further experience.

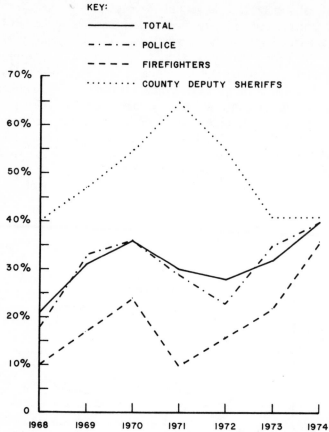

Figure 4-2. Percent of Police, Firefighter, and Deputy Sheriff Negotiations Referred to Mediation, 1968-1974.

Factors Associated with Use of Third-Party Assistance

Responses to questionnaires returned by 71 percent of the parties to collective bargaining relationships under the final-offer arbitration statute and interviews with city and county union and management negotiators generated a long list of factors that help to explain why some disputes are referred to arbitration while others are settled by the parties. The conclusions drawn from interviews with parties who have shown little or no reliance on arbitration are presented first and are followed by those drawn from interviews with the parties in situations where there has been use of factfinding and/or arbitration. It should be kept in mind that these conclusions reflect subjective evaluations of comments made by the people who were interviewed.

Self-Reliant Cities and Counties

The "typical" city that has not used third-party assistance has a population of less than 25,000 and is not located in a Standard Metropolitan Statistical Area (SMSA). Instead, it is located in a predominately rural area, is the county seat and shopping and trade center for the rural residents, and contains the few manufacturing firms in the area. Municipal police wages tend to set the pattern for county police wages in these areas, which, incidentally, are frequently economically depressed. Wages in these cities also tend to be higher than wages paid in the smaller cities in the under 10,000 population category within a radius that may extend from 25 to 50 miles, depending on where in the state the city is located.

Personal Relationships. More often than not, these cities do not rely upon "outside" professional negotiators, but historically have used comptrollers, city clerks who are aides to the major, or part-time city attorneys to provide negotiating assistance to a five-man personnel or finance committee of the city council. It is difficult to identify the management decisionmaker in such situations. Some unions regard the chairman of the personnel committee as the dominant management person; others claim that it is the mayor, even though the mayor took no part in the negotiations. Still others have said that the city clerk or attorney is the key figure because the lay members of the management committee rely upon him for the data used to determine what they consider to be a "fair" wage offer.

Wage and status differences between labor and management seem to be far smaller in these cities than in large metropolitan areas. Personal interrelationships are more widely known; individuals have some conception of how much money their neighbors make—or at least how much they spend. The chairman of the union bargaining committee may be the brother-in-law of a member of the finance committee. A union bargainer may have been a business partner of the city comptroller in a small retail establishment. Public management positions in these communities do not seem to be sufficiently important to the citizenry to demand professionalization of these positions or to justify payment of high salaries in order to attract professionally trained individuals.

The size of the wage increase paid to these management positions seems to depend upon the wage increase granted to municipal employees. Just as salaries of foremen in unionized manufacturing firms may be maintained at a rate just higher than that of the men they supervise, so city and county staff receive only slightly higher salaries than those they supervise. In such a situation, a city clerk may not be a "tough" bargainer in dealing with the police and firefighter bargainers.

In these communities, where the rewards for gaining high public office are nominal and authority is limited because of the extensive participation of lay members of the city and county councils, internal management political power struggles play a smaller role in bargaining than they do in larger cities. The lower personal stakes soften political differences between a mayor and the city council and diminish the ability of the parties to resolve their disputes without reliance upon third parties.

Rural Counties. A similar situation prevails insofar as it concerns the counties in which these cities are located. They tend to be pattern-followers of the major city in the county, to rely upon a county personnel officer or attorney for negotiating assistance, and to vest the negotiating authority in a personnel committee of the county board. Although these county boards may be conservative and, in some instances, anti-union in their dealings with other county employees, they tend to look more sympathetically on the needs of their law enforcement personnel. In these situations, negotiations are rather brief and relations tend to be paternalistic. The deputies emphasize that they "are not a *union*" and usually have found past county proposals to be acceptable.

Firefighters. Firefighter negotiations differ from those of police or deputy sheriffs for several reasons. Firefighters are less likely to compare their own wages with wages of firefighters in the smaller communities because of the use of volunteers rather than full-time firefighters in those communities. The average population of the cities in which firefighters bargain is 50 percent higher than the average in cities in which police bargain. Almost all firefighter units are represented by local unions of the IAFF. In recent years, the state IAFF organization and the national IAFF have offered some assistance to local unions, and there has been some coordination of strategy among the various IAFF locals through their state and national officials.

The factors leading IAFF locals to use arbitration are treated subsequently as a part of the discussion of the experience of cities where arbitration has been used. Those cities that have full-time firefighters but have not used arbitration may have avoided it because of the reluctance of firefighters to break community norms. If other groups are comparing their wages with the wages paid locally and if firefighters have traditionally been paid the same as the police, the firefighters, understandably, may be reluctant to press for higher wages than police even though they are aware that their wages are lower than those paid to firefighters in similar size cities in metropolitan areas.

Immaturity and Cost. Many of the bargaining relationships described above are relatively immature. It can be expected that, as they evolve, they will tend to use mediation and arbitration more often, as has been the case in the larger cities and urban counties. However, cost considerations may dampen the tendency of the small associations to invoke arbitration. Comments during interviews and responses to questionnaires indicated that the per person cost of arbitration is sufficient to act as a deterrent to the use of arbitration in rural counties and in cities of 5,000 population with a police force of five to ten men.

The foregoing description of cities and counties that settle their problems without reliance on third parties does not tell us when or where this stable situation will be altered dramatically. Election of a new mayor or new chairman of a finance committee can change the relationship almost overnight. For example, a new chairman may decide to hire a professional negotiator and give him instruction to hold the line. Or a new police or deputy sheriff association president may decide to hire an experienced labor lawyer to represent the association. Or, what was formerly a docile independent deputy association may vote to affiliate with the Teamsters— an act that would dramatically signal the end of the paternalistic relationship and foreshadow the advent of crisis bargaining and third-party involvement.

Third-Party–Dependent Cities and Counties

We turn now to a consideration of the reasons expressed for the use of arbitration by management and union spokesmen in cities and counties in which petitions for arbitration have been filed. These opinions are based on the relatively short two-and-one-half-year experience under the new arbitration statute and may change as the negotiators gain additional experience.

The Special Problem of the Suburbs. The relatively high use of arbitration in the semicircle of communities around Milwaukee is attributable in part to the spread of unionism from the pro-union city to the far less sympathetic suburbs. In some suburban communities, the management philosophy is set by residents who have lived there many years and during the time the area was rural. They tend to be somewhat antagonistic to bargaining by the protective services associations. Their views are reinforced by some of the newly arrived and relatively affluent management-oriented suburbanites. Although some respondents in this second group stressed in interviews that they believe in unions and bargaining, the prevailing opinion was that one must adopt a firm bargaining stance.

Police and firefighters in these suburban communities are aware of the high wages paid in Milwaukee. They also believe that their suburban communities are less financially pressed than the city and that the income of residents of the suburbs is higher than that of the average city resident. They tend, therefore, to demand larger wage increases than the suburban city mayors and council members believe they should grant. Although differences in what is a fair wage increase are not confined to the groups under discussion here, it is evident that there are other factors present that make it more difficult for these cities to settle without reliance upon third-party assistance.

On the management side, one finds that the professional negotiators are unable to persuade the city councils they represent to make further concessions that might bring about a settlement and avoid the use of arbitration. In some instances, negotiators have stated that they believed such concessions were warranted by economic factors and that this was not an instance in which they believed the union to be unreasonable.

On the other hand, several union spokesmen have argued strongly that the fee arrangements between some Milwaukee suburbs and the law firms supplying the negotiators are not conducive to a quick settlement by the parties and that it is the hard line of the professional that forces them to arbitration. Although conclusions on this point must be highly tentative, it is quite possible that the bellicose attitude of the attorneys about which the unions complained arises because of the need of the attorney to reflect the view of his client. In support of this conclusion, it should be noted that the complaints about attorneys arose more frequently during interviews in the outer, more rural suburban communities that tend to be more conservative than the others.

Use of Attorneys. Arbitration is requested by unions or managements outside the Milwaukee area for a variety of reasons. The "attorney problem" just discussed is present elsewhere, with some union spokesmen suggesting that settlements could have been achieved if the city or county had not been represented by an experienced labor lawyer. Union spokesmen seem to be very sensitive on this point and in one instance implied that the city decision to retain outside counsel as a back-room consultant who did not appear at the negotiating table was an important impediment to settlement and necessitated third-party assistance.

In several situations, the police association fired its attorney after losing a case and blamed him for the decision to take a dispute to arbitration. One of these associations said it had mistakenly hired a general-purpose attorney who didn't understand labor relations and who mistakenly claimed that it couldn't lose before the arbitrator. This association has not replaced the attorney and without professional advice of any sort, succeeded in negotiating the subsequent contract through direct negotiations. In other situations, police associations have switched from relatively aggressive labor lawyers to lawyers in general practice or to more conciliatory labor lawyers.

Although the volume of experience to date with this problem is not sufficient to warrant firm predictions, a general trend is emerging. As independent police and deputy sheriff associations gain bargaining experience, they tend to handle negotiations without legal assistance. Only if they are unable to achieve a settlement through direct negotiations or at the mediation step do they hire an attorney to represent them at the arbitration hearing. Firefighter local unions outside the Milwaukee area handle their own negotiations up to the point of arbitration and then call upon their international union for assistance in the preparation for arbitration and in the hearing. It appears, therefore, that as the parties gain more experience, the possible influence of attorneys, at least on the union side, will be less important in making the determination of whether to use the arbitration procedure.

Role of the Chief Public Safety Officer. Antagonistic relations between the sheriff and his deputies and between a police chief and his men or a fire chief and his men make it more difficult to achieve a settlement without the use of arbitration. Poor relations may exist in smaller cities and rural counties, but the problem emerges much more clearly in the larger cities and urban counties where there are greater salary and status differences between the chief and the men in the unit. City councils and county boards are reluctant to make concessions in bargaining about working conditions, which have been set traditionally on a unilateral basis by the chief, unless the chief is sympathetic to the idea that his rules shall be formalized in the labor agreement and subject to bargaining.

Harmonious relations between the men and the chief tend to reduce the likelihood of arbitration because the chief is usually in a position to offer offsetting noneconomic benefits when a city council has taken a position on a wage increase that might otherwise be unacceptable to the union. For example, one county agreement stipulated that the work week should not exceed 42 hours. The sheriff, who was up for election shortly thereafter, unilaterally reduced the work week from the existing 42 hours to 39 hours without a reduction in pay after the men agreed to accept a county wage offer that fell short of the amount gained by the police in the major city of that county.

Intraorganizational differences can either increase or decrease the tendency to use arbitration. When the chief offsets the hard lines of the council, reliance on arbitration decreases. When the chief takes a hard line, the council may find it politically expedient to let an arbitrator rule against the chief rather than to do it in negotiations, particularly when the council itself is split politically.

Personal antagonisms between the chief and the union leaders cause the parties to turn to arbitration to resolve their differences. In some instances, the union wishes to use the arbitration process to overturn what the members consider to be punitive actions of a chief that were taken in response to the emergence of unionism.

There are remarkably few differences among the police, firefighter, and deputy associations insofar as the above factors concerning arbitration dependency are concerned. Although sheriffs are elected and chiefs appointed and although many independent deputy and police associations are less sophisticated in their approach than local unions of the IAFF, the role of the chief as well as the political nature of the community and the existence or absence of good personal relationships between the union leaders and their chief seem to be equally important to the three groups and seem to influence dependency in the same way.

Economic Factors. Economic factors were mentioned by management and union negotiators alike as important determinants of whether it was easy or hard to achieve a settlement through direct negotiations. In some rural counties and outer-ring Milwaukee suburbs, disputes were referred to arbitration because the association leaders believed that they were entitled to "catch-up" wage increases far in excess of the amount that management was willing to grant. In these situations, a prelude to the request for arbitration was the abandonment of participation in a somewhat paternalistic relationship and the affiliation with the Teamsters or AFSCME.

An equivalent step for local police associations that had been relatively inactive was the joining of either the Wisconsin Professional Policemen's Association or the rival Milwaukee Metropolitan Professional Policemen's Association. When the act of affiliation did not cause city and county managements to revise their wage policies and grant catch-up wage increases, the units involved petitioned for arbitration in order to achieve this goal.

Another economic factor causing unions to petition for arbitration was the substantial increase in the cost of living and the attempt of the larger cities with relatively high wages to grant wage increases in 1974 that were less than the prior year's increase in the Consumer Price Index. Although changes in the CPI were cited by unions in these larger cities when claims were pursued to arbitration, arbitrators ruled against them in most cases because of such other factors as the more modest wage changes in other municipal occupations that had settled first, the failure of private sector settlements in 1973 to keep up with the CPI, and, in some instances, city financial problems.

In one of the larger cities and in several urban counties, however, rising prices discouraged unions from petitioning for arbitration. They believed that arbitrators would not grant automatic cost-of-living escalator clauses because relatively few large cities had such clauses and because most arbitrators would be reluctant to set new patterns through arbitration awards. Instead, these unions mounted public relations programs, which were supplemented in two instances by partial sick-outs and other forms of industrial activity, to achieve their goals. (These actions are discussed below in the section on noncompliance with the statute.)

Other economic factors cited by negotiators that would increase the use of arbitration are the wealth of the community, the tax rate, the wages of private sector workers in the community, and wage changes of public sector employees not covered by the arbitration statute. Less wealthy communities do not have the resources to avoid arbitration by granting higher wages to police and firefighters. Also, police and firefighters press their wage claims more vigorously and possibly to arbitration in communities that have large, high-paying unionized manufacturing plants and that have granted substantial wage increases to other public employees not covered by arbitration and who may have struck or threatened to strike.

Parity. Firefighter local unions are quick to resist the dropping of parity with police wages or the widening of the spread to their disadvantage where parity does not exist. Arbitration was invoked in at least one instance because firefighters believed that they were being treated less well than the police. The reverse situation led police associations to petition for arbitration because they believed that the maintenance of parity or the existing differential was not proper and that their wages should be increased more than those of firefighters and other city employees.

Political Factors. Political factors on either the union or management side were primarily responsible for the referral of several disputes to arbitration. In one large county, the board would not permit the sheriff to make all of the concessions that he deemed proper because of political friction between him and a majority of the county board members. This necessitated the sending of a dispute to arbitration, even though the parties were really not far apart. In another case, a 7-man city finance committee reached an agreement with the union, but the agreement failed of ratification at the city council meeting when a majority of the 14-man council, including some members of the finance committee, upheld the mayor's veto of the proposed contract.

Two points are worth noting about this last dispute. In this instance, under the final-offer arbitration system, the arbitrator chose the union offer, that offer being the contract that had been previously agreed to and then vetoed by the mayor. Almost the same thing happened a year later. The committee reached agreement with the union and recommended it to the whole council. Again the mayor vetoed it, but, given the experience of the previous year, the council this time unanimously overrode the mayor's veto and avoided arbitration. This change of position is explained by the fact that the strong, long-time mayor had decided not to run again and both contenders for his position were council members. Prudent politics dictated that both go along with the negotiated agreement rather than advance a contrary position and then quite probably find this position overturned by an arbitrator shortly before the election.

In one large city in which the IAFF actively supported a mayoralty candidate, the hold-the-budget-line opposition candidate won. When holding the line required a reduction in city personnel, some firefighter positions were abolished and several firefighters were laid off. This situation illustrates the intermingling of economic, political, and bargaining inexperience problems. In addition to the political factor noted above, the city was attempting to break the long-standing parity relationship of police and firefighters. Also, the city made what might have been an acceptable offer on entering the hearing. The firefighter leadership was unable to accept it at that late date, however, because the members were geared up to an all-or-nothing position in support of their stance in the pending arbitration.

Politics on the union side were mentioned in many interviews as a possible explanation for the use of arbitration. Incumbent leadership suggested that previous leaders had not been sufficiently aggressive and that the new leadership was going to remedy this situation by pressing the union position to arbitration. There is considerable turnover among union leaders and, in some instances, this reflected the ascendency of the younger and more militant men over the older and more cautious leaders.

In addition to the age and militancy splits within local unions, interunion rivalry and union financial procedures may be contributing to greater use of arbitration. There is competition among the Teamsters, the AFSCME, and independent associations for the right to represent police and deputy sheriffs in some small cities and rural counties. When a formerly independent association decides to affiliate with one of these unions, it may do so in order to have available to it the financial support and experience of the union for use in arbitration.

A Teamster business agent pointed out that the cost of arbitration—including the supplying of an attorney from the firm that represents the Teamsters nationally—is borne by the larger parent local with which the small group of law enforcement personnel has affiliated and that so far as the police unit is concerned, arbitration itself is free. In turn, AFSCME leadership is pressed by its police and deputy units to supply an equivalent level of service. These factors of union competition and the availability of experienced personnel at no or little cost stimulate use of arbitration. An offsetting factor raised by several local union leaders was that their business agents had discouraged them from petitioning for arbitration because the business agents were too busy to become involved in time-consuming arbitration cases.

Another form of competition that leads to use of arbitration is the rivalry between the Wisconsin Professional Policemen's Association and the Milwaukee Metropolitan Policemen's Association. Each of these groups encourage independent police associations to affiliate with it, and in the Milwaukee suburbs particularly, affiliation leads to an increase in the use of arbitration. The Milwaukee-based "Metro Group" attempts to extend a pattern of benefits from the city to the suburbs and encourages suburban groups to use the Metro's attorney in arbitration proceedings. Historically, the WPPA has supplied its affiliates with wage and fringe benefit information but has not offered bargaining services. The recent push of the Metro group in this direction may lead the WPPA also to offer arbitration assistance and thereby increase the use of arbitration.

Other Factors. Prior to 1972, police in many rural areas did not engage in bargaining because they believed that their managements would not bargain and that it was not worthwhile to petition their employers and possibly resort to factfinding. The passage of the 1972 statute granting full bargaining rights and arbitration stimulated the spread of bargaining into smaller cities and rural counties. There, the threat of binding arbitration awards appears to have been a substantial factor in inducing a far greater willingness to bargain on the part of the employers than had been evident previously.

Another cause for the increased use of third parties in 1973 and 1974 as compared to the years immediately prior to that period is the existence of federal government wage-control programs during the last years in which factfinding was the terminal step. The shift to arbitration occurred shortly after wages were decontrolled, and quite possibly, the increased use of third parties is a reflection, at least in part, of this factor.

A final item in this list of factors that help to explain why the parties turned to arbitration to resolve their disputes is what may be described as "the new toy effect." Some respondents suggested that they went to arbitration in order to try out the new process and to see whether it made any difference. It is hoped that once the novelty wears off, there will be decreasing use of arbitration on these grounds, thus partially offsetting some of the previously discussed factors that may increase the tendency.

Impact of Arbitration upon the Outcome of Bargaining

Regression analysis and the personal interviews were used in order to ascertain the impact of arbitration on the outcome of bargaining. Here the results of the regression analysis are quite revealing, while opinions about factors influencing outcomes that were garnered from personal interviews tended to be somewhat vague and uncertain. Therefore, the regression analysis in the following section is given greater attention than the subsequent analysis of the personal interviews.

Regression Analysis of Bargaining Outcomes

Regression equations were run by using as the dependent variable the monthly maximum base salary of police patrolmen, firefighters, and deputy sheriffs. The independent variables were (1) the number of times arbitration had been used by the city or county in negotiating contracts with the group in question, (2) the weekly manufacturing wage in the second quarter of 1973 in the county (the latest quarter available), (3) the population, (4) the 1970 median family income, (5) the mill rate on the 1971 state equalized property value, (6) the 1973 hourly municipal truck driver wage (chosen because it was a representative semiskilled public sector job for which data were available), and (7) the 1971 state equalized property value.[16]

It was hypothesized that wages of police, firefighters, and deputy sheriffs would be positively related to the income of community members and the wealth of the community as measured by the median family income, the average wage in manufacturing, and the full value of property in the community. The effort that the community made to support public services as measured by the equalized mill rate and the wages paid to other municipal employees also were thought to be positively related to wages paid to the protective service employees. It was further hypothesized that larger cities would require more sophisticated service and that, therefore, city size and salaries of protective service employees would be positively related.

The foregoing hypotheses assume conventional relationships among economic variables. In addition, however, it was hypothesized that use of arbitration would not be positively related to wages and that groups that used the final-offer arbitration procedure would not raise their wages by such a strategy.[d]

---

[d] It should be noted that this hypothesis differs from those considered in Chapter 6 where the effects of the different arbitration systems are compared to ascertain

The results of this analysis are shown in Table 4-3. The maximum monthly base salary of police and firefighters is significantly related to private sector wages and to median annual family income. With controls for the other variables shown in Table 4-3, a one-dollar increase in the weekly manufacturing wage is associated with an increase in the monthly wage of police of $1.91 and an increase in the monthly wage of fire-fighters of $1.64. The regression coefficients for the economic variables are not significant.

This result suggests that the going wage rate in the private sector is the most important determinant of police and firefighter wage levels and that

Table 4-3

Impact of Arbitration and Economic Variables on Bargaining Outcomes: Regression Coefficients and Standard Errors in Dollars

Independent Variables	Police	Firefighters	Deputy Sheriffs
Dependent Variable: 1974 Monthly Maximum Base Wage			
Number of times arbitration used	30.29	28.87	3.74
	(18.75)	(28.51)	(14.53)
Weekly manufacturing wage in			
2nd quarter, 1973	1.91 ***	1.64 ***	0.20
	(0.31)	(0.47)	(0.39)
Population in thousands	0.85	−1.57	−0.05
	(1.09)	(1.34)	(0.05)
Median annual family income in thousands	18.85 ***	14.17 ***	12.16
of dollars, 1970	(0.43)	(7.05)	(7.25)
Mill rate (on equalized value, 1971)	3.70	5.56	a
	(2.08)	(3.45)	
Municipal hourly truck driver wage, 1973	15.10	38.94	a
	(24.95)	(38.80)	
Equalized value of property (in hundred	0.51	25.44	a
millions of dollars, 1971)	(12.83)	(17.06)	
Corrected R^2	.73 ***	.75 ***	.13
Number of cities or counties	78	38	34
Constant	$116.80	$55.20	$646.40
Mean value of dependent variable	$865.62	$865.84	$788.12
	($104.79)	($107.58)	($447.16)

Note: Standard errors are in parentheses.
a County data for these variables were not obtained and therefore these variables were not included in the deputy sheriff regression equation.
*** Significant at the .001 level.

whether the adoption of each system has any effect on protective service employee wages in the particular state, and whether this effect is greater or less than the effect of the different systems used in the other two states. In this analysis, we are attempting to ascertain whether those groups within a state who use arbitration achieve higher wages than those who do not, with controls for differences in economic characteristics of the communities.

factors such as city size, the tax rate, and community wealth (to the extent that it is independent of wages and income) are far less important. It is interesting to note also that "going to arbitration" does not pay off.

The confirmation of the hypothesis that the regression coefficient for use of arbitration would not be significant raises several interesting points. If going to arbitration does not pay off, why do the parties go? One possibility, suggested previously in connection with the analysis of third-party dependency, is that political and personal factors cause the parties to use arbitration and that the explanation is not economic in nature.

A second possibility is that the procedure is used primarily by "outliers" —that is, cities and counties in which either the wage is relatively high and management is attempting to restrain further movement or the wage is relatively low and the union is attempting to catch up. Where the wage is low, presumably the union wins, and where the wage is high, it loses. On the average, therefore, going to arbitration will not show a payoff. The data support this interpretation, as arbitrators had picked management's final offer in 20 of the first 41 cases in which final-offer awards were issued.

A related hypothesis about the impact of final-offer arbitration in Wisconsin is that the enactment of the statute would reduce wage dispersion among all units as well as among those that received awards. It was hypothesized that the existence of arbitration would prevent city and county managements that formerly had been able to use their bargaining strength to depress wages from continuing to do so to the same extent. These managements would grant "catch-up" wage increases, through negotiations in most cases and as a result of arbitration in a few instances. Strong unions would be similarly affected.

In order to test this hypothesis, the percent change and absolute change in wages from 1971 (the last full year of factfinding) to 1974 (the latest year for which wage and arbitration data are available) were chosen as dependent variables and regressed against the 1971 wage. If, as hypothesized, the dispersion is reduced by the existence of arbitration, the regression coefficient for the 1971 wage should be significant and negative. The results of the regression analysis of dispersion are shown in Table 4-4. Essentially, it appears that the hypothesis is strongly supported insofar as wage changes of deputy sheriffs are concerned, partially so in the case of police, and unsupported by the data for firefighters.

A one-dollar increase in the 1971 maximum monthly base police salary is associated with a 2.45 percent decrease in the percent by which 1974 police salaries exceed 1971 police salaries. The regression coefficient for firefighters is not significant. A one-dollar increase in the 1971 maximum monthly base deputy sheriff salary is associated with an 11.66 percent decrease in the percent by which 1974 deputy sheriff salaries exceed

Table 4-4

Wage Dispersion under Arbitration

	Police	Firefighter	Deputy Sheriff
Number of cities and counties	78	38	34

Regression Coefficients and Standard Errors in Percent

Section 4a: Dependent variable is percent change in maximum monthly base salary, 1971-1974

	Police	Firefighter	Deputy Sheriff
Independent variable is 1971 maximum	−2.45 **	a	−11.66 ***
monthly base salary in hundreds of dollars	(0.79)		−1.65
Corrected R²	.10 **	.05	.60 ***
Mean value and standard error of the	17.87%	19.50%	11.84%
dependent variable	(6.76)	(6.47)	(9.40)
Mean value and standard error of the	$736.15	$726.13	$708.67
independent variable	(92.55)	(93.88)	(62.92)

Regression Coefficients and Standard Errors in Dollars

Section 4b: Dependent variable is absolute difference in dollars in maximum monthly base salary, 1971-1974

	Police	Firefighter	Deputy Sheriff
Independent variable is 1971 maximum	a	a	−65.69 ***
monthly base salary in hundreds of dollars			(11.00)
Corrected R²	−.01	−.01	.51 ***
Mean value and standard error of the	$129.48	$139.71	$ 79.45
dependent variable	(43.62)	(40.38)	(56.94)
Mean value and standard error of the	$736.15	$726.13	$708.67
independent variable	(92.55)	(93.88)	(62.92)

Note: Standard errors are in parentheses.
a Not significant.
** Significant at the .01 level.
*** Significant at the .001 level.

1971 deputy sheriff salaries. When the reduction in dispersion is measured in absolute terms instead of as a percentage, the regression coefficients for both police and firefighters are not significant, but the coefficient for deputy sheriffs indicates that a one-dollar higher 1971 salary is associated with an absolute 1971-74 wage decrease of $65.69 per month.

The evidence is particularly convincing insofar as the deputy sheriffs are concerned as the corrected R^2s (coefficient of determination) and significance levels are unexpectedly high for this type of cross sectional wage analysis.[e] Quite possibly this particular effect of arbitration may be strongest in its initial years as weak unions and weak managements "catch

---

[e] It is also of interest to note that when the independent variables of population, median family income, manufacturing wage in the second quarter of 1973, and use of arbitration are included in the regression equations along with the 1971 wage and the same dependent variables (the percent change and absolute change in salary from 1971 to 1974), the corrected R^2s fall from .60 and .51 (as shown in Table 4-4) to .56 and .48, respectively.

up." It is also possible, and seems quite logical, that the conventional wage comparisons made by the parties and the arbitrators will tend to reduce the existing wage dispersions even further.

The distance between the low and the high maximum base salary of police, firefighters, and deputy sheriffs in Wisconsin in 1974 is $385, $426, and $280, respectively.[f] Although these amounts seem rather large, they may reflect in part the wide variations in private sector wages by industry and in which section of the state high-paying industries are located. It is conceivable that the evening-out of wages of protective service employees will tend to even out the wages of other municipal employees and that eventually this trend will have some impact on the private sector. For example, the catch-up obtained by public safety employees in a rural area may spread to teachers and eventually have some impact on private sector wages in manufacturing in the area. Although it is assumed that causality runs from the private sector to the public sector, one possible long-run implication of the use of arbitration in the public sector is an eventual reduction in dispersion of private sector wages.

Participants' Views About the Impact of Arbitration on Bargaining Outcomes

Most management respondents prefaced their views of the effect of arbitration on wage levels and other aspects of bargaining outcomes by indicating that they were speculating because they were uncertain about its impact. Even allowing for this caveat, however, it appears that most managements believe that the existence of the arbitration system increases salaries above the level at which they otherwise might be set. Also, their views provide substantial reinforcement for the idea that the arbitration statute has resulted in a reduction of wage dispersion.

A common management response by representatives from smaller cities and rural counties was that the new statute gives the unions a "hammer" and provides the unions with leverage to increase wages substantially. Some of these representatives suggested that the wages of their protective service employees had lagged behind others in the state, but they thought that the gap was being reduced much too quickly. Union responses in these same environments were to the effect that the law makes the management more reasonable, more willing to bargain, and more willing to establish realistic wage levels.

---

[f] The range in 1974 from the low to the high maximum monthly base salary in cities and counties included in the regression analysis was police, $672 to $1,057; firefighters, $596 to $1,022; and deputy sheriffs, $680 to $960.

In some of the smaller cities and rural counties that as yet have not participated in the third-party processes of mediation, factfinding, or arbitration, management and union representatives understandably were more cautious in their assessments of the impact of arbitration on bargaining outcomes than those who had been involved. They tended to say that they hadn't experienced any change in the bargaining outcome as a result of the passage of the arbitration statute. For the most part, bargaining in these situations is of relatively recent origin and is conducted by local representatives without the aid of outside experienced representatives.

Responses from management and union representatives in two large cities in a rural area of the state provided further support for the idea that the arbitration statute has resulted in the reduction of wage dispersion. In one city that identified itself as a wage leader for its area, the respondents said that arbitration does not affect the size of wage increases. In a second city that had traditionally maintained a lower wage level than the first city, respondents were unanimous in saying that arbitration tends to raise wages in this city toward the level paid in the other city 90 miles away and to the wage level maintained in other cities of the same size in other sections of the state.

Some management spokesmen in larger cities in metropolitan areas where labor unions are relatively strong said that the existence of the statute does not raise wages above the level that, in the absence of the statute, they might otherwise have reached through collective bargaining, threats of industrial action, and increased political activities. This response is more characteristic of the experienced and sophisticated spokesmen. Union leaders in these same large pattern-setting cities tended to agree with their management counterparts and, in some instances, have avoided arbitration for this reason.

Other Aspects of the Impact of Arbitration on Bargaining

The availability of arbitration at the request of either party clearly helps weak unions, and it is assumed that this holds true for conventional arbitration and final-offer-by-issue as well as for final-offer-by-package arbitration. In formulating its bargaining position, municipal management must now take into account the possibility that the union will seek arbitration if the package seems unsatisfactory. Unions that formerly presented suggestions for improvements in wages and other conditions of employment to a finance committee of a city council or county board and then, possibly with some grumbling, accepted the offer determined unilaterally by management, have now forced management to take bargaining more seriously. They meet more often, they exchange proposals, and they modify their positions. Both parties appear eager to settle by themselves rather than to have an outsider make a binding decision on them. Threats of bringing in an outsider are used by the weaker party, however, in attempts to induce changes in the positions of the other party.

In some industrial communities in which the unions are strong, management is petitioning for arbitration. The threat of third-party judgments performs a valuable function in those situations in which elected officials are loath to alienate a potent labor vote. The existence of arbitration may restrain the strong union from pushing as hard as it otherwise might. In a few instances it appears that the stronger party—and this applies equally to unions and managements—is unwilling to compromise on a particular issue and has preferred, as a face-saving measure, that it be resolved adversely to its interests by an arbitrator. Overall, it appears that, since the parties prefer to settle by themselves in most situations, the existence of arbitration helps them to do so, although the terms of settlement may be different from those that would have prevailed in the absence of arbitration.

Another question raised about arbitration is whether unions will comply with the statute or engage in illegal job actions. In Wisconsin, compliance has been almost complete during the first three years the law has been in effect. A possible explanation is that the police and firefighter organizations sought the procedure. They see it as their statute, and this seems to have placed a responsibility on them to abide by it. Unions have engaged in self-help activities in only three negotiations out of the more than 300 that have been conducted. In each of these situations there were sick-outs, picketing, and efforts by the unions to publicize their cases. These actions occurred after negotiations had reached an impasse and were undertaken by the unions instead of their petitioning for arbitration.

In the two-and-one-half-year period prior to the passage of the statute, when factfinding was the terminal step in the procedure, there were three firefighter strikes and at least one one-day sick-out. Although this is a relatively good record, the subsequent experience under arbitration is even better.

In one of the three instances in which unions engaged in sick-outs and picketing, the city management petitioned for arbitration and subsequently won the arbitration case. Although the police involved in this dispute expressed their displeasure with what they regarded as an unfair award, they complied with it and ceased their efforts at self-help. In the second situation, mediation was invoked and a settlement was achieved.

In the third case, a settlement was eventually reached through negotiations, essentially on the union's terms. This dispute, which was mentioned in passing previously, is of interest because it may reflect an attitude of unions about arbitration that is characteristic of strong unions in industrial centers. The basic issue in dispute was the union demand for a cost-of-living clause, a provision rarely included in municipal labor agreements in Wisconsin.

The spokesman for the union thought that an arbitrator would not be willing to innovate and that comparisons with other communities in the area would lead the arbitrator to reject the union demand. He therefore chose instead to initiate an intensive public political education program favoring cost-of-living clauses, supplemented by broad-scale industrial action, not only by firefighters and police, but also by other city employees, teachers, and private sector union workers. Tactics included rallies, picketing of city hall, sick-outs, insistence that all negotiations be public, and inclusion of television and press representatives in union caucuses.

Sufficient pressure was generated on labor-supported public officials to force them to yield to the union demand for cost-of-living protection. It is too early to tell whether this tactic will spread. It is limited, however, to communities in which unions have considerable influence and to issues for which popular support can be mobilized; a cost-of-living clause in an inflationary period seems to be one of the few such issues.

Finally, it should be noted that personal interviews with union and management representatives confirm their preference for final-offer arbitration over conventional arbitration. Some management that had strenuously opposed the passage of the legislation suggested it was working far better than they had believed possible and they had discontinued their lobbying efforts to get the statute repealed. Most managements emphasized that the all-or-nothing aspect of the final-offer system was preferable to conventional arbitration because it forced the parties to take realistic positions and made it easier for them to reach a settlement without third-party help.

A minority position was expressed by several management and union spokesmen who said that final-offer arbitration encouraged gamesmanship and discouraged good-faith bargaining. It was their opinion that the parties attempted to formulate a position that would enable them to win in arbitration rather than one that would enable them to achieve a settlement without arbitration.

The results of the written questionnaire generally corroborated the findings based on the personal interviews, although factfinding was regarded with slightly more favor in the questionnaire responses of the management spokesmen than in the interviews. This may be attributable to an inclination to support the traditional management position when filling out a questionnaire and yet to state in private conversations that it is no longer practical to advocate returning to the use of factfinding as the terminal step in the dispute procedure.

Of the 56 responses from city management, 46 percent expressed a preference for some form of arbitration, 43 percent preferred factfinding, and 11 percent favored the right to strike. Of the 17 responses from county management, 41 percent favored some form of arbitration, 29.5 favored factfinding, and 29.5 favored the right to strike. (This last view was common among rural county boards that were opposed to the whole idea of collective bargaining.)

On the union side it was found that 66 percent of the 59 police negotiators who responded to this question favored some form of arbitration, while 19 percent favored factfinding and 15 favored the right to strike. Of the 39 firefighter negotiators who responded, 80 percent favored some form of arbitration, 10 percent favored factfinding, and 10 percent favored the right to strike. Of the 21 deputy sheriff negotiators who responded, 62 percent favored some form of arbitration, 19 percent favored factfinding, and 19 percent favored the right to strike.

Responses to the questionnaire also showed that although some form of arbitration is favored by most groups, there is considerable disagreement about the merits of final-offer arbitration relative to conventional arbitration. Firefighter and police association negotiators preferred final-offer arbitration over conventional arbitration but were evenly split on the question of whether it should be by issue or by package. Deputy sheriffs favored conventional arbitration over either form of final-offer arbitration. City and county management negotiators favored conventional arbitration over final-offer arbitration by an overwhelming margin—a finding that was in direct contradiction of the findings based on the personal interviews and on the actual practice of the parties.

If the questionnaire responses on this item are reliable, one would expect to find that conventional arbitration had been selected by the parties in many instances and that there would have been some discussion about the deletion of the preferential status of final-offer arbitration when that portion of the statute was amended by the legislature in 1973. For example, when the legislature simplified the procedure for selecting arbitrators, it also could have provided that the petitioner could opt for either procedure and that his choice would be binding on the other party. Or, alternatively, it could have provided that the party which was not the petitioner would be empowered to make the selection of the form of arbitration to be used.

In actual practice, however, conventional arbitration has been used only once in the first 42 cases in which awards have been issued as of March 1, 1975, and, so far as can be determined, neither management nor labor is attempting to persuade the legislature to change the procedure for selecting the form of arbitration. It appears that the questionnaire responses on this item should be discounted and that the opinions expressed during personal interviews are more indicative of the views of the participants.

It is difficult to predict the long-run effect of the statute on bargaining strategy. Going to arbitration one year has an effect on bargaining the next, just as an occasional strike keeps the threat of a strike meaningful. Using the arbitration procedure to induce the opposing party to take a relatively reasonable position, and still challenging it and losing, may occasionally have some advantages to union and management leaders in dealing with rank and file militants or political opposition. The behavioral permutations that final-offer arbitration may occasion are probably innumerable and difficult to anticipate. So far as anyone can tell, however, it has helped rather than hurt the bargaining process.

Summary

Initial reaction of labor and management to the first two-and-one-half years' experience with final-offer arbitration in Wisconsin is favorable. If the statute is evaluated from the viewpoint of such criteria as effect on the process and outcome of bargaining, a similarly favorable impression is gained. Most disputes are resolved by direct negotiations of the parties. There is considerable dependency on mediation, however, with approximately one-third of the disputes requiring some form of third-party assistance. It is hoped that this dependency will diminish as the parties gain experience, but there is no sign as yet of a reduction in the proportion of negotiations in which the services of mediators are requested.

Third-party dependency is explained by a myriad of political factors operating on both sides of the bargaining table and in the relationship of the bargainers to their constituencies. Divided authority among city or county councils and mayors and between them and relatively independent elected sheriffs and civil-service-life-tenured police and fire chiefs contributes strongly to dependency when there are personality differences and political rivalries.

Cities and counties outside Standard Metropolitan Statistical Areas in economically depressed areas are less likely to settle their disputes through arbitration than are major cities or suburban communities. Police tend to compare their salaries with the relatively low incomes of fellow residents and are not inclined to pursue economic goals very militantly. Also, police wage settlements serve as pattern-setters for law enforcement officers in surrounding towns and in the county. By these comparisons, the police believe that they are adequately paid and see no need to press their claims to arbitration. In turn, the law enforcement officers in the county and the smaller towns have not sought arbitration if their wage relationship with the pattern-setter is maintained.

Hard-pressed cities with less financial resources than other cities are more apt to resort to arbitration rather than meet the demands of police and firefighter groups. Firefighters and police tend to press their claims to arbitration more often in communities where there are large numbers of high-paying unionized manufacturing plants and in which other public sector employees receive large wage increases after striking or threatening to strike.

Only about 10 percent of all disputes eventually necessitate the issuance of binding arbitration awards. Although there are no objective standards by which to judge whether this is too many or too few, it is clear that the feared "narcotic effect" has not yet appeared.[17] Perhaps it will take a much longer period of time for this effect to develop. At present, however, the parties have not abandoned bargaining en masse and given decision making to the arbitrators. Of the 192 agreements in effect in 1974, possibly two were reached in a situation in which the bargainers tended to rely on arbitration to a degree that could be regarded as unhealthy.

During the two-and-one-half years that the arbitration statute has been in effect, there have been no strikes by any units covered by the statute, although there have been three instances of partial sick-outs, picketing, and related self-help activities. In the two-and-one-half years prior to the passage of the statute, there had been three firefighter strikes and at least one one-day sick-out. On the whole, it appears that there was substantial compliance with the no-strike provision of the statute when factfinding was the terminal step and that subsequently, after the enactment of arbitration, the record improved. There has been no instance in which self-help was used to set aside a factfinding or arbitration award; noncompliance has taken the form of resorting to job action and avoiding use of these terminal procedures rather than attempting to overturn them.

Regression analysis showed that wages of deputy sheriffs, police, and firefighters were significantly and positively related to private sector wages and median family income. It further showed that, with controls for various economic and demographic variables, cities and counties that had received arbitration awards did not pay significantly different wages than cities and counties that had not received arbitration awards.

Another finding of the regression analysis was that the dispersion in wages of deputy sheriffs was substantially reduced during the first two-and-one-half years that arbitration was in effect. To a lesser but significant degree, this was true also of police wages, but not of firefighter wages. This finding was supported by comments of respondents who believe that in the lower-paying cities and counties, the existence of arbitration raises wages, but that in the higher-paying cities it has no effect, or possibly even tends to dampen wage increases.

Whether or not the effect on bargaining outcomes of final-offer arbitration by package in Wisconsin differs from that of final-offer arbitration by economic issue in Michigan and that of conventional arbitration in Pennsylvania is a question to which attention is directed in the following chapters.

Notes

1. The first three years' experience is analyzed in James L. Stern, "The Wisconsin Public Employee Factfinding Procedure," *Industrial and Labor Relations Review* 20 (October 1966), pp. 3-29.

2. 111.70 (1)(b) and 111.70 (3), 1961 c.663; 1963 c.6, 87.

3. 111.70 (4)(j), 1961.

4. See "Wisconsin Public Employee Labor Relations at the Crossroad," 1970 Supplement to the Report of Task Force on State and Local Government Labor Relations (Chicago: Public Personnel Association, 1971), pp. 41-44.

5. Based on interviews with Durkin. It should be noted that most interviews were conducted on the basis of nonattribution of views to individual respondents, but in this case, with the permission of the respondent, he is identified so that the appropriate "credit" or "blame" can be allocated.

6. Durkin learned about and became favorably disposed to the procedure during a session of the Harvard University special continuing education program for trade union leaders taught by William Simkin, the former director of the Federal Mediation and Conciliation Service.

7. According to William Simkin, there had been discussion about the use of final-offer arbitration on an ad hoc basis over the past 30 years. An article by Carl Stevens, "Is Compulsory Arbitration Compatible with Bargaining," *Industrial Relations* 5 (February 1966), favored its use on theoretical grounds. Widespread attention was drawn to it, however, as a result of its endorsement by President Nixon in 1970 as a method of dealing with disputes in the transportation industry. It was also discussed by witnesses who appeared before the Wisconsin Governor's Advisory Committee on State Employment Relations; see summary minutes of the June 3, 1970, meeting, pp. 65-66 of the Report of the Committee.

8. *Walworth County Deputy Sheriff's Association v. Walworth County,* Prohibited Practice Charge, Case XXI, No. 17434, MP-303, Decision No. 12690, Wisconsin Employment Relations Commission, May 9, 1974.

The claim was subsequently dismissed, but prior to that time, the parties reached agreement through direct negotiations and with the help of WERC mediators.

9. See, for example, *City of Sun Prairie v. Sun Prairie Professional Policemen's Association, IBT,* Declaratory Ruling of the Wisconsin Employment Relations Commission, Decision No. 11703-A.

10. *Milwaukee Deputy Sheriff's Association v. Milwaukee County,* Case No. 585, August term, 1974, Supreme Court of the State of Wisconsin. The circuit court decision was upheld by the Supreme Court in its Decision No. 479, August term, 1974, filed October 1, 1974. Sufficient time has not elapsed for its impact to be felt, however, and therefore the paragraphs speculating about its potential effect have not been changed.

11. *Milwaukee Deputy Sheriff's Association v. Milwaukee County,* Memorandum Decision of the Circuit Court of Milwaukee, Judge Robert N. Curley, December 5, 1973.

12. Letters from Commissioner Morris Slavney, Chairman, Wisconsin Employment Relations Commission, March 1973, to the Honorable Charles C. Deneweth, Mayor, City of Superior.

13. *Waukesha County Sheriff's Union, Local 695, IBT v. Waukesha County,* Wisconsin Employment Relations Commission, Case XXV, No. 17330, MIA-62, Decision No. 12392-A.

14. Frank P. Zeidler, arbitrator, July 26, 1974, MIA-62, *Waukesha County Sheriff's Union, IBT v. Waukesha County.*

15. The details of the estimating procedure followed to derive the number of contracts negotiated each year are available from the author on request.

16. Data sources for the dependent and independent variables were as follows. Salaries of police, firefighters, and deputy sheriffs were obtained from mail questionnaires supplemented by information taken from the annual State of Wisconsin wage surveys and information obtained in personal interviews. The number of times arbitration was invoked with each group is taken from the records of the Wisconsin Employment Relations Commission. The 1973 weekly manufacturing wage is based on unemployment compensation data supplied by the Department of Industry, Labor, and Human Relations. The 1970 population and median family income data were obtained from the 1970 Census figures. The 1971 equalized mill rates and property values were obtained from *Town, Village and City Taxes 1971,* Wisconsin Department of Revenue, and the 1973 hourly wages of municipal truck drivers were obtained from annual State of Wisconsin wage surveys.

17. On the whole, the Wisconsin record from 1968 through 1974 tends to refute the statement made by W. Willard Wirtz at the 1963 meeting of the National Academy of Arbitrators in Chicago. He said: "Experience—

particularly the War Labor Board experience during the '40's—shows that a statutory requirement that labor disputes be submitted to arbitration has a narcotic effect on private bargainers, that they turn to it as an easy—and habit forming—release from the obligation of hard, responsible bargaining." *Daily Labor Report,* February 1, 1963, p. F-2.

5

Views of Mediators and Arbitrators

Two informal conferences, one on mediation and the other on arbitration of public sector interest disputes, were held March 27-29, 1974, at Wingspread, the Johnson Foundation conference center in Racine, Wisconsin.[1] The purpose of the mediation conference was to examine how mediation of interest disputes between public employers and public safety employees —police, firefighters, and, in some states, deputy sheriffs as well—is affected by different statutory arrangements providing for factfinding, for conventional arbitration, or for some type of final-offer arbitration. A majority of the participants were mediators. At the arbitration conference, arbitrators who had had experience as neutrals in such interest disputes evaluated the impact of the various impasse resolution procedures on the process and outcome of bargaining.

Mediation of Public Sector Interest Disputes

Many people familiar with the collective bargaining process and dispute resolution have expressed the opinion that mediation is an art. Most mediators agree, but they also stress that the most skillful and talented mediator can operate most effectively where mediation has a statutory role in the dispute-settlement machinery and where the mediator has some tools with which to work.

The discussion of mediation in the public sector ranged over experience in various jurisdictions, with emphasis on the relation of mediation to the collective bargaining process and the conditions for effective mediation. In particular, the experience in jurisdictions where the law specifies, and possibly emphasizes, mediation as a step prior to third-party resolution of interest disputes was compared with that in other situations where the law specifies compulsory arbitration with no prior mediation.

Statutory Provisions for Mediation

Statutory encouragement of mediation in police and firefighter cases varies from state to state.[a] In Michigan and Wisconsin, mediation is required

---

[a] County deputy sheriffs and traffic officers as well as city police and firefighters are covered by statutes in Michigan and Wisconsin.

before a dispute can proceed to final-offer arbitration. New York City has mediation up to the time that the report of the impasse panel (fact-finders) is accepted. Massachusetts has both a mediation step and a factfinding-with-mediation step in the procedure under its new final-offer arbitration law. Pennsylvania has no provision for mediation nor any board to administer its compulsory (conventional) arbitration law. Canada has only recently added a mediation step to most provincial procedures for the settlement of police and firefighter cases.

Mediation has been a part of the Michigan dispute-settlement system since 1939 when the private sector statute was enacted. Its labor relations legislation is administered by the Michigan Employment Relations Commission (MERC), which has a staff of professional mediators chosen through the civil service system. Since there must be 30 days of mediation before the arbitration process can be set in motion, some parties treat mediation as a legally required prearbitration step and resist attempts to resolve the dispute by mediation. Many of the tripartite arbitration panels (economic issue-by-issue under the Michigan law) also try to mediate an agreed settlement—or as much of an agreed settlement as possible.

Wisconsin stresses mediation to a greater degree than does Michigan. The administering agency is the Wisconsin Employment Relations Commission (WERC), which consists of three commissioners and a staff of mediators. In most situations, there is extensive mediation, and WERC will not certify the dispute to arbitration unless it is convinced that an impasse exists and that no purpose can be served by further mediation. Once an arbitrator is selected, in most instances the parties do not expect him to attempt further mediation. However, if during the hearing, he sees a possibility for an agreed settlement, or for the resolution of some issues, he may persuade the parties to resolve some or all of the issues on their own.[b]

"Settlement is the name of the game" in New York City, and the statutes include criteria that emphasize mediation of all public sector disputes. The mediator is usually selected by the parties from a roster of persons previously screened and approved by the tripartite Office of Collective Bargaining. The impasse panels (factfinders) are specifically authorized by statute to mediate during their hearings, after the hearings are completed, when the report (which may be an interim report) is issued, and right up to the time when the settlement is "accepted." There are no time limits on any step in New York City; the only time-limit problems in the state relate to budgets in some jurisdictions.

Massachusetts has a new final-offer arbitration statute for police and

---

[b] The City of Milwaukee is covered by a separate provision of the statute. See Chapter 4 for details.

firefighters that took effect July 1, 1974. Preconditions for arbitration are (1) the parties must have engaged in mediation for a prescribed period of time; (2) the parties must have participated in a factfinding process, the factfinder must have issued an opinion, and three days must have elapsed since the issuance of the recommendation; and (3) there must be no prohibited practice charge against either party on file with the State Labor Relations Commission. The Massachusetts Board of Conciliation and Arbitration (MBCA) and its small staff of mediators oversee mediation, factfinding, and final-offer arbitration as well as grievance arbitration. Under other Massachusetts labor relations legislation, factfinders are permitted to mediate, and it is presumed that they will mediate under the new law. Only unions may petition for final-offer arbitration, and once the preconditions are met, they must petition; they have no alternative. The petition goes to MBCA whose staff determines whether the preconditions have been met. Arbitration is by tripartite panel. The parties submit their final offers to the panel at the beginning of the hearing and have the right to amend them at the close of the hearing. Final-offer selection is by package, and the award is binding on both parties and the local legislative body. (The parties may agree to final and binding factfinding, but such an award would not be binding on the local legislative body unless it agreed in advance to be so bound.) There is provision for judicial review of the award, but the law is unclear as to the standard for review.

Although there is no provision for mediation in the Pennsylvania statute that specifies conventional arbitration as the terminal step in the procedure, there is some indication that, in practice, the neutral mediates in executive session of the tripartite panel.

On rare occasions, the Federal Mediation and Conciliation Service has been involved in mediating police and firefighter disputes. If the FMCS knows of such a dispute and if there is no state agency to handle it, it can offer its services; or if one party asks for federal mediation and the other party agrees, the FMCS may become involved. The FMCS Director has recently named seven regional coordinators whose assignments will be to concentrate on public sector disputes (primarily federal).

Compulsory conventional arbitration of disputes between police and firefighters and employing government units in most Canadian jurisdictions is required. The procedure is administered by the provincial attorney general who assigns a single arbitrator, usually on an ad hoc basis, to make a final and binding award; a full-time arbitrator for police and fire cases has recently been appointed in Ontario. Originally, there was no provision for mediation in the procedure, but the law has now been amended to add a mediation step—so recently that there has been no opportunity to assess the results. In contrast, the general legislation in Canada gives local government employees the right to strike and requires mediation and conciliation of interest disputes under the administration of the Minister of Labor prior to either a strike or factfinding with recommendations.

Mediation and the Collective Bargaining Process

The mediators' "game" is agreed settlement. They also feel strongly that mediation is and should be not only an integral part of the collective bargaining process but also completely compatible with it, and they believe that this fact should be recognized in any legislation. In their opinion, mediation and collective bargaining can be most effective where the statutes under which they operate stress negotiated settlements and where the procedures allow them maximum flexibility in helping the parties achieve agreement. As one conference participant put it: "If rigidities are built into the procedure, there will be no discretion and the parties to the negotiating process will be frustrated." They oppose any statute with built-in formal procedures, particularly where there is no regard for the effect of such procedures on the collective bargaining relationship. Rather, in their opinion, legislation should be designed to make the parties do the negotiating themselves and to face up to the possibility that they may really get hurt if they fail and that no one is going to bail them out.

Although the prior question of whether collective bargaining has a place in the public sector was hotly debated for many years, and still is in a few states, it is recognized and encouraged in the statutes under consideration here and in the policies of most of the agencies administering the laws. However, the compulsory arbitration and final-offer arbitration statutes are relatively new, and one participant suggested that perhaps the agencies are spending too much time on impasse-resolving procedures and not enough on developing competent people at the collective bargaining table.

Another participant suggested that education can be a useful complement to experience in helping the parties to gain an understanding not only of the collective bargaining process but also of the procedures, and perils, under compulsory arbitration. In Michigan, for example, MERC, employer and union organizations, and the state universities worked together on an extensive education campaign during the first year or so after their public employment relations law was enacted. In the opinion of the speaker, such an effort can be especially rewarding for public employee and employer organizations who are accustomed to lobbying for economic benefits and who, therefore, are unfamiliar with contract negotiations. It can be equally rewarding for the local people with no knowledge of collective bargaining or of the law under which they are negotiating. It was also noted that even though final-offer arbitration laws are several years old, the education process is still going on, as new relationships are established and the older ones gain experience.

Mediators, too, can play an important role in educating the parties about the collective bargaining process: (1) on the scope of bargaining and what issues can and cannot go to arbitration; (2) on what a violation of the law might do to the collective bargaining relationship; and (3) on what the predictabilities and lack of certainties are under a given procedure, including making the parties aware of what other outcomes under the system have been. In this connection, a warning was sounded that sometimes the legal issues on what is or what is not bargainable obscures the efforts to reach an agreement and that under final-offer arbitration, sometimes the legal issues become paramount.

Yet there was general consensus among the participants that final-offer arbitration has encouraged rather than chilled bargaining, although unions' having the right to strike might have a similar effect. One participant was of the opinion that the legislation has stimulated bargaining because the availability of arbitration has created collective bargaining for large numbers of public employees who had never had it before, who had lobbied for wages and benefits, who could not strike, and who had had factfinder's reports ignored by governmental agencies. Further, it was noted that one of the things government does best is nothing, and the threat that some procedure under the law is going to be invoked has resulted in getting both sides down to the business of bargaining.

Conditions for Effective Mediation

Measured in terms of the number of disputes settled by agreement prior to final-offer arbitration, the laws apparently have had the desired effect on the parties of encouraging them to negotiate their own contracts, with or without mediation, according to the mediators who have had experience under the laws. The vast majority of collective bargaining agreements are negotiated by the parties themselves, without assistance. Others are settled with the help of mediators prior to arbitration.

Although those who administer the final-offer arbitration legislation were quick to point out that experience under the laws has been much too limited for them to identify any long-term trends or to make meaningful comparisons with experience under other procedures, they did have some statistics to support their assertions that the legislation has been successful in achieving agreed settlements at some stage.

Of more interest to the mediators were the apparent effects of the final-offer threat in creating a climate for effective mediation, and especially where arbitration would seem to be the better alternative to settlement based on relative economic strength, as has frequently been the case during the past decade—a period during which the public safety employees strongly supported final-offer arbitration legislation and looked to it as a device to be used to enable them to catch up with private sector and some public employees, especially in wages and related economic benefits. It was agreed that mediation is difficult, if not impossible, with parties whose strategy is aimed at arbitration as the terminal point, but it was also suggested that some parties may be using the procedure simply because it was there and, possibly, because they were inexperienced with collective bargaining or with the use of mediators to assist them in reaching a negotiated settlement. In the opinion of the mediators, as the parties gain experience, as the unions achieve their short-term economic goals, and, perhaps, as both sides are "burned" a time or two with unfavorable awards, there will be fewer cases going the arbitration route and more contracts being worked out by the parties themselves, or with the assistance of a mediator on difficult issues in dispute.

One participant noted: "Acceptability and understanding of the process are important. The reality of a dispute settlement process or the possibility of a strike creates a dispute settlement atmosphere. When you have these two realities, then there is an atmosphere for dispute settlement. It doesn't have to be purely a private sector business built upon a strike deadline. It can work in the public sector with the arbitration mechanism."

Acceptability and understanding, and the resulting dispute-settlement atmosphere, are conditions that would ease the way for the mediator in his efforts to help the parties come to an agreed settlement of an interest dispute. A number of others were suggested. For example, in the best of climates, and certainly in the worst, the mediator should be skilled in his "art," including the ability to overcome the parties' disinterest in mediation. He should feel that he is an intimate part of the collective bargaining process and not a third party to it. Over time he will become even more effective as he becomes familiar with his clients and learns to "read their signs." Still another factor, which could be either contributive or destructive of his efforts, is his agency's view of its role—that is, whether it has a commitment to agreed settlements or a preference for "kicking upstairs" the tough cases. At least one of the mediators said that having arbitration in the wings makes it more of a challenge to him to work for a settlement and avoid arbitration.

The parties' uncertainty about the outcome of final-offer arbitration is one of the most important, and positive, factors a mediator can use in cases involving public safety employees. It was generally agreed that the best possible climate in which a mediator could be effective was one in which at least one and preferably both parties have some uncertainty about the consequences of alternative action, although it was pointed out that this condition would be likely to prevail only in situations where arbitration did not seem to the parties to be the better alternative. The presence of an unreasonable demand or demands also provides a lever for a mediator to use to convince the parties to negotiate a "livable" contract rather than to risk ending up with unworkable provisions in the contract under the final-offer procedure.

In the discussion of other methods a professional mediator can, and does, use in convincing the parties that settlement is more attractive than passing the responsibility for determining the provisions of a contract on to a third party, the following were mentioned: (1) an appeal to the parties' pride in being able to settle their differences themselves; (2) stress on logic and the world of reality (what happens if there is no settlement); (3) scare tactics, based on what an arbitrator might do; (4) stress on the cost of arbitration particularly for small units (although cost may not be a factor if the unit's international union wants to go for a substantial economic package in an arbitration award in order to be able to point to it in efforts to organize other small units); and (5) emphasis on the pattern of settlement in the geographic area.

It was frequently mentioned that political as well as economic pressures are at work during the whole dispute-settlement process and in some cases, a mediator may be able to "sell" a solution to the rank and file on either side that the leadership, for political reasons, could not sell. Such a situation frequently obtains where the membership is relatively unsophisticated but where there is good will and a desire for resolution on both sides. However, other mediators said that they found it more difficult to mediate with unsophisticated than with sophisticated people, pointing out that experience with the alternative (arbitration) sometimes creates a condition that makes it possible for a mediator to be effective.

A mediator may be very effective in other cases where he is able to achieve a negotiated settlement between the parties but where they do go to arbitration because one of the negotiators, for political reasons, could not put his name to the settlement and needs the third-party sanction, or "laying on of hands."

With regard to the attitudes of the employee organizations, at least two of the participants suggested that the firefighters seemed to be more interested than were the police in resolving disputes by mediation, possibly because they live together and are accustomed to adjusting their daily differences, whereas the police work alone or in pairs and are accustomed to passing problems on to a third party for resolution in a paramilitary setting.

There was general agreement that in cases where an impasse is unresolved and eventually goes to arbitration, the mediator plays a significant role in resolving some issues, in narrowing others, and in defining the scope of bargaining—that is, by explaining what issues can and what cannot go to arbitration in various jurisdictions. Some mediators complained that they had no "veto power" over a dispute's going to the next level, as they had under factfinding procedures. But in one jurisdiction, the mediator must certify that an impasse exists before the dispute can go to arbitration, which gives him a degree of leverage and some input into the arbitration process. In another, the administrator can refuse to appoint an impasse panel unless the parties bargain down to a reasonable number of issues; in this jurisdiction, there is mediation input throughout the entire process.

Many situations were cited where the role of the mediator is especially difficult, and even chaotic—for example, where one or the other party overdoes the democratic process and the mediator must deal with multiple representatives who often cannot agree among themselves. There are cases where a party may be going for the "last goodie," and if the item is important enough to them, nothing the mediator can do will prevent them from going to arbitration—the "what-have-we-got-to-lose" syndrome. Statutory time restrictions may prevent a mediator from getting back into a case in instances where the parties modify the positions they maintained with the mediator when they formulate their final offers for the arbitrator; these offers might be close enough together for the mediator to be able to effect a "corridor" settlement—and sometimes he does, if there are no statutory bars. There may be cases where the weaker party may simply have to avoid mediation to accomplish its goals and rely upon the generally accepted "wisdom" that arbitration tends to equalize disparity of power to the disadvantage of the stronger party. However, it was argued that there also are cases where the stronger party uses delaying tactics and legal maneuvers to completely frustrate the weaker party. One participant noted that avoiding arbitration with such tactics was getting to be an "art form" in some situations.

Finally, there are cases where the parties feel that the mediator lacks authority and they are looking toward mediation in a tripartite arbitration panel, or some type of "super-mediation." Under procedures where the next steps are either factfinding or tripartite arbitration, or both, parties may tend to hold up some of their cards in mediation so that they will have some to play in the next round. In Wisconsin, where the single arbitrator chooses between the final package offers of the parties, this problem for the mediator does not exist, but it may make mediation especially difficult in other situations.

Conclusion

Conventional wisdom is that compulsory arbitration is destructive of the collective bargaining process because it prompts the parties to take extreme positions in the expectation that the arbitrator will arrive at some midpoint in his award. The theory behind final-offer arbitration is that it will exert a centripetal force on the parties toward a middle ground and thus create a climate for settlement, because the cost of disagreement is so great that they will be more likely to settle than to risk an arbitrator's award.

A question before the conference was the validity of this general proposition in terms of the experience of those who had mediated disputes between police, firefighters, or, in some states, deputy sheriffs and their employers under various compulsory arbitration statutes. A number of the participants were unconvinced that conventional arbitration now is actually destructive of collective bargaining, although it may have been at one time; others were unconvinced that conventional arbitration is compatible with collective bargaining. However, there was consensus that mediation is more effective under final-offer arbitration than under conventional arbitration or factfinding—that it has "more life to it."

Although there was sharp disagreement on whether an arbitrator should attempt mediation, none of the participants doubted that if the parties expected this, the mediation efforts of anyone else prior to arbitration would be minimized. There was some evidence that the arbitrator under conventional arbitration was in a better position to mediate than the mediator. Statutory rigidities also would limit the flexibility that mediators believe is necessary for maximum effectiveness. Also mentioned was the complementarity between mediation and final-offer arbitration in that mediation not only helps the parties reduce the number of issues in dispute but also helps shape final offers so that disasters will not be consequent upon what is finally chosen by the arbitrator. The pressure of risks of final-offer arbitration on the parties seems to be resulting in their mediating themselves to settlement more often than they did under alternative systems.

The mediators were aware that political as well as economic pressures are at work in almost every public safety employee dispute, on both sides of the bargaining table, complicating their efforts toward settlement; they also recognized that inevitably there would be situations in which one side or the other would agree to a settlement in mediation but could not say so publicly, for political reasons. In such cases, an arbitration award would be necessary so that the party could point to it as a third-party settlement, although it might be no more than a "laying of hands" on a previously negotiated contract.

A real need, according to some mediators, is for coordination of formal dispute settlement procedures with informal mediation processes, and an opportunity for mediation throughout the settlement process of disputes that go to factfinding, arbitration, or the courts. One participant noted that under factfinding, in some jurisdictions, there is minimal connection between the mediator and the factfinder or impasse panel, while in others, although the mediator is not an active participant in the factfinding process, he is standing by to assist if there is an indication that the parties are moving toward settlement.

Noted as a possible "side effect" of the introduction of final-offer arbitration is an increase in the number of collective bargaining relationships, as small units who previously felt they lacked the power to force their employers to get down to serious collective bargaining see the law as a "weapon" to be used to force the employer to negotiate wages and working conditions. One result is a shortage of persons knowledgeable about public sector collective bargaining and dispute-settlement procedures. Already there is a need for more people, including mediators and arbitrators, who understand the public sector and the use the parties make of their strengths and weaknesses under the statutes and who will be able to recognize and deal with such issues of the present and future as the "relativities," or parity issues, among the various occupations, the value the public places on those occupations, and the social structure in public employment.

Arbitration of Public Sector Labor Disputes

Five questions were addressed to the participants in the conference on arbitration of public sector labor disputes:

1. Does the availability of final-offer arbitration cause more, less, or the same proportion of impasses and third-party settlements than alternative procedures?
2. Does final-offer arbitration tend to increase, decrease, or have no effect on the size of the economic package?
3. What do the participants in bargaining perceive as the effect of final-offer arbitration?
4. So far as can be determined, does the existence of this procedure damage the chance of achieving success either by the parties or by mediation before the dispute gets to an arbitrator?
5. If it does damage the chances, does it do so more or less than the damage that might be done by the existence of a factfinding statute or a statute providing for compulsory arbitration?

Those who had had experience with final-offer-by-economic-issue or by-package were asked to distinguish, if possible, between the effects of each.

Some of these questions were answered only tangentially, as the discussion ranged over the statutory provisions regulating the resolution of disputes between public safety employees and their public employers in Pennsylvania, Michigan, and Wisconsin, and the very general, and in some cases very limited, experience under those statutes. As the raison d'être for such laws is the avoidance of direct action tactics and interruptions of services, the participants were particularly interested in debating the value of final-offer or compulsory arbitration as an alternative to the strike and its relationship to the collective bargaining process.

One underlying question was whether any kind of compulsory arbitration in a dispute over the interests of employees and their employers was proper in a society where a collective bargaining system is accepted for its social worth. If so, and arbitration was determined by statute to be the only recourse available to public safety employees in the face of a strike ban, should the requirements for a final-offer arbitration procedure be so stringent that the parties would not dare to risk the consequences of arbitration and would, instead, negotiate their own settlement? Or should the statutory provisions for final-offer arbitration be flexible enough to allow either continuation of negotiations during a hearing or in executive session or continued mediation outside the hearing, but under the threat of an imposed settlement?

Pro's and Con's on the Efficacy of Final-Offer Arbitration

Conventional wisdom is that if the terminal point of a procedure is inflexibility fixed and does not include the possibility of a strike, as in the statutes under consideration, the parties will not bargain and will direct their strategy toward that terminal point. Does final-offer or some other type of compulsory arbitration pose sufficient risk for the parties that they will revise their strategy in order to avoid reaching a fearsome terminal point? In other words, how effective is final-offer arbitration in stimulating collective bargaining and a negotiated settlement, and what are the criteria for assessing its effectiveness?

A suggested criterion was acceptability of the *process* by the parties, not necessarily acceptability of the arbitrated settlement. The process must be sufficiently viable that it will not force the parties out into the street, and it must be acceptable enough that they will comply with the law. As an indication that the process might be acceptable to the parties, one participant noted that the firefighters had lobbied hard for final-offer arbitration by package in Wisconsin in order to eliminate the flexibility the arbitrator had under the previous factfinding approach, which they saw as giving them less than what the police were awarded in settlements over the years. In Pennsylvania and Michigan, both the police and firefighters supported compulsory arbitration legislation as a device to enable them to "catch up" in wages with private sector employees and, in Pennsylvania, with public safety employees elsewhere.

Several participants argued that the sole criterion for measuring the effectiveness of a final-offer arbitration procedure was its nonuse, because supposedly the procedure was designed to be so unacceptable that in all cases the parties would choose the bargaining alternative—but acceptable enough that they would not resort to illegal direct-action strikes or sick-leave abuses. One participant suggested that maximum pressure to settle would be exerted on the parties by an arbitration system requiring: (1) total-package rather than issue-by-issue arbitration; (2) both economic and noneconomic issues heard at the same time; (3) one final offer, with no opportunity to revise it, to be submitted at the beginning of the arbitration hearing; (4) single rather than tripartite arbitration (and thus no expectation of further negotiation in a tripartite executive session); (5) no expectation that the arbitrator would mediate (but outside mediation constantly available); and (6) selection of one of the two packages by the arbitrator, with no written opinion.

Others argued that the final-offer provision might be called successful in achieving its purpose if only one or two well-defined issues, economic or political, ultimately went to arbitration, where it did not matter to the parties which way the settlement went. Under final-offer arbitration, what should be assessed is not the quality of the arbitration award but the quality of the behavioral activities of the parties under the statutes.

Some participants who were dubious about the whole concept of final-offer arbitration suggested that perhaps it was only a current vogue or panacea that might be worthy of a trial but was of questionable value in achieving the desired results of settlement through negotiations without third-party intercession of any kind. What is important in the assessment, one participant again emphasized, are the behavioral implications of the process. Will the parties consider the process a sort of Russian roulette, where the risk is so great that they will get back to the business of bargaining? Or does it introduce a "gaming problem," especially in the package approach, where a party's strategy might be to take a position on the major issues that would "convert" the arbitrator and then throw in some costly items "that the arbitrator may not notice" because of the complexity of the package? In the latter case, a party's total strategy might well be directed toward the terminal point—arbitration—with the result that good faith bargaining would be undermined, as occurs under the Rhode Island compulsory arbitration law, according to one participant.

A comment was made that some arbitrators seem to feel that they can fashion better awards than either of the choices before them in multiple issue cases. Yet, this critic continued, the theory behind final-offer arbitration is that an arbitrator's decision should constitute so great a risk to the parties that they will negotiate their own agreements rather than go the final-offer route. Arbitrators who see themselves as dispute-settlers apparently are troubled by the final-offer process, and their orientation toward explanation, rationalization, and self-justification has colored how they look at the whole final-offer idea. They appear to be frustrated by their inability to come up with a "magical [compromise] package."

Although there was general agreement among the arbitrators that effective mediation is an important ingredient of any dispute-settlement procedure, there was a wide variety of opinion about such questions as who would do the mediating and at what point in the procedure it should start and end. Finally, the point was made that final-offer arbitration is not a true substitute for the strike because in a strike situation negotiations proceed until a settlement, while under a strictly run final-offer arbitration system there is no room for further negotiations after each party submits its final offer to the arbitrator.

The Pennsylvania Experience

Pennsylvania has had a compulsory conventional arbitration law for police and firefighters since 1968.[c] It requires tripartite arbitration of impasses, but there is no provision for mediation nor criteria for arbitrators to use in making their awards.

According to those at the conference who had had experience under the law, the majority vote problem gets the panel into a situation not unlike several rounds of final-offer arbitration by issue, where the neutral tries to move one or both parties to a position he believes is equitable. However, the potential for inducing the parties to modify their positions (the final-offer weapon) is lacking. There was general agreement on the strengths of the Pennsylvania system:

1. It is acceptable in terms of compliance; there have been no strikes.
2. It is useful in getting at the real issues and strengths of positions, although there is some evidence of arbitration being used for internal political purposes by one side or the other.
3. It protects against introduction of the "zinger" (extraneous issue) better than does final-offer package arbitration.
4. Decisions can be made in terms of the realities of the situation; for example, a pension issue can be considered in terms of the effects of a change on other employees of the municipality.

Those describing the Pennsylvania experience seemed to feel that in essence arbitration under the law often is a tripartite bargaining session,

[c] State police and public safety employees in Allegheny County only are also covered by the statute.

which raised the recurrent question of whether the arbitrator's proper role was to mediate and/or to manipulate the parties to his (third-party) position. Should the arbitrator properly assume the larger role of dispute-settler? It was suggested that if the parties give any hint that they might settle, he should give them a reasonable opportunity to explore the resolu-ion by taking the dispute off the table. There was general agreement that a settlement with the parties' own signatures at the bottom was superior to a third-party settlement.

Other conference participants maintained that some coercion necessarily obtains in tripartite arbitration—that the parties go along with the neutral because they know that he has to come down on one side or the other eventually and that there is a risk that he will go the other way if they don't move. Thus, the procedure in Pennsylvania is similar to the Michigan tripartite final-offer-by-economic-issue process.

Some participants argued that the neutral's role in tripartite arbitration is not mediation because he has a point of view, which raised the question of whether or not he should represent the "public interest." Others count-ered that a point of view was not necessarily synonymous with the "public interest."

Although most arbitrators seemed to be "comfortable" with the Penn-sylvania system, some of them cited situations that made them uncom-fortable: (1) the parties talking off-the-record outside the executive session —at a panel's informal dinner, for example; (2) pseudo-negotiated settlements, where negotiations take place in executive session and the arbitrator is simply someone to "lay hands" on the final product; (3) situ-ations in the executive session where the partisans have compromised on an issue to an agreement with which the arbitrator disagrees, and he must decide whether to go along, in a unanimous decision, or dissent; and (4) situations in which the arbitrator, once he is into a case, has the feeling that the only reason the arbitration is taking place is so that the lawyers can collect fees.

It was claimed that, in general, arbitration has not had a chilling effect on collective bargaining in the smaller jurisdictions in Pennsylvania: "They have gone in and out of arbitration. They have been offended by an award and have gone to negotiations after arbitration." The large jurisdictions have tended to go to arbitration more frequently than have the smaller units. The medium-sized cities are in and out of arbitration. There was con-jecture that Pennsylvania was past the "learning" and "catch-up" period and that there was some feeling on the part of the unions that now not as much can be "squeezed out of arbitration." However, the observers felt that movement in and out of arbitration would continue. They believed that the unions had accomplished what they saw as the purpose of the law, namely, catch-up; that most of the arbitrators are comfortable with their awards; and that the parties are generally satisfied with the process.

The Wisconsin Experience

The general law covering public employees in Wisconsin has been in effect since 1962 and calls for factfinding with recommendations if the parties reach an impasse in their negotiations. In 1972, a final-offer arbitration statute was enacted to apply to impasses between police, firemen, and deputy sheriffs and their employers (see Chapter 4 for exceptions). Under this law, a single arbitrator (unless the parties request a panel) is restricted to making a choice between the final-offer packages submitted by each of the parties. The parties may opt for conventional arbitration of their dispute, but they seldom do.

One strength of the procedure, or success criterion, as judged by those who have had experience under the law, is that they find they are making their decisions within a narrow framework. They reported that fewer issues come to the arbitrator than were presented to them when they served as factfinders, possibly because the parties have gained a degree of sophistication in their previous experience with factfinding, because prior mediation has succeeded to a degree in resolving some issues, or because the parties recognize the perils of a "grab bag" in final-offer. Another participant pointed out that the system avoids giving the parties what they don't want, which sometimes happens in conventional arbitration if the arbitrator refuses to go along with either party.

A number of problems inherent in the Wisconsin procedure were noted:

1. An arbitrator has difficulty making a choice when a "zinger" is in the package submitted by one side or the other. Does the presence of such an extraneous issue compel the arbitrator to reject the whole package?
2. Should an arbitrator decide what he sees as a public policy issue, if such is included in the package? Does he have an alternative?
3. What does the arbitrator do in cases where the package contains both wage items and managerial items?
4. What does he do if there are many (too many) issues submitted to him for decision? It was suggested that a case in which a great many items remained unresolved provides evidence that bargaining or mediation has failed, or has been chilled, and that conventional arbitration would be the preferable method for resolution. In any event, the arbitrator

would have to try to reduce the number of issues before proceeding with his efforts to arbitrate.

5. What happens if the overriding issues go in opposite directions and cannot be settled by any technique except to give an overwhelming advantage to one side or the other? What happens if only totally unacceptable packages, in terms of contract administration, are submitted to the arbitrator? One suggestion was that if an unworkable arrangement is the only solution, the dispute should be returned to the parties to work their own way out of it.

6. A more general problem, which applies to any arbitrated settlement, is that the arbitrator seldom knows what happens in the labor-management relationship after he has left the scene.

On the question of whether there should be a written opinion, one participant expressed his judgment that there is a need to comment on each issue. He said that he usually found that there was one or several issues on which the parties were not far apart and thus played no part in his decision; he made his decision on the basis of one or two overriding issues and made this known to the parties. Another participant said that he felt a need to demonstrate, in a written opinion, that he took account of the statutory criteria.

The proposition that the parties, under this particular kind of compulsory arbitration, would direct their strategies toward the terminal point to the neglect of any serious bargaining or mediation was discussed at some length. The question posed was "Would it not be a rational strategy for a party to identify what the arbitrator would consider to be the overriding issue, to make an offer as close as possible to what the arbitrator might choose, and then to add as many other items as possible?" It was pointed out that there was a danger that this strategy, by hitching a number of what might be minor items to the overriding issues, might lead to a substantial advantage for one side. In response, one participant argued that the proposition was based on the questionable assumption that at least one party to the dispute was structuring its whole case to get the best advantage in final-offer arbitration; in practice, he and others have found that the parties have tended to bargain to an agreement, or at least to narrow the issues. A comment related to strategy was the suggestion that municipalities might tend to take a "reasonable," but conservative, approach in their offers and unions might opt for more risk, on the premise that they would not lose much—that is, they would get a "reasonable" settlement—and might gain a lot.

It was agreed that there has been too little experience with final-offer arbitration in Wisconsin to be able to identify trends with regard to city size and frequency of arbitration.

The Michigan Experience

The Michigan legislature enacted an experimental law in 1969 that required arbitration of interest disputes between public safety employees and their employers. In 1972, the law was renewed but amended to provide for final-offer arbitration, issue by issue, of only the economic issues in dispute; noneconomic issues are handled by conventional arbitration. Arbitration is by a tripartite panel, and the panel makes the decision on whether an issue is economic or noneconomic.

Conference participants who have arbitrated under the system see it as an extension of collective bargaining, not as a chilling of it. They report that as many cases are going to final-offer arbitration as went the arbitration route under the previous law, but that almost twice as many settlements are being reached without an award.

A number of positive factors associated with the Michigan system were noted:

1. Hearings are shortened.
2. The parties are forced to hone their demands; thus the issues are reduced or narrowed down.
3. The noneconomic issues are separated out, item by item, and handled by conventional arbitration methods.

It was pointed out, however, that these noneconomic issues are not examined in the abstract; rather, they are considered in relation to each other and to the economic issues, which enables the panel to formulate a reasonable package. Apparently, however, the system allows maximum flexibility. For example, one arbitrator described the process as not unlike the well-known device of "med-arb," where he indicates his views and has the power to cajole the parties and bring them closer together toward a settlement even though, in the end, the award is the final offer of one party or the other on each economic issue. He claims that, in the executive session, he can get from the partisan members of the panel an idea of the parties' priorities and thus can put together the final package with the items weighted accordingly. He sees the essential structure of final-offer being preserved and more settlements being achieved than under compulsory arbitration, possibly because there is an opportunity for noneconomic items to be traded off for economic items in order to reach an agreement in the executive session.

In contrast, another arbitrator, who also has had a number of final-offer cases in Michigan, said that although the statute does, in some cases, invite mediation in the tripartite panel, he does not mediate. Instead, he exercises the options of sending the parties back to mediation or simply telling them to go back and think over their final offers because he will not allow them to modify their positions after an executive session—but adding that he is willing to incorporate any agreement they might reach on various issues into the award. He believes that the issue approach allows him to get a consensus from the two parties on what looks like a good contract while allowing either party to dissent on parts it does not like. The first arbitrator does not write opinions; the second arbitrator does.

On the question of whether there were any differences between the Michigan final-offer-by-issue procedure and conventional arbitration, some participants agreed that the systems are quite similar but that structural variables exist: (1) whether or not the board is tripartite; (2) whether final-offer arbitration is to be defined as with mediation or without it. There was no consensus within the group on the question.

A question also was raised as to whether the Michigan issue-by-issue system is really final-offer arbitration. In response, one of the arbitrators pointed out that he uses the partisan panel members throughout the hearing and tips them off that if they do not modify their positions, he will decide against one side or the other. Thus, he induces the parties to move in the direction of settlement of the economic issues—a technique not unlike that used by some neutrals in tripartite grievance arbitration.

With regard to use of the final-offer procedure, disputes in some large cities go to arbitration every year; others are in and out. Use does not seem to depend on the sophistication of the parties, but the cost factor seems to affect use in disputes in smaller governmental units.

The experience in Eugene, Oregon, is not unlike that described by one of the Michigan arbitrators in that the two whole-package final offers allowed each party in multi-issue disputes and the tripartite arbitration panel structure create a climate for mediation in the executive session.

Summary

It was agreed that it is difficult to identify a sharp dichotomy between what is called final-offer arbitration and conventional arbitration, although there are several dimensions along which the schemes may differ. Among these differences are (1) how much mediation gets done; (2) who does it; (3) where it is located within the structure; (4) whether or not the parties participate in the decision making; and (5) whether the award is issue-by-issue or package. What really needs to be examined is the consequences of the system for collective bargaining rather than what happens during each process.

There seemed to be agreement among the participants that settlements take place in different ways, with different laws, and with different people administering them. Tripartism seems to be effective in mediating and negotiating settlements under the Pennsylvania and Michigan procedures; in operation, the Michigan system does not seem to be unlike the conventional arbitration system in Pennsylvania. Written opinions with the awards seem to be less essential in those states than in Wisconsin where the arbitrator has to choose between two packages. The system in Wisconsin, and possibly also in Michigan, seems to result in a narrowing of the issues, the position of the parties, and the number of issues that ultimately go to arbitration, but the Wisconsin package approach may result in inequities no matter which final offer the arbitrator chooses. Other problems faced by arbitrators of interest disputes at one time or another were cited: (1) lack of sophistication on the part of some parties who may not realize the dangers of maintaining their positions, no matter what the mediators may have told them; (2) attempts to undermine the process by some parties who, not for lack of sophistication, deliberately maintain their positions, resort to delaying tactics, and appeal awards to the courts; and (3) a kind of "creeping incrementalism" whereby over a period of years the parties may be able to get the arbitrator to choose a side that adds in rather small segments to their position.

One participant reviewed the discussion from the perspective of how the variations in procedures under final-offer arbitration might have an impact on the collective bargaining process and how they might affect the role of the arbitrator working under these procedures. In his analysis, he identified a series of alternative provisions in final-offer systems and made a judgment of which would be the more stringent or the more flexible, and thus more effective, in exerting the maximum pressure on the parties to settle their own differences:

1. The choice between final-offer package and issue-by-issue would be the one that permits the analysis of the components in a fashion most readily geared to being used as a lever to get the parties to come to their own resolution of the dispute.
2. The choice between separating out economic issues or including both economic and noneconomic issues in the consideration would be the one that best results in a narrowing of the issues in dispute.
3. The choice between one final offer or two or more would be the one that permits revision in positions as late as possible and, therefore, permits the greater movement toward mutuality prior to the issuance of any award.
4. The choice between having the final offer at the beginning or at the end of the hearing would be the one under which it would be easiest to work out an adjustment prior to receiving the parties' final offers and, hope-

fully, where the final offers would become a mere rubric for compliance with the law and in forming the award.

5. The choice between a procedure where the arbitrator is expected to mediate or one where he lacks the statutory authority to do so would be the one that gives the neutral the most leverage in getting the parties to resolve their dispute, whether it be mediation by a mediator or by an arbitrator.

6. The choice between a single arbitrator or a tripartite panel would be a function of where the strong partisans are. Tripartite arbitration might be preferable because it provides an opportunity for bringing the parties together—if the partisan members of the panel are the strong spokesmen for each side. A single arbitrator might be able to accomplish the same end by mediating with the two strongest spokesmen.

7. Hopefully, there would have to be no choice between having or not having a written opinion. No written opinion would be necessary if the arbitrator is a successful mediator under any procedure, unless, of course, an opinion is needed by one side or the other to enable a partisan member of a tripartite panel to dissent "for the record," although concurring in fact.

Avoidance of the end result—the choosing of one or the other final offer by an arbitrator—seems to be the prime objective of final-offer arbitration procedures. The question remains whether under any compulsory procedure it is detrimental or salutary for the collective bargaining process in the long run to have mediation to a compromise done by a mediator or by an arbitrator.

In sum, it was agreed that low usage of the procedure is preferable to high usage, reduction of the number of issues to a few is preferable to multiple issues, and a narrowing of the gap between the parties on any specific issue is desirable. However, it must be recognized that the parties are heterogeneous, and a system that may be successful in terms of acceptability and compliance for the large units and sophisticated parties may not work at all for the small units and unsophisticated parties, and one that works well now may not have the same results a few years hence. The participants agreed that thus far there has not been enough experience under any of the statutes to come to firm conclusions on viability or on the key question of whether final-offer arbitration procedures are less chilling to collective bargaining than any other form of compulsory arbitration. A warning was raised of the possible danger of some inexperienced party's insisting on court interpretations of the ambiguously worded statutes in Michigan and Wisconsin, which might result in limiting the flexibility of the arbitrator in his attempts to help the parties reach a workable solution to their dispute.

Final-Offer Arbitration as Viewed by Arbitrators in
Wisconsin, Michigan, and Pennsylvania

To supplement the views of the participants at the Wingspread conference and to obtain the judgments of other arbitrators about their experiences with final-offer and other forms of arbitration, questionnaires were sent to arbitrators with recent experience under the Wisconsin, Michigan, and Pennsylvania statutes. The returns, which were received from 39 arbitrators, covered a total of 71 cases—that is, in Pennsylvania, 25 cases (12 arbitrators); in Wisconsin, 14 cases (7 arbitrators); and in Michigan, 32 cases (20 arbitrators).

What Procedure Do Arbitrators Prefer?

Arbitrators in each of the states were asked to rank their preferences among the various dispute-settlement procedures: final-offer-by-package, final-offer-by-issue, conventional, and factfinding. The responses must be viewed in light of the respondents' experience. Wisconsin arbitrators typically had experience with factfinding and final-offer-by-package, and perhaps with conventional arbitration. Michigan arbitrators typically had experience with final-offer-by-economic-issue, factfinding, and conventional, but not with final-offer-by-package. Pennsylvania arbitrators tended to have experience with conventional arbitration and factfinding, but with neither type of final-offer arbitration.

Wisconsin arbitrators clearly favor some type of binding procedure over factfinding. They responded favorably to final-offer-by-package arbitration and several made it their first choice. One arbitrator who favored conventional arbitration gave final-offer-by-package as his second choice. Two arbitrators speculated that final-offer-by-issue might be preferable and ranked final-offer-by-package next; one indicated his displeasure at not being able to compromise between the parties' positions in final-offer-by-package. He also articulated his fears about being confronted with ". . . a case where one party had an eminently reasonable position except for one outlandish part, while the other party had a generally less reasonable position but one that the arbitrator would greatly prefer not to select." None of the Wisconsin arbitrators ranked factfinding as their preference.

Michigan arbitrators also indicated a strong preference for binding procedures. They gave a mixed, though generally favorable, assessment of final-offer arbitration by economic issue. Of nine who ranked this procedure, two ranked it as most preferable, three ranked it second, two ranked it third, and two ranked it last. One arbitrator who ranked it last commented: "The piecemeal selection between 'final offers' on each issue lets the panel come up with any package (in terms of cost to management) it wants. Thus, there is no threat to the recalcitrant party that he may lose 'big' if he remains unreasonable. . . ."

Another Michigan arbitrator also was critical: "I am not convinced as yet that most parties fully understand and apply final-offer concepts. As a result, positions are often far apart and tend to place an even greater burden on the impartial third party than existed in conventional. . . ." He shared the concern that the final-offer-by-package arbitrator might have to select one of two inequitable economic packages.

This fear of having to select from among unreasonable alternatives was cited by several Michigan arbitrators as the reason for their assigning a low ranking to final-offer-by-package arbitration. One ranked it first and five ranked it last; none of the six had had experience with the procedure. Two arbitrators expressed a preference for conventional arbitration and two for factfinding. One said there was no difference between the two.

Of the Pennsylvania respondents who indicated their preferences, two chose conventional arbitration over factfinding, and two preferred factfinding to conventional. One who preferred factfinding said: "The [parties] tend to bargain and tend to accept factfinding recommendations. . . ." He contrasted this to conventional arbitration wherein "they tend to take extreme positions hoping the arbitrator will decide somewhere in the middle." The two Pennsylvania arbitrators who ranked final-offer procedures preferred "issue" to "package," but they placed "issue" third and "package" fourth. Neither had had experience with final-offer procedures.

The responses suggest that parties tend to favor procedures with which they are familiar. Except for the clear preference of Wisconsin and Michigan arbitrators for their respective final-offer procedures, there was no consensus among the respondents. Conceivably, preferences would have emerged if they had been supplied with criteria on which to base their rankings—for example, the arbitrator's comfort in the decision-making role, his view of what is best for collective bargaining, his view of what procedure will be used least, and so forth. As is evident from the summary of the Wingspread conferences, it is difficult to arrive at preferences where there is no agreement on the criteria on which to base judgment.

The Effect of Arbitration on Bargaining

The arbitrators were asked to indicate which procedure they thought would be most effective in narrowing the bargaining positions of the parties prior to third-party decision making. This question was deemed relevant because one success criterion for an arbitration procedure may be the extent to which prearbitration bargaining is successful.

Michigan and Wisconsin respondents agreed that more effective bargaining resulted from binding procedures than from factfinding. One Wisconsin arbitrator said of final-offer-by-package, ". . . the parties appear disposed to eliminate the less consequential issues and put emphasis on the one or more which they deem important." Another said, "Final-offer seems to generate maximum pressure for narrowing differences."

A Pennsylvania arbitrator thought that factfinding had produced more bargaining than had conventional arbitration. He pointed out that the Pennsylvania factfinding law applies to teachers—a group that has not been reluctant to back up bargaining demands with strikes—while the conventional arbitration law applies to police and firefighters—groups that are less apt to strike. This respondent's observation raises the question of whether the potential for a strike may be just as important as the statutory terminal dispute-settlement procedure in determining what the degree of bargaining will be.

Michigan respondents were of the opinion that final-offer arbitration either "probably" or "definitely" increases the parties' incentive to concede in negotiations. As one arbitrator said: "Final-offer seems to force them to define their areas of disagreement with greater precision and thus they prepare more specifically and carefully."

Final-Offer Arbitration and Equitableness of Awards

The Michigan questionnaire asked arbitrators to indicate whether they thought final-offer arbitration resulted in equitable awards, in comparison with other arbitration procedures. There was general agreement that final-offer would result in awards that would not be as equitable as those under conventional arbitration—for example, "[I]t forced me to resolve issues in a manner I felt was wrong. . . ." The inquiry did not supply any criteria for determining "equitableness," so the responses may simply indicate the arbitrators' belief that exercising their own sense of equity is fairer than having to choose one party's position without altering it.

Arbitrators as Mediators

A question debated by students of industrial relations and practitioners alike is whether arbitrators should attempt to mediate in disputes in which they are appointed as "interest arbitrators." The questionnaire responses indicated generally that the mediate-no mediate decision is made on practical grounds rather than on high principles concerning the proper role of an arbitrator. Views of the arbitrator's role ranged from those who said it is not their role to mediate, or those who said they may mediate under some circumstances (for example, "I believe in arbitrators' sticking to arbitration in the absence of some pretty clear signals from the parties or some highly unusual circumstances"), to those who feel arbitrators should not hesitate to mediate (for example, "resolution is the order of the day and arbitrators should afford many opportunities for that process to function").

On the basis of the questionnaire response, it appears that arbitrators attempt to mediate in 30 to 40 percent of the cases. When the interactions of tripartite panels are counted as mediation, as in Michigan and Pennsylvania, the percentage is probably considerably higher. Several respondents indicated that they used these panel sessions either for mediation or for "med-arb." Several Michigan arbitrators indicated that they did not ask the parties to state their final offers until close to the end of the hearing so that the parties could maximize their opportunities for resolving their own differences with or without the aid of the arbitrator or tripartite panel.

The arbitrators gave various reasons for their decisions to mediate or not to mediate; these reflected a combination of an arbitrator's view of his role, his experience and/or self-confidence in a mediation role, the attitude of the parties toward mediation (or further mediation), and the nature of the remaining issues and whether they lend themselves to mediation. Thus, it is not unusual to find an arbitrator attempting to mediate in one case and not in another.

It is difficult to evaluate success of the arbitrators' mediation efforts from the questionnaire responses. The responses indicate that mediation efforts are occasionally successful in obtaining a settlement, and in other cases they succeed in moderating the parties' positions and allowing the arbitrator to get a better understanding of what might make an acceptable arbitration award. In still other cases, they are unsuccessful.

Suggestions for Improvements

The arbitrators in each of the states were asked for their suggestions for improving the arbitration statutes. There was little response to this question, which indicates perhaps that there is as yet not enough experience under the prevailing laws to enable individual arbitrators to make judgments about them.

One Michigan arbitrator did suggest that the statute give the arbitrator an option: "Let the arbitrator reject both offers if he thinks it advisable and direct the parties to submit new offers more in line with his judgment." In a sense, this is done now by some Michigan arbitrators since the statute enables the arbitrator to remand the dispute to the parties for an additional three weeks of bargaining.

Conclusions

The questionnaires did provide some additional insights into arbitral opinion concerning the operation of final-offer procedures, but responses were not in any material way different from the views expressed by arbitrators at the Wingspread conference. Arbitrators who have participated in final-offer procedures are basically satisfied with their experiences. Those who have not participated generally have reservations about final-offer. It may be that conclusions about which procedure is preferred will have to wait until a substantial number of arbitrators have had a half dozen or more cases under each type of procedure and have thereby acquired a better basis for making a judgment.

Notes

1. The conferences were sponsored by the Industrial Relations Research Institute, University of Wisconsin-Madison, in cooperation with the Johnson Foundation. Morris Slavney, Chairman of the Wisconsin Employment Relations Commission, served as chairman of the sessions on mediation, and David B. Johnson, Professor of Economics, University of Wisconsin-Madison, chaired the arbitration conference.

Conference participants, in addition to the authors of this volume and the session chairmen, were as follows: Arvid Anderson, Chairman, New York City Office of Collective Bargaining; Commissioner Howard S. Bellman, Commissioner Zel S. Rice II, and George R. Fleischli, Wisconsin Employment Relations Commission; Commissioner Robert G. Howlett and Howard Case, Michigan Employment Relations Commission; Richard I. Bloch, University of Detroit; Arlen C. Christenson and Edward B. Krinsky, University of Wisconsin-Madison; Peter Feuille, University of Oregon; J. Finkelman, Chairman, Public Service Staff Relations Board of Canada; Walter J. Gershenfeld, Temple University; Larry Holden, Massachusetts Board of Conciliation; Myron L. Joseph, Carnegie-Mellon University; Mark L. Kahn, Wayne State University; Herbert J. Lahne and Thomas M. Phelan, U.S. Department of Labor; Philip G. Marshall, attorney; Joseph S. Murphy, American Arbitration Association; A. Howard Myers, Florida Atlantic University; Carl M. Stevens, Reed College; Martin Wagner, University of Illinois at Urbana-Champaign; Dean Ernst John Watts, National College of the State Judiciary; Hoyt Wheeler, University of Wyoming; Richard A. Williams, Federal Mediation and Conciliation Service; and Arnold M. Zack, arbitrator. Observers were Anita Schoomaker, University of Michigan, and June Gertig, Stephen Rubenfeld, Norman Solomon, and Joseph Tremiti, University of Wisconsin-Madison.

The conference reports were prepared from transcripts of the proceedings. The participants knew that their remarks would be treated confidentially, that no remark would be attributed to anyone, and that the tapes and transcribed record would be destroyed after being used in the preparation of the summary reports.

6

Measuring the Impact of Final-Offer Arbitration on Salary Outcomes

The purpose of this chapter is to provide an empirical analysis of the impact of final-offer arbitration on the salaries of police and firefighters in Wisconsin and Michigan. Some reference will be made to Pennsylvania, which maintained a system of conventional arbitration from 1969 to 1974 and could be regarded as a "control group" in an experiment.

The statistical results are properly viewed as rough estimates of the true underlying relations since they lack the precision one expects from sophisticated data and well-honed theory. Many of the impressions and insights reported in the previous chapters on the individual states are supported by the quantitative results, but our conclusions must be appropriately regarded as tentative because of both the very limited experience with final-offer procedures and inevitable problems that arise from using data generated by special surveys.

This chapter begins with a brief review of the asserted expectations underlying the final-offer process. Second comes an analysis and discussion of the theory of the final-offer awards. Third, there is an extended statistical analysis of the effect of the final-offer arbitration process on salary outcomes, and finally a brief review of the implications of this work for the development of public policy.

The Nature of the Final-Offer Process

The support for final-offer arbitration has come from labor-management neutrals and other observers of labor relations in the public sector who see the procedure as a substitute for a work stoppage with its own pressures to resolve impasses. The expectation is that there will be as much pressure on one side as on the other to make concessions so that the existence of the opportunity to seek final-offer arbitration will not affect the outcome in any *systematic* manner. We leave to a later section an analysis of the question as to whether the process is in fact neutral with respect to outcomes.

Arbitration, whether conventional or final-offer, has the effect of suppressing (not eliminating) the use of raw economic and political power so that the terms of settlement emphasize other matters. The effect of shifting from an alternative procedure to a process of arbitration of disputes over interests will tend to improve the short-run position of the party that is relatively weaker in terms of power. The consequent equalizing of "bargaining" strength may produce wage changes of a "once-and-for-all" nature whereby the wage level takes a step upward (or downward) and thereafter resumes rising at a normal rate. In a study that examines the impact of final-offer arbitration on outcomes within an entire state, the estimate of the impact is a measure of the average effect—that is, final-offer in any given instance may either raise or lower wages relative to the absence of final-offer.[a]

The "disarmament of economic and political power" does not depend on whether either conventional or final-offer arbitration is available nor whether the parties decide to seek an award. The mere existence of an alternative means to determine the terms of employment tends to deprecate the economic and political strengths of the parties and to bring them into the negotiation process as relative equals.

One other point we would make here is that the parties' drive to make "reasonable" demands and offers, which stems from the need to convince the arbitrator, leads to an increased similarity of results. If comparability is the name of the game, then there will be a tendency to group around a typical settlement—what may be termed a regression toward the mean. One effect will be to change markedly the distribution of police and firefighter salaries within a state. Unusual circumstances and unusual arrangements will become increasingly difficult to maintain and defend. The very high and the very low salaries will tend over time to be pushed toward the middle and the distribution will tend to be less spread.

This result is best illustrated by the behavior of the wages of Wisconsin police from 1969 to 1974. Table 6-1 shows that the dispersion of starting or base salaries across Wisconsin municipalities rose each year from 1969 to 1972, but that in 1973, the first full year when final-offer was available to all the parties, the dispersion declined. The dispersion is measured by the coefficient of variation (V), which is the ratio of the standard deviation (s) of the base salaries for police among the Wisconsin cities divided by the mean base salary $(\bar{X})$. Thus, the coefficient of variation rose from 0.1285 in 1969 to 0.1420 in 1972, and then turned around in 1973 and fell to 0.1344. It continued to fall in 1974—to 0.1266. This behavior indicates that the distribution was squeezed after final-offer began and is consistent with our expectations.

The data for the Wisconsin firefighters' base salary show some of the

---

[a] If this line of argument is correct, it is possible to argue that any empirical estimate of the effect of final-offer on outcomes may be regarded as a general measure of the relative weakness of the parties at a time preceding the adoption of final-offer legislation.

Table 6-1

Means and Distribution of Wisconsin Salaries (Base), 1969-1974

	Police			Firefighters		
Year	Mean ($\bar{X}$)	Standard Deviation (s)	Coefficient of Variation (V)	Mean ($\bar{X}$)	Standard Deviation (s)	Coefficient of Variation (V)
1969	$554	$71.2	0.1285	$551	$ 76.6	0.1390
1970	598	80.1	0.1339	600	78.5	0.1308
1971	647	88.7	0.1371	643	90.9	0.1414
1972	676	96.0	0.1420	676	94.5	0.1398
1973 [a]	716	96.2	0.1344	718	94.4	0.1315
1974	739	90.6	0.1226	741	101.9	0.1375

[a] First full year of final-offer-by-package.

same general tendencies, but the picture is not as clear. The variation reaches a peak in 1971 and begins to decline in 1972 when final-offer became available to some of the parties.

The Theory of Final-Offer Arbitration by Package

In the next few pages we shall discuss the nature and theory underlying a final-offer-by-package award, such as exists in Wisconsin. Our concern is with the effect of an award on the nature of the package rather than the effect of the opportunity to seek an award on the negotiation process. We are interested in the effect of the award relative to what settlement the parties would have reached by themselves as well as the effect of the packaging aspect of the award on the size and shape of the package.

Some notation will be useful. Define the union's initial demand on a given item as X_1^i and the city's initial offer on that item as Y_1^i. The result of collective bargaining on that item when final-offer is not available is denoted as X_2^i.

We may assume that the negotiated outcome with respect to the item is determined by the relative economic and political strengths of the respective parties, such that

$$X_2^i = Y_1^i + \lambda i (X_1^i - Y_1^i),$$

where λ is a measure of the relative economic and political strengths of the employer and the union with respect to the ith item. We would expect that the parties would place differing values on the various items on the bargaining table; some items are more important than others to one side.

Thus, a negotiated package will reflect different degrees of compromise on the various items, so that the observed λ's will vary.

Under final-offer arbitration (by package) the results will almost surely be different from what the parties would have come to themselves. Define $X_3{}^i$ as the award that an arbitrator would make for the ith item. If an arbitrator awards a package of items, i through n, $\Sigma_i{}^n X_3{}^i$, so as to minimize the difference between the package and his judgment of a "reasonable" outcome, he implicitly imposes a constant value of zero or one for the λ on each of the n items on the table. The differences between the parties on all items is judged to reflect an identical arbitral λ on all matters, rather than the various values for λi's that the parties would have negotiated.

Practitioners have already raised in the literature some of the problems arising from this constancy.[1] Two are worth noting here. Arbitrators involved in final-offer-by-package have complained that they do not feel comfortable in having to give all items to one side when they would rather "do justice" by picking and choosing items from those on the table. In our terminology, this is the same as saying that the λ judged appropriate by the arbitrator is discomfortingly different from the one he is forced to use on some items when he delivers a package award. But it is almost certain that in every award there will always be some implicit λ's that do not reflect the arbitrator's atomistic views of the items, and so arbitrators will always feel that final-offer-by-package yields an award that is in some part uncomfortable to them. The discomfort is necessarily less, of course, where there is final-offer-by-*issue*, since the difference between the arbitrator's value of the items and that of each of the parties can be minimized.

The problem of the "sleeper" item or "zinger"—recognized as an unusual demand that would almost surely be denied if it were evaluated on its own merits by the arbitrator but is still of so little import that it does not offset the basic attractiveness of the party's final position—is an extreme example of a divergence between the "appropriate" λ and what the arbitrator must award. While the parties have worried about the frequency of such occurrences, it is still too soon to say whether the sleeper issue will become a serious problem.

Some aspects of the theory of winning a final-offer arbitration suggest that the sleeper will not become common because its cost to the proposing party is apt to be too high. Since the arbitrator is asked to determine the more reasonable package based on both stated and unstated criteria, the process places pressure on each side to be more reasonable than the other. But the pressure is to be *marginally* more reasonable since that should be sufficient to win the award. Since the sleeper item is, by definition, far from reasonable, the only way the party can hope to win the award (and the sleeper) is to lower its sights on other, presumably important, items by a distinguishable amount. Thus, the cost of winning a package that includes a sleeper is apt to be so high in terms of forgone opportunities on other items that few sleepers will be demanded and even fewer accepted. Of course, if the party believes that it is likely to lose the arbitration, it will be under no compulsion to trim its demand, and sleepers may proliferate. On occasion it may make political sense to lose "big" rather than to lose by a small margin.

The effect of a final-offer award on an item is rightfully judged by a comparison of an outcome within a final-offer environment with an outcome where final-offer was absent. Two "control" groups quickly come to mind. In one case the comparable outcome would have been reached in an environment that provided no opportunity for final-offer; in the other case, there would be an opportunity to use final-offer although the parties were able to settle without it. The meaning of the phrase "the effect of final-offer" would differ in the two cases. The former would yield an estimate that would incorporate measures of both the effects of the final-offer process on the negotiations and the arbitrator's award itself. The effect of final-offer would be the difference in outcomes described by $X_3{}^i - X_2{}^i$, where $X_2{}^i$ reflects an environment without final-offer legislation—for example, final-offer versus factfinding.

In the latter case, the effect of final-offer can be examined only within an environment where final-offer is possible. The fact that final-offer was available in both bargains may have affected both settlements—even the one that was negotiated without recourse to a final-offer award. Thus, the effect of final-offer as a process cannot be identified since its effect may be "hidden" in both agreements. This measure of the effect of final-offer would describe the effect of using final-offer relative to doing without it even though the process was available. We could denote the effect of final-offer in this case by $X_3{}^i - X_2{}^i$, where $X_2{}^i$ represents a settlement achieved in an environment where final-offer arbitration was a realistic means of dispute resolution but was not requested.

The best measure we can derive of final-offer's effects necessarily relies on observed behavior. There is no unambiguous way of estimating what parties would have done in circumstances that did not or could not exist. Moreover, the accuracy of measures taken from observed behavior depends critically on how well we can isolate the other determinants of bargaining outcomes.

The Effect of Final-Offer Arbitration on Salaries

A Model of the Wage Determination Process

In order to estimate the effect of final-offer on salary levels, it is necessary to construct a model of the wage determination process so that the impact of final-offer can be identified. We assume that the primary demand and supply determinants of salary are similar as between police and firefighters and in Wisconsin and Michigan.[b] The demand for public services is, of course, a function of the community's income, population, interest in providing such services, and the cost of obtaining equivalent service from alternative sources, such as a private contractor. The effect of each of these variables on the demand for services and the wage of police (firefighters) is expected to be positive. Variables that are unique to the demand for the uniformed forces in our study are discussed at length later. (The symbols for all variables used in the study are defined in Appendix D.)

The supply of police (firefighter) services is largely a function of alternative employment opportunities, but also depends upon the nature of the work and the announced requirements for the job. The supply will be larger (and wages lower) the less attractive and less available the alternative opportunities. Specific features, such as whether the police (firefighters) must live within the community's boundaries, will also affect the supply.

Although it is possible to estimate the effect of the final-offer arbitration process on wages from a multi-equation demand and supply system, it will suffice for our purposes to estimate the effect of final-offer from a single reduced-form equation for salaries. The single equation should not bias the measure of the impact of final-offer, although it may affect other parameter estimates.

The survey produced information about both base and maximum monthly salaries as well as on scheduled hours of work, so we were able to consider three different variables as alternative outcome measures: the base, maximum, and hourly wage rate (base divided by hours of work). The maximum monthly salary (M) tended to rise a bit faster than the base (B), but generally both variables seemed to depend on the same economic and political forces. As a result, we use the models for M and B almost interchangeably in estimating the effect of final-offer. Scheduled hours of work changed so little from 1969 to 1974 and the intrastate variance was so small that the use of an hourly wage rate as the dependent variable did not add much to our understanding. Separate regressions are reported for police and firefighters.

The data were obtained primarily from two sources: questionnaires sent to all cities (in the three states) that bargain with either their police or firefighters and the 1970 Census. Salary data were reported by both city

---

[b] We found enough small differences after examining the data in a variety of ways to encourage us to abandon the strict adherence to this assumption.

and union representatives. Their responses did not differ much—as little as $6 difference for the mean in Wisconsin for some years—and the distributions, as measured by the variance, were also very similar. Since the response rate was almost always higher for the city management than for the respective unions, we used the salary levels reported by the city as the dependent variable(s).

The use of the salaries reported by the cities provides a common link between our models for police and firefighters that would otherwise be absent. Further, it will enable the reader to compare our results with those of earlier studies of the salaries of municipal employees,[2] particularly firefighters,[3] which used salary data taken from published sources, which are often derived from the reports of municipal governments.

Our basic model of a city's demand for police (firefighter) services described the base (or maximum) salary (B) (or M) for police (firefighters) in a given year in a given state as a function of the city's wealth, measured by its median family income in 1970 (I) and taxable real property in 1971 (R); its willingness to tax itself, measured by the 1971 effective property tax rate (T); its felt need and interest in providing safety services, measured by the number of public (alternatively, safety) employees per capita in the city (N); the proportion of families with incomes below the "official" poverty line in 1970 (D) or, alternatively, the ratio of the number of families with annual incomes above $15,000 to the number of families in poverty (D') to attempt to capture the effect of poverty and income distribution on the need for safety employees; population (S) and land area (A) in 1970, together with their ratio to measure urban density $(U = S/A)$; a dummy variable if the city is located in an urban area (C) to take some account of the fact that costs of living are often higher in urban areas; and the scheduled number of hours in a regular work week (H) in a given year.

Two additional demand side variables are included to reflect the unique circumstances involved in municipal police-firefighter negotiations. In some cities there is a tradition, rule, or other agreement to pay police the same monthly salary as firefighters so that there is parity between the two forces. Unless the demand and supply for firefighters and police are identical, the rule of parity may have the effect of twisting the "market" wage structure between the two services. Since it is common for a city to have far more applicants for firefighter jobs than for police work, one may infer that the demand and especially the supply are not identical between the two occupations. Thus, in order to take into account the "twist" in salaries, we included a dummy variable (E) for those cities that in 1973 paid firefighters at a parity with their police, as reported in the city's questionnaire. The variable took the value of one if the city had parity, and zero otherwise.

Second, we recognized that even if parity is absent, settlements reached with one party may not be independent of bargains either reached earlier with other municipal organizations or negotiations yet to be completed. Both the unions and the city were asked if they regarded their negotiations as pattern-setters, pattern-followers, or independent of other negotiations. The responses indicate that the unions see their own negotiations as pattern-setters less often than do cities. This difference may result from using different references for comparison. The unions may have been looking to settlements for safety forces in other cities, while the cities may have looked to settlements of other municipal employees within the city.

Our interest in the pattern-setter question stems from an expectation that cities may bargain harder if they regard a specific set of negotiations as pattern-setting, since the marginal cost of a settlement with a pattern-setter will be higher than the wage increase granted at the time. Such increases, by definition, will spill over to whatever other organizations the city engages in bargaining. Thus, a city may devote special resources to limit the wage increases of pattern-setters with the result that their wages may be lower than they would otherwise be. We use the cities' answers to the pattern-setter question to determine which bargains were pattern-setting since cities are the units of observation for our analysis. We constructed a dummy variable (P) that took the value of one if the city regarded its 1973 negotiations with the union as pattern-setting, and zero otherwise.

The major variable on the supply side was the salary that police and firefighters might be able to obtain in alternative employment. There is no one occupation that can be said to be the predominant alternative for persons who work in the safety forces. They are recruited from many lines of work. As a measure of the level of wages that would be earned elsewhere, most of the models used the hourly wages earned by municipal truck drivers for a given year (W) except for 1974 where the data were not available. In Pennsylvania those data were not available, so for models that included the Pennsylvania cities, we used the average weekly manufacturing wage. The use of W is unlikely to entail any systematic bias and has the advantage of being another municipal occupation where males predominate. We measured the availability of alternative jobs by the 1970 rate of unemployment in the city (L). Last, we used the proportion of workers employed in manufacturing (G), a highly unionized private sector, as a proxy measure for the public support that the safety forces have for their collective bargaining with the city.

Not all of these variables were used simultaneously. The essence of our model can be outlined by the statement

$$B_{xy} = B(I,T,D,U,C,H,N,E,P,W,L,G;Z),$$

where the dependent variable is the base salary for either police or fire-fighters (x) for a given year from 1969 through 1974 (y). The variable Z, which we do not attempt to estimate, represents the effect of an arbitration award on the salary level.

Our expectations, stemming from earlier studies of municipal employee wages and our implicit theories, about the relation between the independent variable and salary can be summarized as follows. Salaries are hypothe-sized to vary positively with I and T on the grounds that the richer the community and the more willing it is to tax itself to provide for services, the greater the demand for and wages of the uniformed employees. We expect that, taken by itself, an increase in the incidence of poverty (D) in a city will lead to an increase in demand for uniformed forces and, there-fore, their wages, since the conditions of poverty are often associated with the need for safety forces. We have in mind matters such as crime and substandard housing. Economic crimes, such as robbery, may reflect a disparity in the distribution of income, so we hypothesized that the ratio of the number of more affluent families to the number in poverty (D') might measure the city's felt need for police.

It seemed clear that as a city's size increased, whether in terms of popu-lation (S) or land area (A), its demand for safety forces would increase. But it seemed that there would be an even clearer relation with the city's congestion, complexity, or density, so that the greater the number of per-sons per square mile (U), the greater the demand for safety forces. We thought that urbanization would also be associated with differences in costs of living and, since the dependent variables, salaries, were always meas-ured in money terms, it would be appropriate to take into account dif-ferences in prices between cities in urban and nonurban areas. Thus, the dummy variable C takes on a value of one for cities in urban areas and zero for cities in nonurban areas in an attempt to make a rough adjustment for the market-basket value of the salary levels.

We felt it necessary to include weekly hours of work (H) in the model because it seemed possible to establish "trade-offs" between higher salaries and fewer hours, and because it was important to make sure that any higher salary levels we observed were something other than compensation for a longer work week. In point of fact, there was very little change in the average hours worked for police between 1969 and 1974—less than a 1 percent (about a half-hour) decline in Wisconsin and Michigan. In Pennsylvania the average work week for police, according to our survey, fell by 0.9 hours during that five-year period. The situation with respect to firefighters was not much different although they are on duty many more hours in a week. In Wisconsin, for example, the average hours of work per week fell from 57.7 in 1969 to 56.5 in 1974; in Michigan the decline was from 55.7 to 55.4 hours. In addition, the variance across cities in any given year was extremely small, which suggests that changes in hours of work was seldom used as compensation to offset salary.

We expect that the more interest the city has in public services, the greater its demand and the higher the wages of its public employees. Cities with little taste for public services and public employees will have lower demands for the uniformed services and, therefore, will be able to offer lower wages. Salaries, therefore, are expected to vary negatively with our variable N, which measures the number of persons served by each city employee.[4]

The use of the pattern-setting dummy variable may deserve further discussion. Most of the empirical literature on the determination of public employees' salaries ignores the relationship among the settlements of the various groups that bargain with the city.[5] The estimated wage increases gained, say, by the sanitation workers appear to have no forward or backward linkages with bargains struck or to be struck with other groups of city employees. No one would accept that proposition, but it is usually very difficult to isolate the spillover effects from one bargain to another. Since the survey asked city negotiators whether they regarded their negotiations with police and firefighters as pattern-setters, we were able to include that kind of a relation in our models. We expected that new salary levels might be lower than otherwise if the city thought that it might be able to put itself in a position of granting similar increases to all its employees. Certainly, the incentive would be there for the city to bargain as hard as it possibly could. The sign of this dummy variable (E) was expected to be negative.

We thought that the effect of the adoption of parity between the wages of police and firefighters (P) would twist the wage structure, but we had no firm expectation with regard to whether the effect would be to lower the wages of police, raise the wages of firefighters, or both. Given the evidence that at the same salary or wage rate relatively more persons prefer to be firefighters than police, it follows that if the demands for the two services are identical, the market clearing wage for police is larger than that for firefighters. The rule of parity, therefore, reduces the salaries of police relative to those of firefighters. (Parity may have an effect on the size and quality of the police force, but the basic model assumes that the quality is not much lower.)

On the supply side, we expect that the higher the expected wage in alternative employment (W), the higher the salary for the safety forces. The expected wage may be defined as the going wage in alternative employment adjusted by the relevant unemployment rate. The alternative wage should be one in an occupation that is demonstrably attractive to the employees of the police and fire departments and has the same promotional structure. No single occupation is a good substitute for each potential applicant to the police and fire departments. The selection of the municipal truck drivers' wage for a variable is properly viewed as a *measure* of the wage an applicant might earn in alternative work; there is no implication that truck driving is the only source of alternative employment. We do expect the variable to capture the important elements in the supply of labor for municipal employment.

It is permissible to view the unemployment rate (L) as the probability of a given worker's securing employment. The higher the unemployment rate, the less the chance of securing a job and the more people competing for the same job. (The effect on quality of new entrants is, again, ignored, but it is worth observing that in certain common circumstances these quality effects are biased in an offsetting direction compared to those mentioned two paragraphs above.) All else equal, the salary will vary negatively with the unemployment rate and positively with the going wage rate.

Finally, it seemed that public support of collective bargaining for the police and fire forces may be an important element in enabling them to reach their goals. We assumed that persons who were union members might be somewhat more sympathetic on the average to union demands of the safety forces, and that the safety forces might be able to translate this sympathy into support. On the grounds that manufacturing is a highly unionized sector and is dispersed over the whole state, we included the percent of the city's labor force employed in manufacturing (G) as an independent variable with the expectation that it would have a positive effect on salaries.

Determinants of Firefighter and Police Base Salaries in Michigan and Wisconsin

In order to examine the effect of the final-offer process, we shall develop a number of statistical tests to enable us to make direct and indirect inferences about the effect of the process. Basically, however, there are two types of tests. First, given that the model is adequately, if not perfectly, specified, is there a tendency for wages to rise in a state after final-offer is instituted, as evidenced by an upward shift in the intercept term of the regression equation? Second, if the data over two and three years are pooled and dummy variables for years when final-offer was fully available are introduced, are the dummy variables for final-offer significant, and what do they suggest about the short-run effects? We seek to ascertain whether final-offer affects salaries, and if it does, whether that effect is likely to be cumulative over time. Since theory alone could not tell us whether, for example, D or D' would be a more powerful predictor in a particular model, our parameter estimates reflect more than a little trial-and-error. Rather than report all the regressions behind each of our findings, we shall present only representative equations to illustrate the nature of the results and the robustness of the coefficients.

In the first instance, we employed a stepwise regression procedure and noted the combination of variables that tended to produce the most explanatory power. Those models are displayed in Table 6-2 and suggest the following generalizations.

1. Salaries are positively associated with our measures of the cost of living, city incomes, density, public support of collective bargaining, and alternative employment opportunities.
2. Since the variables for the incidence of poverty, parity, and scheduled hours of work measure forces that determine salaries in Wisconsin but not in Michigan, the model seems to be a slightly better predictor of salaries in Wisconsin than in Michigan.
3. The basic model accounts for a greater proportion of the variance in the salaries of firefighters than of police and indicates that the basic model underlying the salary determination of the two occupations may differ.
4. There is no consistent tendency for an upward shift in any of the dependent variables after the adoption of final-offer, although some of the regression coefficients do seem to float upward, even if only by statistically insignificant amounts.
5. The 1973 intercepts for Michigan firefighters and Wisconsin police point toward an upward shift in salaries, although the intercepts for the Michigan police and Wisconsin firefighters do not.
6. The model has slightly less explanatory power in 1973, after the introduction of final-offer, than earlier, thereby raising the possibility that final-offer may have been a determinant of 1973 salaries.[c]

Thus, it would appear to be fair to conclude that the evidence is ambiguous, at best, with respect to the wage-raising tendency of final-offer arbitration.

The statistical tests are almost always two-sided because we are estimating a reduced-form model and some variables arguably enter the model from both the supply and demand sides. This is a good point to alert the reader that in all the regression equations we present we shall indicate variables that are significant at the .10 level as well as the more customary

---

[c] The unemployment rate never became statistically significant and, even when it had the expected sign, its t-value was less than 1. As a result, it was not considered further.

Table 6-2

Selected Models of the Determinants of Police and Fire Salaries, Michigan and Wisconsin, 1969, 1971, and 1973

	Dependent Variable					
	Firefighters				Police	
	Base Salary 1969	Base Salary 1971	Base Salary 1973	Base Salary 1969	Base Salary 1971	Base Salary 1973
				Michigan		
Intercept	172.196	108.961	930.612	824.563	109.914	281.042
C	101.591 *** (17.993)	118.550 *** (24.270)	123.744 *** (27.546)	86.789 *** (24.183)	150.630 *** (28.043)	178.288 *** (27.758)
G	1.588 ** (0.543)	2.406 *** (0.679)	2.346 *** (0.814)	2.005 ** (0.834)	1.041 (0.887)	1.460 (0.885)
I	0.00789 ** (0.00312)	0.01244 *** (0.00407)	0.01090 ** (0.00454)	0.01352 *** (0.00372)	0.01379 *** (0.00431)	0.02462 *** (0.00721)
W	68.580 *** (23.729)	83.636 *** (25.732)	56.672 ** (25.714)	31.574 (33.208)	73.385 ** (32.943)	
U	0.00629 * (0.00321)	0.00590 (0.00412)	0.01161 ** (0.00468)	0.00632 (0.00419)	0.00938 * (0.00473)	0.01063 ** (0.00437)
D						4.485 (4.303)
O			−6.946 ** (3.104)		1.731 (1.873)	1.896 (1.886)
E	13.750 (15.043)					
H				−12.752 ** (5.670)		
$\bar{R}^2$	.7854	.7598	.7141	.6137	.6786	.7162
Observations	38	64	63	78	81	76

Table 6-2 (continued)

	Dependent Variable					
	Firefighters			Police		
	Base Salary 1969	Base Salary 1971	Base Salary 1973	Base Salary 1969	Base Salary 1971	Base Salary 1973
			Wisconsin			
Intercept	316.895	450.390	293.917	888.784	365.511	1136.264
C		44.841 ** (17.714)	83.161 *** (23.618)		46.032 ** (18.707)	83.932 *** (20.464)
G		0.8655 (0.6571)	2.002 ** (0.869)		1.424 ** (0.689)	2.659 *** (0.733)
I	0.00500 * (0.00279)		0.00720 * (0.00387)	0.00849 *** (0.00270)	0.01156 *** (0.00350)	0.01266 *** (0.00372)
W	123.907 *** (22.679)	102.745 *** (20.254)	60.627 ** (30.06)	57.318 *** (20.013)	61.466 *** (20.028)	
U	0.00607 * (0.00317)	0.00508 (0.00342)	0.00468 (0.00526)	0.00667 * (0.00376)	0.00584 (0.00353)	
D	−5.414 (3.468)	−7.603 ** (3.583)		−12.764 *** (2.974)	−6.910 * (3.963)	−6.928 (4.407)
O	0.570 (0.396)					
E						−40.596 * (23.943)
H	−2.186 * (1.165)	−3.285 * (1.748)		−11.552 ** (5.132)		−13.159 ** (5.159)
$\bar{R}^2$	.7975	.8069	.6948	.7551	.7227	.6955
Observations	36	40	35	59	64	68

Note: O = percent of eligible employees who are members of the union. See text and Appendix D for definitions of variables.
* Significant at the .10 level on a 2-sided t-test.
** Significant at the .05 level on a 2-sided t-test.
*** Significant at the .01 level on a 2-sided t-test.

.01 and .05 levels. Readers may not want to dismiss out of hand those variables that do not meet stringent significance tests because the construction of our data tends to increase the size of the standard errors. Not infrequently data were missing or not available for some variables in an observation. If the missing data were from the dependent variable—for example, salary level—we eliminated the observation. If the missing data were from an independent variable, we substituted the mean value of the sample run. The effect of this procedure is to leave the estimated parameter unbiased, but to increase the standard error,[6] so one may want to make a mental adjustment to consider variables that appear to lack a high level of significance.

Within-State Effects of Final-Offer Arbitration

A second way to test the hypothesis about the impact of final-offer is to define the dependent variable over two years and include a specific variable to account for the year (or instance) when final-offer was available. The variable *FO* would take the value of one for salary levels determined in a year when final-offer was available and zero when it was not and could properly be added to the basic model that is being estimated, which would enable us to compare, say, 1972 with 1973. If the new dummy variable were significant and positive, it would indicate that salaries had received a thrust upward from a source independent of the remaining variables in the equation. Illustrative results of this test using 1972 and 1973 base salaries of Wisconsin police are:

$$
\begin{aligned}
(1) \quad B_{72} = \ &678.938\,^{***} - 41.071E\,^{***} - 9.540H_{72}\,^{***} + 52.736C\,^{***} \\
&\ (119.531) \quad\ (15.421) \qquad\ (1.309) \qquad\quad (13.897) \\
&+ 1.174G\,^{***} + 0.00600I\,^{**} + 0.510D + 68.270W_{72}\,^{***} \\
&\ (0.453) \qquad\ (0.00262) \quad\ (2.774) \quad\ (12.355) \\
&+ 0.006270U\,^{**} - 0.011O + 35.6080FO\,^{***} \qquad \bar{R}^2 = .7155 \\
&\ (0.00245) \qquad\ (0.800) \quad\ (9.121)
\end{aligned}
$$

(*, **, *** are defined as in Table 6-2).

There is no need to discuss each of the coefficients since the parameter estimates coincide with those we discussed earlier.[d] (The new variable, *O*, is the proportion of eligible workers who are members of the police union. Although it is theoretically interesting, it is not statistically significant. Its lack of statistical significance may result from its negligible variation since

---

[d] Note that this procedure requires using all the observations for some variables twice.

almost all unions reported 100 percent membership and no union reported less than a 90 percent membership.)

We regard the significance of the *FO* variable as important and infer from it that, all else equal, monthly base salaries were nearly $36 ($35.608) higher in 1973, when final-offer was available to all parties, than in 1972, which was a year of transition. It is not possible to assert that it was only final-offer that raised the average base salary by that much; it is possible to think of alternative explanations—for example, inflation, union militance, and so forth. We hope that the income and (especially) the wage variables are sensitive enough to include within themselves the general inflationary pressures that increased the wages of all employees.

In order to better understand the implications of Equation (1) we ran Equation (2), which is similar to Equation (1) except that the dependent variable was 1973 and 1974 salaries; thus, the *FO* dummy variable allows a comparison of salaries in those two years. If the estimate for the 1973 dummy in Equation (1) were the result of an upward pressure on wages coming from a variable that the model omits or from a general inflation of all police salaries, we would expect to find that the 1974 dummy in Equation (2) is also significant. If that dummy is not significant, then it is appropriate to conclude that something raised salaries in 1973 above the 1972 level that did not further raise them in 1974 above the 1973 level. The most likely candidate to fit that explanation would be the adoption of final-offer.

$$
\begin{aligned}
(2) \quad B_{73} = {} & 922.659\,{***} - 48.585E\,{**} - 12.011H_{73}\,{**} + 70.904C\,{***} + 1.976G\,{***} \\
& \;(243.750) \qquad (23.594) \qquad (4.648) \qquad\quad (18.720) \qquad\;\; (0.660) \\
& + 0.00423I - 0.113D + 70.982W_{73}\,{***} + 0.00164U - 1.251O \\
& \;\;(0.00405) \quad (4.078) \quad\; (20.911) \qquad\qquad (0.00381) \quad (1.182) \\
& + 15.377FO \qquad\qquad\qquad \bar{R}^2 = .6433 \\
& \;\;(16.848)
\end{aligned}
$$

(*, **, *** are defined in Table 6-2.)

Thus, since the *FO* dummy is not significant here, we are inclined to suggest that the independent force that operated in 1973 but not in 1974 was final-offer. It probably raised police wages by about 5 percent [= 36/676] in 1973 relative to 1972. The insignificance of the 1974 dummy raises the possibility that final-offer may have a once-and-for-all effect—that is, raising wages when initially instituted and thereafter having no cumulative impact on wage levels.

The results for Michigan police indicate the same relation—an exogenous upward thrust in 1973 compared with 1972, but nothing further from 1973 to 1974. The results for Wisconsin firefighters show the same once-and-for-all result, but the results for the Michigan firefighters indicate an additional effect in 1974. The parameter estimates for the *FO* dummy are significant for both 1973 and 1974, although the 1974 effect is smaller than in 1973. These results are displayed in Table 6-3. Taken together, they do provide some hard evidence that final-offer had the effect of raising salaries for the safety forces.

Effects of Final-Offer Arbitration Measured Across States

Yet another way to test the (null) hypothesis that final-offer had no effect on wages is to pool all the data for the years 1972 through 1974 and establish new dummy variables for 1973, 1974, and the specific state. These variables, appended to the basic model, will enable us to view the entire effects at once and allow a comparison of the two years when final-offer was fully available with the year of transition.

The dependent variable is base salaries of both Michigan and Wisconsin police (firefighters) in the years 1972 through 1974, and the new independent variables are FO_{73} and FO_{74} for salaries determined in 1973 and 1974, respectively, and MI for the Michigan salaries. The two equations appear below (police first).

$$
\begin{aligned}
(3) \quad B_P = \ & 296.735^{***} - 20.968E^{**} + 101.290C^{***} + 1.741G^{***} + 0.00554I^{***} \\
& \ (39.634) \qquad (10.422) \qquad (10.291) \qquad (0.321) \qquad (0.00180) \\
& + 55.651W^{***} + 0.00973U^{***} + 13.684P - 0.1183N^{***} \\
& \ \ (11.060) \qquad\quad (0.00193) \qquad\ \ (8.922) \quad\ (0.0401) \\
& + 41.780FO_{73}^{***} + 73.493FO_{74}^{***} + 47.213MI^{***} \qquad \bar{R}^2 = .6621 \\
& \ \ (8.416) \qquad\qquad (10.035) \qquad\qquad (7.825)
\end{aligned}
$$

$$
\begin{aligned}
(4) \quad B_F = \ & 179.817^{***} + 9.913E + 105.620C^{***} + 2.060G^{***} + 0.0103I^{***} \\
& \ (55.601) \qquad (10.890) \quad (12.397) \qquad\ (0.385) \qquad\ (0.0026) \\
& + 63.864W^{***} - 0.028D + 0.380T^{**} + 0.0102U^{***} + 1.730P \\
& \ \ (12.664) \qquad (1.819) \quad (0.149) \qquad (0.0023) \qquad (12.101) \\
& - 0.2100N^{**} + 42.840FO_{73}^{***} + 73.981FO_{74}^{***} + 41.915MI^{***} \quad \bar{R}^2 = .7354 \\
& \ \ (0.0868) \qquad (9.525) \qquad\qquad (11.415) \qquad\qquad (9.702)
\end{aligned}
$$

(*, **, *** are as defined in Table 6-2.)

We infer from these results that, inter alia, the institution of final-offer in 1973 was associated with a rise in the base salary level of police of about $41-42 in 1973 and an increase of about $73-74 when comparing 1974 with 1972. These results estimated over both states (Michigan offers $47 and nearly $42 more for police and firefighters, respectively, than Wisconsin) bridge the first estimates about the impact of final-offer.

We are now inclined to the view that final-offer does cause an "immediate" increase in salaries after the first year and that the effect tapers off in subsequent years. Both FO_{73} and FO_{74} are statistically significant (relative to the 1972 situation) at better than the .001 level in each equation, and

Table 6-3
Determinants of Base Salary Levels Estimated from Two-Year Pooled Data

			Equation			
	4.1	4.2	4.3	4.4	4.5	4.6
Dependent Variable [a]	Michigan Police 1972-73	Michigan Police 1973-74	Michigan Firefighters 1972-73	Michigan Firefighters 1973-74	Wisconsin Firefighters 1972-73	Wisconsin Firefighters 1973-74
Intercept	322.65 (300.514)	360.139 (452.410)	-109.301 (530.049)	758.110 * (404.162)	446.505 ** (197.301)	415.499 (306.44)
E	-4.758 (15.638)	-15.489 (19.131)	24.151 (15.083)	10.878 (18.820)	-9.713 (18.764)	-13.520 (32.749)
H_y	-2.694 (6.246)	-3.373 (10.532)	17.053 * (8.644)	1.292 (5.199)	-2.354 (2.254)	-1.546 (3.252)
C	113.431 *** (17.660)	122.327 *** (21.435)	133.475 *** (18.706)	136.225 *** (22.723)	42.331 ** (19.047)	84.264 *** (25.145)
G	1.363 ** (0.566)	1.980 *** (0.671)	2.014 *** (0.571)	2.276 *** (0.659)	0.965 (0.692)	1.855 * (0.936)
I	0.0144 *** (0.0042)	0.0090 (0.0061)	0.0156 *** (0.0046)	0.0139 ** (0.0054)	0.0052 (0.0040)	0.0048 (0.0061)
D	6.044 ** (2.617)	3.3746 (3.3472)	3.494 (2.647)	3.294 (3.175)	-4.352 (4.079)	-2.858 (6.152)
W_y	34.281 (21.576)	69.616 *** (22.549)	22.881 (20.981)	55.965 ** (22.153)	73.624 *** (17.423)	71.800 ** (33.217)
U	0.0116 *** (0.0030)	0.00872 ** (0.00383)	0.0120 *** (0.0030)	0.00978 ** (0.00396)	0.0110 *** (0.0035)	0.0037 (0.00566)
O	0.587 (1.205)	0.167 (1.337)	-5.914 *** (2.092)	-6.440 ** (2.508)	-0.357 (0.425)	-0.132 (0.707)
FO	43.616 *** (12.281)	18.181 (16.041)	41.206 *** (12.604)	31.632 ** (15.459)	44.860 *** (11.667)	28.137 (19.320)
$\bar{R}^2$	.6295	.6459	.7356	.7214	.7362	.6047

Note: The standard errors of the coefficients are in parentheses.

[a] H_y and W_y are the hours and wages, respectively, taken in the first year.

*, **, *** are as defined in Table 6-2 above.

FO_{73} and FO_{74} themselves differ at the .05 level. In other words, there is strong statistical evidence that salaries were significantly higher in 1973 and 1974 compared to 1972 by about 4.6 percent and 8.2 percent for police, respectively, and 5.7 percent and 9.9 percent for firefighters. Certainly the other parameter estimates in Equations (3) and (4) are well enough behaved and the explanatory power sufficiently large that we can have confidence in the results.

As an aside, we note that the small differences in the models of Equations (3) and (4) reflect our judgment that the model that best explains the salaries of police is not the best predictor of the salaries of firefighters.

Testing for Bias in Parameter Estimates

It is possible that our parameter estimates for the *FO* variables in Equations (3) and (4) contain bias because the state effects may not have been fully separated. To examine that possibility, we ran a set of regressions that used the same dependent variables as in Equations (3) and (4), but created separate dummy variables for the states and years. As a result we have six distinct variables for the three years of Wisconsin data and the three years of Michigan data; the reference variable is 1972 Wisconsin. The estimated coefficients appear in Table 6-4.

The discussion is confined to an analysis of the effects of final-offer. The most significant conclusions to be drawn from the estimates in Table 6-4 are that final-offer tended to raise both police and firefighter salaries by slightly more than \$40 when it was adopted and that its impact the second year was noticeably less than the first.

Consider the police salaries first: The variable F_1 is a measure of the difference in Wisconsin salaries between 1972, the transition year, and 1973, the first full year of final-offer. It is statistically significant and indicates a \$41 increase. The effect of final-offer in Michigan can be approximated by taking the difference between the dummy for Michigan salaries in 1972 (conventional arbitration), F_3, and the Michigan dummy for 1973 (final-offer), F_4. This difference is slightly more than \$42 (= \$88.26 − \$45.95) and is statistically significant at the .02 level.

The same exercise for firefighters yields similar conclusions. The year of the adoption of final-offer in Wisconsin is associated with a rise in salaries of \$45, and in Michigan with a rise of \$41, statistically significant at the .01 and .05 levels, respectively.

The inference that the effect of final-offer tapered off after the initial year and is not cumulative stem from two comparisons of the second year effects. The first is arithmetical; the second statistical. The simple arithme-

Table 6-4

Police and Fire Salaries with Pooled Regressions and Final-Offer Effects, Wisconsin and Michigan, 1972-1974

Independent Variable [a]	Dependent Variable	
	Police Base Salaries, 1972-74	Firefighter Base Salaries, 1972-74
Intercept	297.090 ***	178.233 ***
	(39.985)	(56.143)
E	−21.063 **	10.491
	(10.466)	(10.974)
C	101.251 ***	105.743 ***
	(10.322)	(12.441)
G	1.744 ***	2.050 ***
	(0.323)	(0.387)
I	0.00555 ***	0.0104 ***
	(0.00181)	(0.0026)
D	not run	0.0102
		(1.8263)
W_{73}	55.713 ***	63.352 ***
	(11.097)	(12.743)
T	not run	0.3829 **
		(0.1493)
U	0.00972 ***	0.0102 ***
	(0.00193)	(0.0023)
P	13.672	10.695
	(8.948)	(7.674)
N	−0.1184 ***	−0.1453 **
	(0.0402)	(0.0348)
F_1	41.107 ***	45.282 ***
	(12.502)	(15.935)
F_2	71.362 ***	83.823 ***
	(15.242)	(20.399)
F_3	45.947 ***	46.121 ***
	(12.158)	(14.399)
F_4	88.264 ***	87.560 ***
	(12.280)	(14.478)
F_5	121.085 ***	115.587 ***
	(14.158)	(16.042)
$\bar{R}^2$	.6602	.7335
S.E.E.[b]	71.777	67.549

Note: The standard errors are in parentheses.

[a] F_1 (Wisconsin 1973) equals 1 if the variable was from Wisconsin, 1973, 0 otherwise; F_2 (Wisconsin 1974) equals 1 if the variable was from Wisconsin 1974, 0 otherwise; F_3 (Michigan 1972) equals 1 if the variable was from Michigan 1972, 0 otherwise; F_4 (Michigan 1973) equals 1 if the variable was from Michigan 1973, 0 otherwise; F_5 (Michigan 1974) equals 1 if the variable was from Michigan 1974, 0 otherwise.

[b] Standard error of estimate.

** Significant at the .05 level on a 2-sided t-test.

*** Significant at the .01 level on a 2-sided t-test.

tic difference betneen F_1 and F_2 (a measure of the second year effect of final-offer) is \$31 for Wisconsin police and about \$38 for Wisconsin firefighters. Both estimates are smaller than the first-year effects, F_1. In Michigan, a comparison of the difference between F_4 and F_5 with the difference between F_3 and F_4 shows that the former are smaller for both police (\$33 versus \$42) and firefighters (\$28 versus \$41).

If we follow the principles of statistical inference, it may be reported that none of the second year effects are different from zero at the .10 level —that is, a test of whether, for example, F_2 is equal to F_1 in the police equation yields a t-statistic of 1.53, which permits rejection of the hypothesis of equality at only the .13 level (which is insufficient to meet the usual standards of significance). Thus, conventional tests of statistical significance would indicate that the second-year effects of final-offer are no larger than the first-year effects. Taken together, the arithmetic and statistical tests provide strong evidence that the effect of final-offer tends to taper off over time.

One other inference worth making from the models in Table 6-4 can

Table 6-5

Estimated Effects of Final-Offer on Salaries, 1972-1973

	Wisconsin				Michigan			
	From				From			
	1972		1973		1972		1973	
	Police	Fire	Police	Fire	Police	Fire	Police	Fire
To 1973	\$41 **a	\$45 **a	—	—	\$42 **a	\$41 **a	—	—
	(6.7)	(6.7)			(5.5)	(5.5)		
To 1974	\$71 **	\$84 **	\$30	\$39	\$75 **	\$69	\$33	\$28
	(10.5)	(12.4)	(4.2)	(5.4)	(9.9)	(9.2)	(4.1)	(3.6)

Note: Estimates derived from Table 6-4; percent increase is in parentheses.
** Significant differences at the .05 level.
a Best estimate of the effect of a full year of final-offer.

be derived from an examination of F_3. That variable measures the difference between salaries paid in Michigan and Wisconsin in 1972, when Michigan operated under a procedure of conventional arbitration and Wisconsin had factfinding and some final-offer. If one is reasonably satisfied with the specification of the salary determination models, it would be appropriate to conclude that conventional arbitration raised the salaries of both safety forces by about \$46 relative to the combination factfinding/final-offer that existed in Wisconsin. Table 6-5 summarizes these effects of final-offer.

*Relative Effects of Final-Offer Arbitration on Firefighter
and Police Salaries*

Finally we developed regression equations to allow comparison between
the cities in Wisconsin and Michigan, on the one hand, and Pennsylvania,
on the other. Throughout the period under consideration, Pennsylvania
remained with a procedure that provided for conventional arbitration. As a
result, it should be possible to examine the wage changes in Wisconsin and
Michigan from 1972 to 1974 relative to the changes in Pennsylvania
during those years to estimate the impact of final-offer procedures. If we
assume that the same economic and demographic forces are at work in all
three states, it is appropriate to conclude that differences in wage changes
between Pennsylvania and Wisconsin/Michigan resulted from differences
in their dispute settlement procedures. However, since we cannot assert
that our models capture all the determinants of salaries correctly, the
estimates of the effects of final-offer should not be taken as definitive.
This, nonetheless, is the strongest test of the impact of final-offer.

The independent variables in the model that we used include the effects
of parity (E), the proportion of persons employed in manufacturing (G),
urbanization (C), family income (I), city density (U), pattern-setting
(P), and number of persons served by each city employee (N). In place
of the wages of municipal truck drivers, we substituted the average weekly
wage in manufacturing (W'). Pennsylvania did not have sufficient data on
the municipal truck drivers' wage, and it is possible that such wages may
be "tied" to the safety forces' wages in something less than a causal
manner.

The dependent variables are the base salaries for police and firefighters,
respectively, in the cities of Wisconsin, Michigan, and Pennsylvania for
the years 1972, 1973, and 1974. Each equation has eight state-year
dummy variables: Wisconsin 1972 (D_1), Wisconsin 1973 (D_2), Wisconsin 1974 (D_3), Michigan 1972 (D_4), Michigan 1973 (D_5), Michigan
1974 (D_6), Pennsylvania 1972 (D_7), and Pennsylvania 1974 (D_8). The
salaries in those instances use the salaries in Pennsylvania 1973 as the
reference measure, so the regression coefficients for the dummy variables
are to be interpreted as the effect in each instance relative to the Pennsylvania 1973 experience.

The results, reported in Table 6-6, are less straightforward than those
using only Wisconsin and Michigan, which are reported in Table 6-4. The
economic and political variables tell the same story for firefighters as in
Table 6-4. Their salaries are positively related to urbanization, extent of
manufacturing, income, pattern-setting, city density, and wages in alternative occupations (this time, manufacturing). The t-statistic for W'
is slightly in excess of 2, statistically significant at the .05 level but much

Table 6-6

Estimated Regression Coefficients Pooled over Wisconsin, Michigan, and Pennsylvania, 1972-1974

	Dependent Variable	
Independent Variable [a]	Police Base Salaries, 1972-1974	Firefighter Base Salaries, 1972-1974
Intercept	425.540 ***	309.475 ***
	(32.845)	(38.902)
E	0.5311	21.276 *
	(7.416)	(11.598)
C	141.406 ***	149.323 ***
	(8.223)	(13.163)
G	1.295 ***	2.110 ***
	(0.307)	(0.399)
I	0.0007487	0.0105 ***
	(0.0006985)	(0.0025)
W'	13.0253 ***	8.594 **
	(3.3788)	(3.933)
U	0.0003185 ***	0.0003906 ***
	(0.0001022)	(0.0000984)
P	27.454 ***	19.900
	(9.212)	(13.783)
N	0.0005897	−0.0135 ***
	(0.0008595)	(0.0037)
D_1	39.486 **	32.343
	(18.252)	(27.654)
D_2	80.550 ***	78.462 ***
	(18.097)	(27.860)
D_3	109.757 ***	115.112 ***
	(20.991)	(31.546)
D_4	95.937 ***	91.687 ***
	(17.585)	(26.210)
D_5	139.077 ***	132.433 ***
	(17.695)	(26.262)
D_6	165.363 ***	157.473 ***
	(19.525)	(27.354)
D_7	−31.179 *	−36.385
	(16.650)	(31.522)
D_8	54.955 ***	40.267
	(17.424)	(32.962)
$\bar{R}^2$	.5294	.6412
S.E.E.[b]	86.481	80.367
Number of observations	522	291

Note: The standard errors are in parentheses.

[a] D_1 = Wisconsin 1972; D_2 = Wisconsin 1973; D_3 = Wisconsin 1974; D_4 = Michigan 1972; D_5 = Michigan 1973; D_6 = Michigan 1974; D_7 = Pennsylvania 1972; D_8 = Pennsylvania 1974.

[b] Standard estimate of error.

* Significant at the .10 level on a 2-sided t-test.
** Significant at the .05 level on a 2-sided t-test.
*** Significant at the .01 level of a 2-sided t-test.

less than the t-value of 5 for W in Table 6-4. The effect of the variable that measures the number of persons served by each city employee still has a negative effect on salary levels. The parity variable, E, has a positive effect on the salary levels of firefighters and is statistically significant at the .10 level. As compared with the results in Table 6-4, the predicted effect of E is both larger and more significant (since the standard error of the variable is of about the same magnitude as before).

As might be expected by the inclusion of a third state of observations, the $\overline{R}^2$ is lower (.64 versus .73) and the standard error of estimate larger (80.37 versus 67.55) than in the firefighter model of Table 6-4.

We turn now to a discussion of the effect of final-offer as measured by the dummy variables D_1-D_8 and begin with the unexpected results for Pennsylvania, D_7 and D_8. Those two regression coefficients are of the right signs (negative for 1972 and positive for 1974, relative to 1973) and of roughly the correct magnitude, but neither is statistically significant at even the .10 level. Thus we are unable to reject the hypotheses that the 1972 and 1974 salary levels of Pennsylvania firefighters are equal to the 1973 levels. As a result we are left with the lame assertion that salary levels did not change from 1972 to 1973 and 1973 to 1974. (Of course, our best guess is that they *did* change, by \$36 from 1972 to 1973 and \$40 from 1973 to 1974. We shall return to this "unsophisticated" reasoning later.)

With the exception of D_1 (Wisconsin 1972), all the remaining dummy variables are significantly different from zero. But in order to test for the effect of final-offer, we must determine whether wages rose more from 1972 to 1973 in Wisconsin (Michigan), which had final-offer, than in Pennsylvania, which did not. Above, we conceded that there is not strong evidence to support the assertion that Pennsylvania salaries were significantly higher in 1973 than in 1972. A comparison for Wisconsin and Michigan involves testing whether $D_1 = D_2$ and $D_4 = D_5$, respectively. The t-statistics for the 1972-73 Wisconsin difference is 1.17 and for Michigan it is 1.10, which indicates that those differences were not statistically significant either. For 1973-74, comparing D_3 with D_2 and D_6 with D_5 obtains results that are even less significant. For Wisconsin, the t-statistic is only 0.87 for D_3 and D_2; for Michigan, 0.66 for D_6 and D_5. Thus, none of the year-to-year differences within any of the states reaches a level of statistical significance that exudes confidence.

These results simply do not indicate that final-offer had any effect on salaries relative to conventional arbitration. We came to this conclusion, it must be recognized, after finding that no statistically significant changes had occurred in year-to-year wage levels beyond those accounted for by the major economic and political variables in the model.

If the parameter estimates are taken at face value as the single best estimate of the state-year instance, the coefficients lend (very weak) support to the assertion that final-offer provided a small additional upward push to salaries when it was initially adopted. While salaries in Pennsylvania rose by $36 from 1972 to 1973, they rose by $46 ($= D_2 - D_1$) in Wisconsin and by $41 ($= D_5 - D_4$) in Michigan. Given the relative salary structure of firefighters in Wisconsin and Pennsylvania, the $46 raise in Wisconsin may be judged large relative to the $36 in Pennsylvania.

The large increases in the final-offer states were not maintained in the following year, though. In 1974, Pennsylvania firefighters' wages were probably $40 higher than in 1973, but 1974 Wisconsin salaries were only $37 higher than they had been a year earlier. Michigan, with final-offer in 1974, observed only a $25 increase over 1973. This evidence, to be sure, is consistent with our earlier statement that the effect of final-offer tapers off in the second year, but we did not expect that it would in fact yield increases *less* than conventional arbitration.

The results for police are similar to those we have just discussed for firefighters. The model for police yields a lower $\overline{R}^2$ than the earlier model with only two states (.53 versus .66) and the standard error of estimate is larger (86.48 versus 71.78). The differences in the effects of the economic and political variables are that now parity, family income, and population per city employee are no longer statistically significant, but pattern-setting is and has a positive effect. The new wage variable, W' is significant at a higher confidence level for police than for firefighters, although its consequent t-value is smaller than that of W in the two-state model.

The state-year dummies may be interpreted as follows. D_7 is statistically significant at the .10 level, so we infer that salaries for Pennsylvania police were about $31 higher in 1973 than in 1972. The D_8 variable is significant at the .01 level and indicates that 1974 salaries were about $55 higher than in 1973. Those estimates serve as the bases for our judgments about the impact of final-offer in Wisconsin and Michigan.

For Wisconsin, the data indicate that police salaries rose by about $41 ($D_2 - D_1$) from 1972 to 1973 when final-offer was fully available. The t-value for the difference is 1.60, which is statistically significant at the .12 level. For 1973-74 ($D_3 - D_2$), salaries rose by an estimated $29, which is a statistically insignificant amount. Note again the pattern of a smaller increase (in terms of dollars as well as percentages) during the second year of final-offer than during the first.

A comparison of the "best estimates" for Wisconsin and Pennsylvania suggests that when final-offer was adopted, it raised police salaries by more than those salaries increased where only conventional arbitration was available. The relative effect in favor of Wisconsin the first year likely evaporated in the second year and may have worked to the relative disadvantage of the Wisconsin police.

For Michigan, with final-offer-by-issue, we estimate that police salaries rose by \$43 $(D_5 - D_4)$ from 1972 to 1973. This difference yields a *t*-value of 1.73, which is statistically significant at the .09 level. Thus, we infer that salaries in both Michigan and Pennsylvania increased by statistically significant amounts, that the dollar increase was larger in Michigan, that the increase was 38 percent (43/31) larger—greater than the relative base salary levels in the two states. From these facts, we gain the impression that *something* happened in Michigan to raise salaries (by less than a statistically significant amount) that did not happen in Pennsylvania.

For 1974, Michigan police salaries rose by an estimated \$25, whereas in Pennsylvania, as we said above, salaries increased by about \$55. While this difference is not statistically significant, it is obvious that it would stretch reason to assert that the assumed effect of final-offer in Michigan was to raise salaries by more than they increased in Pennsylvania. There is no good evidence to indicate that, relative to the Pennsylvania experience, final-offer, as such, raised Michigan police salaries in 1974.

In sum, it would be better to speak of impressions gained from an analysis of the data rather than hard findings based on statistical principles. The data suggest that final-offer had a small positive effect on wages during the first year, but no effect—perhaps even a negative effect—the second year. If hairsplitting is permitted, we could argue that the positive effect is somewhat larger for Wisconsin, where there was final-offer-by-package, than in Michigan, where there was final-offer-by-issue. If final-offer-by-issue is regarded as a procedure that is part way between final-offer-by-package and conventional arbitration, then the rank order of estimated salary effects is as one would expect from high to low.

Consider, for example, the following argument. Police salaries rose in Pennsylvania by \$31 from 1972 to 1973 according to our best estimate in Table 6-6. Since they averaged about \$633 per month in 1972, one could argue that in the absence of final-offer police salaries tended to increase by about 4.9 percent. In Wisconsin, however, police salaries increased by 6.1 percent (= \$41/\$676). The 1.2 percent difference may be the consequence of the adoption of final-offer in Wisconsin.

In Michigan, police salaries tended to rise by 5.7 percent (= \$43/\$757). The difference between that and 4.9 percent is a measure of the effect of final-offer in Michigan—that is, 0.8 percent of salary.

If changes in hours of work were felt to be necessary to any conclusion, it is worth observing that average hours of work per week fell by much more in Wisconsin (by 0.7 hour [e]) than in either Michigan or Pennsyl-

---

[e] The fall in average hours worked per week from 41.0 to 40.3 may be an overestimate of the true decline since the 41-hour work week in 1972 is greater than the estimated work week in 1971 and 1970—both 40.6 hours.

vania, where they fell by 0.1 and 0.2 hours, respectively, from 1972 to 1973. The main effect of incorporating hours of work into the analysis would be to raise the estimated effect of final-offer in Wisconsin, so that it might be as much as 2 percent.

Effect of Final-Offer Arbitration Awards

So far we have been concerned solely with the impact of the final-offer process, or the availability of final-offer, on the level of salaries. It is also possible to estimate the impact of final-offer awards on the salary outcomes of a given occupation in a given state. One such test would use the models we displayed earlier to ascertain whether cities that paid "high" or "low" wages demonstrated a pronounced tendency to use final-offer more often than cities that offered salaries more in accordance with the predictions of the models. In other words, one could divide the residuals from one of the regressions into two groups according to whether the city was involved in a final-offer award. The test would be to determine whether the mean *absolute* size of the residuals from the "awarding" cities was larger than that of the cities that did not get an award. A further test would be to determine whether the final-offer awards tend to move salary levels toward the mean. This latter test is similar to the test we discussed at the opening of this chapter that pertains to the effect of the final-offer *process* on the distribution of salaries. However, the scarcity of awards together with the problem of missing data preclude us from carrying out either test at this time because the number of cities for which we have both an award and a salary level in any year is less than 10 percent of the sample; at the most, six or seven observations are available.

Summary and Conclusions

Although all the evidence does not point unambiguously in one direction, the preponderance of evidence makes it reasonable to conclude that the institution of final-offer arbitration tended to raise the salaries of the police and firefighters in Michigan and Wisconsin by more than 1 but less than 5 percent and that the positive effect was much smaller, if it was present at all, in the subsequent year. This estimate must be accepted only cautiously because there is some evidence that final-offer had no effect even in the initial year. The ambiguity probably results from the fact that the basic model is not as well specified as one would like, which results in the appearance of coefficients that are sensitive to the specific model used in the estimation. Obviously, it is difficult to measure the relative effects of alternative procedures. The instability of the regression coefficients should be taken as a warning that the estimates are not robust.

The data indicate also that the effect of final-offer-by-package is slightly larger than the effect of final-offer-by-issue.

The parameter estimates in Table 6-4 are highly significant and well behaved. The test is powerful and the coefficients are reasonable. The estimates in Table 6-6, which use Pennsylvania as a "control," tell roughly the same story. Moreover, those results are in accord with the theoretical expectations developed in the first part of this chapter wherein we outlined the nature of the effect of final-offer on salaries. If the theory is correct, one might expect that the magnitude of the effect of final-offer would depend on the nature of the initial procedures. The more similar those initial procedures were to final-offer, the smaller the expected impact of final-offer. The change in Wisconsin, from factfinding to final-offer-by-package, would seem to be sharper than when Michigan went from conventional arbitration to final-offer-by-issue on economic matters. Thus one would expect the effects of final-offer to be greater in Wisconsin than they were in Michigan, and the estimates in Tables 6-5 and 6-6 indicate that the gains in Wisconsin were relatively larger.

It is beyond the scope of this study to determine whether gains of this magnitude are desirable. That kind of analysis would have to take into account whatever costs (including those of lost services) would be incurred if the parties were to resolve their disputes with some other procedure. It is possible, also, that gains such as this would be regarded as acceptable for some occupations and not for others, or during some time periods and not others.

If the system of final-offer is maintained so experience and data accumulate, it will, ironically, be possible to provide better estimates of the effect of final-offer and to make more reasoned judgments about its value in resolving disputes.

Notes

1. See Fred Witney, "Final-Offer Arbitration: The Indianapolis Experience," *Monthly Labor Review* (May 1973), pp. 20-25.

2. For example, Hirschel Kasper, "The Effects of Collective Bargaining on Public School Teachers' Salaries," *Industrial and Labor Relations Review* 24 (October 1970), pp. 57-72; Donald Frey, "Wage Determination in Public Schools and the Effects of Unionization," in Daniel S. Hamermesh, ed., *Labor in the Public and Nonprofit Sector,* (forthcoming); and Ronald G. Ehrenberg, "An Economic Analysis of Local Government

Employment and Wages," University of Massachusetts, 1972. Unpublished mimeo.

3. See Orley Ashenfelter, "The Effect of Unionization on Wages in the Public Sector: The Case of Fire Fighters," *Industrial and Labor Relations Review* 24 (January 1971), pp. 191-202; and Ronald G. Ehrenberg, "Municipal Government Structure, Unionization, and the Wages of Fire Fighters," *Industrial and Labor Relations Review* 27 (October 1973), pp. 36-48.

4. Ronald G. Ehrenberg correctly observed (in private correspondence) that this variable may merely reflect the downward sloping demand for public employees.

5. One exception is Ronald G. Ehrenberg and Gerald S. Goldstein, "A Model of Public Sector Wage Determination," *Journal of Urban Economics* (forthcoming).

6. See Jan Kmenta, *Elements of Econometrics* (New York: Macmillan, 1971), pp. 336-45.

7 Conclusions

In this final chapter, the findings of the separate state studies are considered as a whole, and conclusions are presented concerning the effect of using arbitration to resolve disputes about the terms of labor agreements covering law enforcement personnel and firefighters. An attempt is also made to determine the impact of final-offer-by-package arbitration relative to that of conventional arbitration and final-offer arbitration by each economic issue. Finally, the results of these studies are used as a foundation for speculative generalizations concerning the use of arbitration procedures in other areas of the public sector as well as in the transportation industry and other basic industries subject to the national emergency provisions of the Labor Management Relations Act.

Arbitration—Is It the End of the Line?

An important consideration, which has not been emphasized either in this study up to this point or in most other studies of arbitration, is that legislation providing for arbitration was sought by employee organizations only after they had become dissatisfied with a procedure terminating in nonbinding factfinding recommendations. In both Pennsylvania and Michigan, police and firefighters had access to factfinding from 1947 to 1968 and 1969, respectively, when arbitration was adopted as the terminal step. In Wisconsin, factfinding was the terminal step from 1962 until 1972.

The Pennsylvania and Michigan factfinding provisions had been included in general public sector antistrike legislation that was considered to be repressive by the labor movements of those states. In Wisconsin, however, factfinding was introduced much later as part of a bill providing bargaining rights for public employees. In this last instance, it was sought by unions as a first step toward ending unilateral management determinations. And, as has been noted, the initial Wisconsin experience with factfinding was appreciably better than that of the other two states. Even so, in all three states, after a decade or more during which factfinding was the terminal step, firefighter and police organizations chose to replace the advisory procedure with binding arbitration.

During this same period, other public sector unions were at first considering and subsequently clamoring for the right to strike rather than for arbitration. It seems clear that the different route taken by police and firefighter unions reflects the essential nature of their services, the traditions of their organizations, and appraisals by these organizations of public reaction to the few but highly publicized instances in which there were police and firefighter strikes.

The Union View

After six years' experience in Pennsylvania, five in Michigan, and two in Wisconsin, police and firefighter unions are quite satisfied with the arbitration statutes that they have obtained. None of them is lobbying for drastic changes in the legislation, and noncompliance with the law has been minimal. The satisfaction with arbitration reflects the present belief of these organizations that the threat of arbitration makes municipal employers treat them fairly.

One factor contributing to the favorable evaluation of arbitration is the belief that the availability of arbitration has stimulated bargaining in many smaller municipalities of under 10,000 population. Also, initial arbitration awards reflected wage "catch-up" and were more favorable to unions than were subsequent awards. More recent awards, particularly in the larger cities, have not been as favorably received, and a word of caution should be introduced about the possibility that the present satisfaction is not permanent.

In an era in which the cost of living is rising rapidly and estimates of what is a fair wage increase are also rising, the time lag associated with settlements reached only after extensive negotiations and arbitration proceedings may mean that awards that might have been acceptable at an earlier stage are now considered unsatisfactory. This is particularly true in the situation in which all but one of the public employee unions in a city have settled by direct negotiations, and then, some six months later when prices are up by another 5 percent or more, the last group receives an award identical with what had been negotiated earlier by the other groups.

Although the integrity of the bargaining process is preserved by awards that confirm patterns set previously, the satisfaction with the arbitration procedure, expressed earlier, tends to be greatly reduced. As one police association negotiator announced to a reporter after receiving an award under the circumstances just described, "It will be a cold day in hell before we go to arbitration again." [1]

It is quite possible that the negotiations for agreements effective in 1975 may reduce the dissatisfaction noted here by providing for substantial wage increases, either through negotiation or arbitration. If real wages are protected through escalator clauses or large catch-up increases, the arbitration system may continue to be popular with the employee organizations. If real wages are not protected, the previously expressed sentiments about being treated "fairly" will be repudiated, and whatever dispute resolution system is in effect at that time will be blamed for the changed circumstances. Assuming, however, that real wages are not eroded further, the general consensus of employee organizations about arbitration is likely to remain quite favorable.

The Employer View

Employers opposed arbitration originally and still have not grown to like a system under which a third party tells them how much to pay their police and firefighters. Even so, with the increased militance of other public employees, particularly teachers, management's aversion to arbitration of labor disputes in the essential services has diminished. Most management negotiators do not regard a return to factfinding as a practical alternative, and when faced with a choice between a system that permits strikes and one that ends in arbitration, they reluctantly come down on the side of arbitration.

Some managements espouse the heretic position—"Let 'em strike." This minority view is advocated privately by several municipal managements who have had first-hand experience with police and/or firefighter strikes in the period prior to the adoption of the arbitration statute. They have indicated that it is possible to provide emergency protection through use of a skeleton standby police or firefighter force made up of supervisory employees of the department concerned and supplemented by supervisors of other public services. These same managements have suggested, however, that it is not politically feasible for elected municipal officials publicly to favor such a position, and they doubt that city managements will sponsor legislation providing for this option.

Although many managements express a preference for factfinding in place of arbitration, they create the impression that this is a yearning "for the good old days" rather than a goal they will actively pursue. They recognize that you can't turn back the clock and that unions that have negotiated agreements under statutes permitting them to invoke binding arbitration unilaterally will engage in strikes and other forms of direct self-help rather than return to a system under which an advisory opinion is the terminal step. Some managements also note that the lack of finality of factfinding caused them some problems, as unions sometimes found such recommendations partially unacceptable and attempted further negotiations in order to improve the proposed settlements. In summary, the general consensus among management negotiators seems to be that arbitration is here to stay and that, although undesirable, it has not proved to be as bad as they originally thought.

The View of Arbitrators and Mediators

Mediators and arbitrators also expressed satisfaction with the use of arbitration to resolve public sector disputes of police and firefighters. Mediators believe that they have more "clout" when rejection of the mediator's recommendations leads to arbitration rather than factfinding. The reasoning advanced in support of this view is that the parties are more apt to moderate their positions in order to avoid a subsequent binding decision by a third party than to avoid a subsequent advisory opinion.

Although the logic of this position is strong, it should be noted that no statistical evidence was found in any of the three states to support it. Furthermore, in Michigan, the parties who arbitrated tended to discount the value of the prearbitration state mediation services. In general, it appears that mediators in Michigan and Wisconsin are resolving many of the disputes referred to them, but it cannot be determined from the statistics whether the proportion of mediated settlements is greater when followed by arbitration of one sort or the other than it was when followed by factfinding.

It should also be noted that many other factors have changed over the years and that the comparison of mediation statistics in the two periods does not take these into account even though they may have substantial influence on the likelihood of a mediator's being able to resolve a dispute. Such factors include deterioration of the financial position of many large cities, increased militance of public employees, and the provision of full bargaining rights along with arbitration.

Many of the arbitrators who have extensive private sector grievance arbitration experience are somewhat uneasy with their new role when vested with the authority to determine the terms of a new agreement in the public sector. They are well aware that legislatures granted them powers usually reserved to management, or to management subject to bargaining with the union.

Arbitrators recognize that their decisions not only determine directly the wages of the police or firefighters involved in the case, but also indirectly affect the level of service that will be offered, the tax rate in the community, and quite possibly the wages of other public employees in the same and in neighboring communities. Even so, however, the arbitrators end up in much the same posture as union and management representatives. They may have qualms about the propriety of being vested with such authority, but, in comparison with the alternatives of strikes or unilateral action or advisory recommendations that are not followed, arbitrators also are satisfied with the use of arbitration to resolve disputes of firefighters and police.

Several points should be noted about the views of arbitrators summarized here. Agreement on the notion that the system is working satisfactorily does not mean that the arbitrators are in agreement about the mechanics of the bargaining system of which the arbitration step is just one part. As will be noted subsequently in this chapter, arbitrators—and labor and management spokesmen as well—hold a wide variety of views about such matters as the method of triggering arbitration, whether or not the arbitrator should mediate, whether or not there should be a single neutral arbitrator as opposed to a tripartite panel, and whether or not the forms of arbitration should be conventional or final-offer by issue or by package.

The Mechanics of Arbitration and Their Effects on Third-Party Dependency and Bargaining Outcomes

We turn now to comparison of various aspects of the arbitration procedures in the three states studied and the effect of these elements on the bargaining process and outcome.

Cost of Arbitration

The cost of arbitration may serve as a deterrent to use of the process in some of the smaller cities where the per capita cost to the members in 5- and 15-man bargaining units outweighs the possible gains to be achieved through arbitration. Complaints about the cost of the process were voiced to a greater extent by union negotiators than by management negotiators. Even so, only a minority of union representatives believed that costs acted as a very important deterrent to use of arbitration.

The cost-sharing arrangements differ in the three states: in Pennsylvania, the management pays the full cost of the neutral arbitrator; in Michigan, the state lightens the direct load on the parties by paying one-third of the cost of the neutral and requiring the union and the management to divide evenly the remaining two-thirds; in Wisconsin, the full cost of the neutral is borne by the parties, with each paying half. On the basis of these procedural arrangements, unions face the largest costs in Wisconsin, less in Michigan, and still less in Pennsylvania. Other procedural arrangements, however, contribute to costs, and in actual practice, the relative cost in the three states appears to be reversed.

In Wisconsin, the arbitration proceedings are shorter than those in Pennsylvania and Michigan because Wisconsin uses single arbitrators while the other two states use tripartite arbitration panels. Tripartite arbitration facilitates mediation—a factor that is discussed subsequently—but usually requires executive sessions of the panel and will involve greater expenditures of time by the neutral. For this reason, the actual costs of the neutral in Wisconsin, which average about $350 for each party, are about half as much as those paid in Michigan.

Although unions in Pennsylvania bear no part of the costs of the neutral, they and the unions in Michigan pay the full cost of the partisan union representative on the arbitration panel. This may increase costs appreciably. In Pennsylvania, where the parties recently have tended to choose attorneys or other experienced professionals as their arbitration panel members, the fees of these men outweigh the union's share of the neutral's cost in Wisconsin and in Michigan. In addition to the above factors, there are the costs in all of these states that each party must bear in preparing and presenting its case.

The process of final-offer-by-package arbitration may reduce costs as compared to final-offer-by-economic-issue or conventional arbitration. If the Wisconsin procedure reduces the dimensions of the controversy to a greater degree prior to arbitration than is the case under the other two procedures, hearing time would be shortened and costs reduced. Unfortunately, however, the cause of the cost reduction cannot be attributed to the use of final-offer-by-package arbitration rather than the other two procedures because these forms of arbitration are part of procedures that differ in such other respects as the role of mediation and the use of tripartite panels instead of single neutral arbitrators.

In general, the cost of arbitration has only a minimal effect on the bargaining process and does not deter usage appreciably except in very small bargaining units. Even so, union representatives express considerable concern about what they consider to be the high cost of arbitration. Management representatives tend to express far less concern, probably because the cost represents a much smaller share of employer expenditures than of union expenditures. The discussion of cost by management and union representatives runs parallel to the continuing debate about the cost of grievance arbitration. It is possible, therefore, that in the future there will be attempts to reduce the cost of interest arbitration by the use of experiments patterned after similar efforts to reduce the cost of grievance arbitration.

Mediation Prior to Arbitration

Prearbitration mediation is emphasized in Wisconsin, is used in Michigan but given less emphasis, and is almost totally absent from the Pennsylvania procedure. Mediation occurs in about one-third of the Wisconsin negotiations. Precise data from Michigan are not available, but it appears that a slightly higher percent of negotiations are referred to mediation and that a slightly lower percent of these disputes are settled at that step. No evidence was found that the existence of the mediation step in either Michigan or Wisconsin had an adverse effect on the bargaining procedure despite the relatively heavy reliance on it, in comparison with the use of mediation in the private sector.

In Michigan, the parties were more critical of the efforts of state mediators than were Wisconsin parties. Failure to reach a settlement in mediation may reflect a lack of skill on the part of unions, managements, or mediators, or may be caused by other factors. If the parties in Michigan anticipate mediation in the executive sessions of the tripartite arbitration panel, they may be less inclined to settle at the mediation step than in Wisconsin where the arbitration procedure is less conducive to further mediation.

In any event, since mediation is advisory and does not involve the imposition of a settlement on the parties by an outside third party, frequent recourse to mediation has not been considered violative of "free" collective bargaining. This point is raised here, however, because of the absence of a formal prearbitration mediation step in Pennsylvania and the question of whether this makes any difference. A larger percent of disputes are referred to arbitration in Pennsylvania than in Michigan or Wisconsin, a development that may be caused by the absence of mediation in Pennsylvania, or instead may be caused by the differences in the arbitration procedures in the three states.

Theoretically, the use of final-offer arbitration in Michigan and Wisconsin will deter the parties from using the procedure to a greater extent than they would if conventional arbitration were the terminal step. In this instance, however, it is impossible to determine whether the greater dependency on arbitration in Pennsylvania is attributable to the absence of a mediation step or to a lesser deterrent effect of conventional arbitration. It would be desirable, if a model can be constructed and data obtained, to determine precisely by mathematical means what proportion of the greater usage of arbitration in Pennsylvania should be attributed to absence of mediation and what proportion to the form of arbitration used and to other factors that differ from state to state.

In any event, it should be noted that the absence of mediation is associated with greater resort to arbitration in Pennsylvania than in Michigan or Wisconsin, although this may be caused by other differences in procedure. Occasionally it has been suggested that the Pennsylvania statute be amended to provide for a mediation step, but the question has not been sufficiently important to cause legislative action.

"Med-Arb" and Tripartite Panels

In all three states, the request for arbitration, either subsequent to state mediation or without such a step, does not mean that the dispute is pursued automatically to the point of an award. The request for arbitration may be used as a bargaining tactic by either side to induce a change in position by the other. The request tends to emphasize the determination of the petitioning party to proceed to arbitration unless a further compromise is offered by its adversary.

In Pennsylvania, the request for arbitration leads directly to the appointment of the partisan panel members and their selection of a neutral, usually from panels furnished by the American Arbitration Association. In Michigan and Wisconsin, the parties first go through mediation and then become involved in arbitration. In Wisconsin, the parties select a single neutral by alternately striking names from a panel furnished them by the Wisconsin Employment Relations Commission. In Michigan, the Michigan Employment Relations Commission usually appoints the neutral arbitrator and the parties each select their own partisan representative on the tripartite arbitration panel. In all of these states, the parties may avoid these procedures by agreeing upon a neutral.

Union and management negotiators sometimes resolve their impasse while selecting the neutral and abort the procedure at that point. If the dispute has not been resolved by the time the arbitrator is appointed, the parties in all three states can encourage him to act as a mediator, but differences in the statutes make mediation by the arbitrator most feasible in Michigan, less so in Pennsylvania, and least in Wisconsin.

Mediation by the neutral arbitrator in Michigan is enhanced by the statutory requirement that, on each economic issue, he must pick the offer of one side or the other but cannot select a compromise position. In executive session of the arbitration panel, the neutral can suggest to the side he believes should make a compromise that he is leaning toward the position of the other side and that he regards the present position of the first side as an unreasonable one. This suggestion has coercive power since the party to whom it is addressed recognizes that failure to move will result in the arbitrator's selection of the other party's position on this issue.

When the potential loser has adjusted his position accordingly, the arbitrator can then turn to the other side, if the parties are still apart, and suggest that this movement by the first party has persuaded him that the position of the second party is now the more unreasonable one and that the second party also should consider making a compromise. Then, assuming that the parties have "voluntarily" reached agreement upon this issue, the arbitrator can turn to the remaining issues and follow the same procedure. If he is successful on each point, he will have mediated the impasse in its entirety, and the case is resolved either with or without the issuance of an agreed-upon award, depending upon the wishes of the parties.

Under the tripartite panel format in Pennsylvania, the neutral can follow the same strategy as the Michigan neutral and may also be successful in disposing of many of the items in dispute. On the whole, however, he faces a more difficult task because the statute does not prohibit the neutral from taking a compromise position. If either party believes that the arbitrator is going to "split the difference," it will resist mediation attempts by the arbitrator and will maintain its point of view in an attempt to persuade the neutral to come closer to its position.

In Wisconsin, the use of a single neutral instead of a tripartite panel acts as a barrier to mediation. The arbitrator can invite the parties to an informal prehearing conference, presumably for the purpose of discussing procedural matters, and then, while they are there, he can attempt to mediate the dispute. By this time, however, the parties are mentally geared up for arbitration and may have lost the flexibility that is needed if mediation is to succeed. Furthermore, the arbitrator knows that he is engaging in an activity without specific statutory blessing and may therefore be less aggressive in his mediation efforts.

The statutory arrangements in Wisconsin also favor a judicial-type process under which the arbitrator considers evidence in support of total packages that have been amended no later than five days before the hearing. In actual practice, some arbitrators have deviated from this position in efforts to reduce the number of unresolved issues and to give the parties an opportunity to reach a settlement on their own. Even though these attempts by the arbitrator may include such devices as interpreting the time limits for amending proposals to mean within five days after the actual hearing rather than before it, relatively few of the cases heard by arbitrators are resolved by mediation.

A comparison of the Wisconsin and Michigan procedures clearly illustrates the different value judgments that have been made by the respective legislatures. In Michigan, arbitrators can refer disputes back to the parties for further negotiation. Also, the executive session of the tripartite panel is conducive to mediation. If the deterrent effect of arbitration is weakened in the process of mediation, this is not regarded as a defect that is of sufficient importance to offset the value of agreed-upon settlements relative to imposed settlements.

If "med-arb" is regarded as more desirable than judicial-type arbitration, the Michigan procedure facilitates this arrangement more than do the procedures in the other two states. It should be noted, however, that there are arbitrators in Michigan who favor the judicial approach and follow it, even though it can be argued that the statute favors mediation. It is ironic that some arbitrators with a penchant for mediation serve as arbitrators in Wisconsin where it does not have preferred status and that the reverse is true in Michigan. Perhaps this aside provides an insight into the reasoning of those supporters of final-offer arbitration who favor this procedure, not for its claimed deterrent effect, but because it prevents the arbitrator from innovating and fashioning what he is wont to view as a sensible compromise.

Arbitration Dependency

Arbitration has not caused the demise of collective bargaining by public safety employees in the three states studied, but instead has served as a stimulus to union organization and the spread of collective bargaining to geographic areas where formerly it did not exist.

Relatively powerful managements in the rural areas have been forced to take into account the possibility that unions will petition for arbitration and have demonstrated that they prefer to make any changes by direct negotiation rather than to have them imposed by an arbitrator. Unions also, for cost reasons as well as on the grounds of self-determination, have shown that they prefer negotiated settlements to arbitration awards.

In Michigan, Pennsylvania, and Wisconsin, the majority of settlements have been achieved through direct negotiations without third-party assistance through either mediation or arbitration. Settlements achieved through agreement after the arbitration hearing had begun or through issuance of arbitration awards ran from about 12 percent in Wisconsin to about 30 percent in Michigan and in Pennsylvania. Most labor and management spokesmen emphatically deny that the possibility of arbitration on the motion of either side destroys the incentive to settle through collective bargaining, although there are exceptions to this generalization.

The finding that Wisconsin has the lowest use of arbitration supports the theoretical underpinnings of final-offer-by-package arbitration. Presumably the greater risk under this procedure makes the management and the union more willing to compromise in order to avoid losing everything through arbitration. The limited experience on which the extent of dependency estimates are based suggests, however, that these findings are in no sense definitive.

It is interesting to note that in Michigan, where the parties had several years' experience with conventional arbitration before changing to a modified final-offer system, the number of requests for arbitration is about the same under the new system as it was under the old one. The significant change has been the sharp reduction in the percent of cases in which it has been necessary to issue awards. In three years, under conventional arbitration, awards were issued in an estimated 61 percent of the cases referred to arbitration. In the first year and a half under final-offer-by-economic-issue, awards were issued in only 36 percent of the cases.

This suggests that in Michigan the effect of the change in procedure was to increase the use of "med-arb," but that the incentive to settle directly without petitioning for arbitration was unchanged by the move from conventional to final-offer-by-economic-issue arbitration. Quite possibly the parties' knowledge that they would have the opportunity to engage in mediation and change their positions after petitioning for arbitration may have seriously weakened the deterrent effect of final-offer arbitration. Also, under a final-offer-by-economic-issue system, either or both parties can maintain unreasonable positions on issues that they are willing to lose and, by so doing, may strengthen their hands on other issues that are more important to them.

Although it may be a coincidence, it is important to note that the percent of cases settled by issuance of arbitration *awards* in Michigan is about the same as in Wisconsin, despite the fact that the percent of disputes referred to arbitration is about twice as high in Michigan as in Wisconsin. If one accepts the percent of disputes settled by awards as the significant figure for measuring arbitration dependency and ignores settlements achieved through successful "med-arb," the Michigan final-offer-by-economic-issue system does as well as the final-offer-by-package system in Wisconsin. If, however, one regards the number of settlements achieved through "med-arb" as an indication of greater third-party dependency than an equal number of settlements achieved through mediation before submission of a dispute to arbitration, then there is a substantial difference between the two procedures.

As has been indicated in the separate state studies, arbitration dependency is attributable to a variety of factors that exist in all three states. Weak leadership and inexperience on either side contributes to the use of arbitration. A desire by either side to change a traditional relationship will generate a dispute that is referred to arbitration. If a city has many small bargaining units, it is more difficult to settle with all of them without resort to arbitration.

Finally, in connection with the degree of dependency on arbitration, it should be noted that overall statistics may conceal differing trends. In Pennsylvania, for example, suburban Philadelphia areas rely less on arbitration than they did several years ago, but this downward trend is offset by the rising use of arbitration in the smaller cities in rural areas. The existence of these many variables that cause changes in the degrees

of dependency on arbitration makes one aware of how difficult it is to at-
tribute differences in dependency in the three states to particular factors
such as differences in the form of arbitration.

The Splitting-the-Difference Syndrome

One popular indictment of arbitration is that the arbitrator will split the
difference between the positions of the parties and that, therefore, it is
wise to maintain an extreme position rather than to make compromises
that might possibly lead to a settlement. One of the claimed advantages
of final-offer-by-package arbitration over conventional arbitration is that
the parties know that they may be penalized heavily if they do not formulate realistic positions. Theoretically, the parties will reach settlements
more often under such a system and, in cases where agreement is not
reached, they will be closer together so that the arbitrator will have less
room for error.

One measure of the deterrent effect, which has been discussed already,
is the percent of cases in which it is necessary to use the arbitration
process. Another measure of the relative effect of each form of arbitration
is the average number of issues in dispute in each case in which an award
is issued and the total amount by which the proposals differ.

When measured by the criterion of number of issues in dispute, the
final-offer-by-package arbitration system used in Wisconsin tended to
bring the parties closer together than did the systems in the other two
states. Seven of the first 22 Wisconsin awards involved only one issue;
another four involved only two issues. Only five of the 22 cases involved
six or more issues. The criterion of number of issues is not particularly
significant, however, unless the importance of each issue is known.

An analysis was made of the difference in wages between the proposals
of the parties and of the difference in total compensation. Values attributed
to differences in fringe benefits are difficult to calculate accurately and
therefore the estimates are not precise. The differences found in Wisconsin
compared to the other two states are so large, however, that it is doubtful
that they are affected appreciably by the estimating procedure.

Based on the first 33 awards in Wisconsin, the average wage gap between the offers of the parties was only $16 per month. The average gap
in the value of the fringes was $25, which brings the average gap in total
compensation to $41 per month. The average wage gap in Michigan, based
on a sample of 12 awards, was $78 and the average wage gap in Pennsyl-
vania, based on 18 cases, was $80. Estimates were not available for calcu-
lating the average gap in the value of the fringes or total compensation.

Although the evidence is very slim, it appears that final-offer-by-package arbitration brings the parties closer together than do the procedures in the other two states. There is insufficient evidence to say very much at this point about any possible differences between final-offer-by-economic-issue and conventional arbitration because of the lack of fringe benefit data and small sample size, but no difference between the two was detected.

In Michigan, the average wage gap in nine conventional arbitration cases was $77 and in three final-offer-by-economic-issue cases it was $80. Although the sample is very small, it strengthens the suspicion that where "med-arb" doesn't work, the gap in the cases that end in awards is about the same under conventional arbitration as it is under final-offer-by-economic-issue arbitration. This impression is supported by the similarity of the wage gap in Pennsylvania and that in Michigan under either system.

One other criticism of final-offer-by-package arbitration *and* of final-offer arbitration by economic issue that runs completely contrary to the implications of the charge that arbitrators split the difference is that these systems prevent the arbitrator from splitting the difference when he should do so. If, in his judgment, the legislative criteria justify a wage increase of 8 percent, but the management is offering only 6 percent and the union is demanding 10 percent, then the legislative prohibition against his splitting the difference means that the final settlement, regardless of which he picks, does not meet the criteria for wage-setting enumerated in the statute to the same degree as the settlement he would have imposed had he been allowed to select a compromise position.

Critics who believe that arbitrators split the difference and should be prevented from doing so should also recognize that, by implication at least, they are suggesting that one or the other of the extreme positions is more sound than a middle-ground position. Theoretically, it is doubtful that this can be substantiated.

Noncomparable Multiple Issue Cases

One theoretical objection to final-offer-by-package arbitration is that in multiple issue cases, either or both sides may include in their final offers an unsound proposal that an arbitrator will be forced to grant because he must choose an offer in its entirety and is statutorily prevented from modifying it. For example, the arbitrator may believe that the union's economic proposals are slightly more reasonable than those of management, but he disapproves of the union proposal to include a clause in the agreement that would prevent management from changing past practices without the prior consent of the union. He may find that the management offer is also marred by some proposal such as its opposition to an agency shop in a situation in which it is clear that most employees favor it and in which management has granted an agency shop to other groups of its employees.

It is no wonder that arbitrators complain bitterly when faced with such Hobson's choices. Defenders of the final-offer-by-package system have no answer for the arbitrator who is placed in this position. He can be assured only that the fault lies with the parties for including such proposals and that the cure for the problem lies in ruling against the party with the most atrocious proposal. Losing the case should deter the party from presenting unsound proposals in the future. Also, it should be noted that fear of this result supposedly persuades the parties not to formulate such packages in the first place.

The Wisconsin experience to date suggests that this defect in the final-offer-by-package system does not come into play very often. For the most part, the parties withdraw outrageous proposals prior to arbitration, and only in about three or four cases out of the 173 agreements negotiated in 1973 did this problem arise. Although this is a dramatic and well-advertised possible drawback to adoption of a final-offer-by-package arbitration system, the Wisconsin experience shows that the problem is overrated and of no great policy consequence.

A related and possibly more important practical and theoretical drawback of the final-offer-by-package arbitration system, not found in an issue-by-issue final-offer arbitration system, is that it is very difficult to balance the merits of reasonable proposals on dissimilar issues in a case that involves two or three issues. For example, assume that a case involves wages and whether or not there should be a residency requirement. Reasonable men differ about both of these questions, and an award that gives one issue to each side in a situation may appear to be more equitable to an arbitrator and to legislative observers. Balanced against this criticism, however, is the notion that the possible loss in equity that this problem represents is outweighed by the claimed greater deterrent effect associated with the all-or-nothing package system and the high value placed on settlements achieved voluntarily by the parties.

Impact of Arbitration on Bargaining Outcomes

The findings of the statistical analysis in Chapter 6 about the impact of arbitration on wages and the more subjective findings reported in the chapters on the separate states should be regarded as initial tentative estimates. Until several more years of experience are accumulated and until the sample is extended to other states with arbitration statutes as well as to states without provisions for arbitration, it will not be possible to make a definitive statement about the relative effect on wages of each form of arbitration. These tentative findings are summarized below and some of the problems in generalizing from these data are discussed.

In each of the state studies, arbitration was reported to be responsible for the "catch-up" effect and awards in the initial years of operation were greater than awards in subsequent years. In Pennsylvania, it is estimated that the catch-up period ran approximately from 1968 to 1971. In Michigan, it occurred during the 1969-72 period when conventional arbitration was in effect, and in Wisconsin, it occurred in 1973. Data were not available to test these subjective impressions thoroughly, and the few statistical tests that were run partially corroborated, but in some cases contradicted, these impressions.

The regression equations in Chapter 6 that sought to estimate the magnitude of the effect of final-offer arbitration relative to alternative systems of dispute settlement suggest that final-offer raised salaries by a slight amount when it was first adopted. With various social, economic, and political influences on salaries taken into account, the data indicate that final-offer raised Wisconsin police and firefighter salaries in 1973 by somewhere between 1 and 5 percent more than they would have been increased under factfinding or conventional arbitration and that the effect in Michigan was less.

The model that uses the 1973 Pennsylvania experience as a base indicates that the Wisconsin final-offer procedure raised police salaries by slightly more than 1 percent above what would otherwise be expected, and that the Michigan final-offer-by-economic-issue system raised 1973 police salaries by something less than 1 percent relative, also, to Pennsylvania's conventional arbitration. The estimated coefficients indicate also that in neither state was there a further increase in 1974 beyond what would be normally expected. As a result, the final-offer effect may have the characteristics of a "one-shot" affair. The model that takes the 1972 Wisconsin experience as the basis for comparison also indicates that the effect of final-offer on 1974 salaries was negligible. That model suggests that final-offer, taken alone, raised Wisconsin police salaries by approximately 5 percent in 1973, but by nothing further in 1974. The model indicates that the effect in Michigan was less than 5 percent.

The difference in the estimated effects between the two models may be attributed to one or both of two important considerations. In the model that yields the approximately 1 percent measured effect, Pennsylvania's 1973 experience is used as the basis for comparison, whereas in the model that implies a 5 percent effect, Wisconsin's 1972 mixed factfinding and final-offer system served as the control. Thus, the 1 and 5 percent effects reflect different bases of comparison and so are less inconsistent than they appear at first blush.

A second difference is the alternative specification of the wages that are assumed to determine the salaries for the police and firefighters. In the model yielding a 1 percent final-offer effect, it is implicitly assumed that the police and firefighter salaries are determined by wages in the private sector; in the model implying a 5 percent final-offer effect, it is assumed that the wages of public workers are the relevant determinant of the salaries for the uniformed safety forces. The correct specification is important in obtaining accurate estimates, as was observed in Chapter 6, but the theory of wage determination in the public sector is sufficiently recent that one cannot take a dogmatic view on the best measures of the relevant determinants.

If changes in hours of work are incorporated into the analysis of bargaining outcomes, the impact of Wisconsin's final-offer procedure appears larger while that for Michigan declines. Thus, relative to Pennsylvania in 1973, Wisconsin's police may have had upward of a 2 percent combined wage-hour advantage as a result of final-offer, but Michigan police may have gained as little as 0.5 percent.

It can be argued that the appropriate base line for the measurement of the effect of different forms of arbitration should be wages and wage changes in states such as Ohio and Illinois that do not provide for arbitration of police and firefighter wages. The choice of a base line depends on the specific question one wants to ask, because the subsequent statistical inferences are made with respect to that base line. Ohio, for example, would be a good base line if one wanted to ascertain the effect of final-offer relative to what would occur in an unstructured system since Ohio has no legislation to guide the settlement of disputes. The use of Pennsylvania's 1973 experience as a base line means that we have studied the effect of final-offer relative to conventional arbitration.

One other problem that remains, however, is that it will be difficult to isolate the impact of different aspects of the arbitration systems unless a sufficient number of states with arbitration systems are added to the study in order to control for such other elements of the arbitration systems as absence or presence of mediation and use of tripartite arbitration panels rather than single arbitrators.

The statistical analysis in the Wisconsin state study does not address itself to the question of the relative effect of different forms of arbitration, but instead is addressed to the question of whether, with controls for size, wealth of the community, tax rates, and public and private sector wages, those units that used the arbitration process raised wages by this effort in comparison with those who were eligible to use the process but instead settled on their own. Regression analysis showed that those who received arbitration awards did not raise wages by pursuing claims to arbitration. This result may occur because of the primacy of wage comparisons in arbitration cases. In those communities with high police and firefighter wages, arbitrators may be less sympathetic to the organizations' wage claims than in communities in which their wages are much lower than the average in the state. Impressions of management and union negotiators in Pennsylvania and Michigan also lend support to this interpretation of the data.

From an overall subjective view, it appears that enactment of legislation providing for arbitration will help the lower-paid workers to catch up in situations where lack of bargaining strength formerly hampered such efforts. In pattern-setting cities, however, the introduction of arbitration in a few states may have little or no effect on wage changes. It appears that wage settlements in major private sector negotiations provide the bench marks for public sector settlements in the major cities and that major city settlements, in turn, provide guides for the smaller cities. The interpretation of the mass of comparative wage data by an arbitrator in a major city is not likely to vary greatly from the settlements agreed upon in other major cities and may actually reflect the settlements based on political power and threat of economic action in major cities in which the parties settled by direct negotiation, regardless of whether arbitration was provided for by statute, as is now the case in New York City, or whether there is no statute, as is the case in Chicago.

The Noncompliance Problem

In the first few years that the arbitration systems have been in effect in Pennsylvania, Michigan, and Wisconsin, noncompliance with the statute has been rare and, so far as can be determined, there has not been a single instance up until the end of 1974 in the three states in which public safety employees have engaged in strikes or other forms of direct action in order to overturn an arbitration award. Losers have grumbled about awards, but no employee organization has struck to change an award. Noncompliance occurred in connection with bargaining in a few instances, as a substitute for the use of arbitration.

For example, in Wisconsin, a union launched a community-wide education and harassment campaign in support of its attempt to gain a cost-of-living escalator clause in its agreement—the first such clause for public employees in that immediate geographic area—and it was successful. The union doubted that any arbitrator would have granted the union demand and defended its action on that basis. However, it can be argued that this union claim is not correct and that arbitrators will award cost-of-living escalator clauses on the grounds that private sector employees have such protection. In any event, as each successive round of negotiations is completed, it seems logical to predict that a few of those leaders who wish to innovate may occasionally decide that the best strategy to follow is one of arbitration avoidance and the use of economic pressure instead. Sick-outs, picketing, and appeals to private sector unions and other public sector unions for a community solidarity program may be invoked in order to achieve some new benefit.

This type of action reflects a traditional private sector union view that arbitration is essentially a comparative process and would work to the disadvantage of pattern-setters. Even though it may be correct insofar as private sector pattern-setters are concerned, its extension to the public sector does not appear equally valid, and it is doubtful that this view and the noncompliance it engenders will spread. A basic criterion in the legislation of many states is that wages of public employees should be comparable to those of workers in the private sector. Therefore, for the most part, public sector workers are pattern-followers.

It should be noted also that the claims of strike-free environments in those states that have passed arbitration statutes is one that needs more thorough exploration than has been done to date. Statistics about illegal strikes are difficult to gather, particularly when they are partial strikes, rolling strikes, or strikes of short duration and are called by other names such as "blue flu." Management also is occasionally guilty of noncompliance with an award, although its resistance usually takes the form of a legal challenge rather than economic action. In each state, there are municipalities that have made clear that they oppose the statute, and in some instances, they have invoked legal challenges that delay the effective dates on which awards are implemented.

Regardless of whether or not there is perfect compliance with the statute or an occasional example of noncompliance, the basic point is that the arbitration procedure cannot be faulted on the grounds of noncompliance. Very few statutes achieve the degree of compliance associated with the arbitration statutes in the three states included in this study.

Extension of Arbitration to Other Public Sector Employees and to the Private Sector

The generalizations set forth in this section are speculative in nature. To some degree they reflect value judgments of the authors and are not buttressed by data. To some degree they also reflect the lessons learned in the study of police and firefighter bargaining and arbitration systems. It is recognized that public safety employees are very different from other public sector employees and private sector employees in basic industries.

Therefore, readers should be aware that the principle of not extrapolating beyond the limits of the data is being consciously violated.

The Consent of the Governed

Noncompliance with arbitration awards is not a problem in police and firefighter negotiations because the employee organizations reject the right to strike and believe that arbitration is the proper method of resolving their disputes. The opposition of public sector management to enactment of the arbitration statutes may have sharpened the unions' realization that arbitration is their chosen tool and that noncompliance with awards they do not like will weaken the entire system that they strongly favor.

To the degree that other groups share similar values and wish to reject the right to strike and to rely instead on arbitration, it is likely that such groups also will abide by arbitration awards and eliminate most problems of noncompliance. Although one cannot say with certainty how many public employees prefer arbitration to the right to strike, it appears that this view is widespread, particularly if the group concerned is able to express its view on the matter and to have that view determine the procedure to be followed.

Popularly, this is known as the Canadian system under which each bargaining unit of Canadian federal employees elects, prior to the start of bargaining, to have either the right to strike or the right to invoke arbitration if it cannot reach agreement with its employer. The legislation supported in Congress in 1973 by the American Federation of State, County, and Municipal Employees and the National Education Association is similar in nature. It provides for factfinding and further specifies that the recommendations will be binding upon the parties if the union so notifies the employer prior to the issuance of the recommendations. If the union does this, it voluntarily gives up the right to strike. In Canada, about 90 percent of the bargaining units have chosen the arbitration route in preference to the right to strike. It seems likely that the same sort of preferences would be expressed in the United States.

Gaining Employer Cooperation

Employer groups tend to indict this choice-of-procedure approach under which a weak union may choose arbitration and a strong one will choose the right to strike. Insofar as compliance with an arbitration award is concerned, however, it is logical to let the employees select the procedure.

This does not mean, however, that such a system would not tip the balance of power toward the employees, as employers charge. It probably would, although the impact of such a move may be much smaller than is imagined by employers who oppose this option.

Even if the economic position of the employer is not adversely affected to the degree that the employer fears it will be, a system of employee choice of procedures deprives the employer of any voice and seems unfair on grounds of political democracy and equal participation by both sides. One method of reducing the employer complaint of unequal treatment is to give him the power to choose the form of arbitration. When the union selects the right to arbitrate, the employer then could be given the right to specify whether it will be arms' length judicial-type arbitration or "med-arb," whether the arbitration will be conducted by a single neutral or a tripartite panel, and whether it will be conventional arbitration, final-offer-by-issue arbitration, or final-offer-by-package arbitration.

Although the employer's choices may seem relatively inconsequential and may be characterized as variations on a theme, the variations are significant. The employer will be determining whether there will be an adjudicatory court-type model or a collective bargaining "med-arb"-type model. Even further, the value of involving the employer in the selection of the form of arbitration is considerable. To some degree, the employer will also evaluate the result of the process in terms of his participation in it. Just as employees who lose an arbitration case may wonder whether they might not be better off choosing the right to strike in the next round, so the employer who loses may opt for a different arbitration mechanism the next time around.

Application to Other Public Sector Employees

If the bargaining and arbitration systems presently followed by police and firefighters are offered to other public sector employees, on an optional basis in place of the right to strike, it seems likely that most unions in smaller cities and rural areas will opt for arbitration. In an atmosphere in which arbitration is the prevailing method of dispute resolution, as opposed to collective bargaining under the threat of a strike, it is conceivable that views about the process could change dramatically and that dependency upon arbitration will increase.

So long as the private sector settlements act as pattern-setters, however, and so long as private sector bargaining dominates the scene, this general shift in views may not take place. In any event, unless and until there is such a general change in views, the expansion of arbitration to cover all public employees, if they so desire, should not spell the abandonment of collective bargaining. There is no reason why the desire to settle by them-selves in preference to third-party dictation should not be as strong, if not stronger, among these groups than among public safety employees.

Arbitration as a process may seem more rational than the strike to groups with higher average levels of education. White-collar, middle-class, professional employees such as accountants, nurses, and lawyers working for public employers may have a value system that biases them strongly in favor of arbitration rather than the right to strike.

Nonessential employees, of which the librarians are cited as the arche-typical group, prefer arbitration because the right to strike is meaningless when the cessation of services causes no great inconvenience, at least in the short run. Other groups of public employees who opt for the right to strike may well find that their services are not so essential as they have assumed, and they also may turn to arbitration.

The Wellington-Winter argument about the inelasticity of government services may prove to be overstated.[2] Use of government services may be postponable, or they may be curtailed without great harm to the consumer, once the consumers have made psychological adjustments to the possibility of service interruptions caused by strikes of public employees. As this change in attitude occurs, more and more groups of public employees will give greater consideration to the use of arbitration.

It should be reemphasized that this shift to a system under which em-ployee groups can opt for arbitration does not imply a greater percent of awards to settlements than was found among firefighters and police. The drift, under a choice-of-procedures plan, will be one under which a union is able to invoke arbitration, but presumably will not desire nor deem it necessary to do so more often than has been the case among fire-fighters and police. Experience of the Canadian unions in the federal sector provides support for this opinion, as only about 18 percent of the cases in which the unions opted for arbitration required the issuance of awards.

Application of Arbitration to the Transportation Industry

An ingredient essential to a successful transfer of an arbitration system to the transportation industry is the desire of the unions in that industry for such a plan. This desire is conspicuously absent, however, and it is the employers who would welcome such a procedure. Under these circum-stances, it seems sensible to devise an arbitration system that is more palatable to the unions than the present state of affairs where stoppages in the industry are decried and the parties are subjected to both statutory and ad hoc delaying tactics until they have tired of the battle and are willing to settle because of the possibility of congressional action.

For example, if management is given the right to invoke arbitration in the transportation industry, after meeting a variety of governmental mediatory requirements, the unions might be given the right to specify the form of arbitration—the reverse of the public sector system, but consistent in that the nonpetitioner determines the character of the arbitration procedure. Unions still might opt for noncompliance, however, but the costs of nonparticipation become greater.

Alternatively, given the present union opposition to arbitration, the National Emergency provisions of the Labor Management Relations Act might be amended to provide that in national emergency disputes in the transportation industry, either party could petition for arbitration and the other side could opt to either choose the form of the arbitration procedure or veto the petition and thereby automatically activate the next step in the current procedure. Under such a plan, the union may be willing to try the new option if it believes that the results may be more desirable than those that will eventually flow from the present procedure. If the unions decide against the option, no great damage will have been done to the existing procedure.

In closing this section about the application of arbitration to other sectors of the economy, the reader should be warned again that these notions are speculative. A system that works well in one industry or in small cities may not work well in another industry or in large cities. It is worth noting, however, that both management and union negotiators prefer the system they have lobbied for or are familiar with to the ones used by others. To the degree that the plans are custom-made by the parties for their own use, the possibility of improving dispute resolution procedures is increased.

And finally, a word to those readers who are skeptical of the possibility of extending arbitration to any industry in the private sector: Don't forget about baseball! This industry designed its own arbitration plan with many unique features. It is a form of final-offer arbitration, limited to disputes over salaries, in which the arbitrator must choose the salary demanded by the player or the salary proposed by the club. The arbitrator does not render an opinion; he simply selects the figure that he believes more nearly approximates the criteria that the players and the owners have agreed upon.

Apparently this system is working well and bargaining has not been abandoned. Of the approximately 500 major leaguers eligible to use arbitration in 1974, about 125 players had not signed their contracts as the deadline for signing or arbitrating approached. Fifty-four players and owners continued to disagree to the point of having arbitration hearings scheduled. Of these, 25 were settled by further adjustments of the parties subsequent to submission of the dispute to arbitration. Only 29 cases remained to be disposed of by arbitration—of which the player's proposal was chosen in 13 instances and the owner's proposal was chosen in the other 16.[3]

If, five years ago, one had been asked to predict the likelihood of such a system being introduced into baseball, and of its working well, it is doubtful that it would have been given a higher probability than would be assigned today to the chance that a custom-made arbitration system has of being introduced into the railway, trucking, or longshore industry within the next five years. It may not happen in transportation, but long-shots occasionally do come through, and the possibility of extending systems that work to other sectors of the economy should not be discarded out of hand.

Conclusion

In conclusion, it can be stated that legislated arbitration works where the unions demand the adoption of such a system. Prearbitration mediation reduces the number of disputes referred to arbitration, but the system will work even in the absence of a prearbitration mediation step. The cost of arbitration is more bothersome to unions than to managements, but it is not a very important deterrent to the use of arbitration except in small bargaining units where the per capita cost is very high.

The desire of union and management negotiators to reach negotiated settlements is sufficiently strong to prevent constant referral of problems to arbitration. Both sides prefer to make their own mistakes rather than to transfer the power to do so to an outsider. Most negotiators think that the arbitrators are competent, although many union and management spokesmen believe that there are particular individuals who are not. Even so, the parties are understandably hesitant to transfer their decision-making power to an arbitrator if they can avoid doing so. This strongly held preference for self-determination has, so far at least, prevented arbitration from undermining the collective bargaining process. As one management negotiator phrased it, "My fear of itinerant philosophers making judgments of policy determinations will likely keep my feet to the fire even longer than my fear of a walkout."[4]

Arbitration changes the balance of power and raises wages of workers in weaker unions in rural areas relative to the wages paid in metropolitan areas where unions have strong political support. It is not clear, however, that arbitration raises wages in pattern-setting large cities over what they would have been in the absence of an arbitration statute. The militant actions of public sector unions in large cities prior to the enactment of arbitration statutes suggest that threats of economic force and occasional use of it gave rise to substantial wage increases. Substitution of arbitration for such tactics does not seem to generate higher wage increases and may even generate lower ones, although the larger ones in the earlier stage may have reflected the need to catch up with the private sector rather than the differential effect of using economic force rather than arbitration.

Noncompliance with arbitration is rare in those situations in which the union has sought the enactment of the arbitration statute. As yet, however, there has not been sufficient time for resentment to build up against a succession of awards that the employees believe to be unfair. If this were to happen, the relatively unblemished record may tarnish and the arbitration system may become useless. It is important to keep in mind that leadership changes may reflect changes in attitudes toward arbitration and that the current endorsement of arbitration by the present public safety union leaders may be superseded in future years if or when new leaders who prefer the right to strike are elected.

Industrial relations systems are in constant turmoil—adjusting to changes in technology as well as a variety of economic, social, and political factors. There does not seem to be a procedure that represents a long-run equilibrium position to which the parties gravitate. Instead, the situation is more aptly described as a dialectic in which use of particular impasse procedures grows and declines because of the continuing changes in economic, social, and political factors and the resulting changes in the attitudes of the leaders and their constituencies. The procedure that is regarded as ideal today may have a life-span of a decade or two and as such should be considered successful. When it is replaced by another alternative, it should not be forgotten forever, for its time may come again.

Interest arbitration was relied upon to some extent before grievance arbitration gained widespread acceptance. Then its use declined as the right to bargain and to strike was protected by national labor legislation. Today, in the public sector, interest arbitration is emerging as a politically acceptable means of resolving impasses, endorsed by those unions with the greatest power to disrupt the health and safety of the community. It has not had an adverse economic effect so far as can be determined, nor has it damaged the bargaining process. The evidence suggests that it would be wise to consider its adoption in other areas in which there is dissatisfaction with alternative methods of dispute resolution.

As for the precise form of arbitration that should be selected, it will depend on the values of the parties. If they wish to emphasize the deterrent effect of arbitration and encourage a judicial, arms' length approach in cases that are arbitrated, the single-arbitrator final-offer-by-package system of Wisconsin would fit their needs. If they wish to emphasize the agreed-upon settlements through "med-arb," the Michigan approach, which uses a tripartite panel with authority to mediate but the need to choose the final offer of either party on each economic issue, would be the choice. If there is fear of "gimmicks" and a desire to establish a framework that is applicable only to dispute resolution and that does not fit into a statute providing for full regulation of bargaining, the Pennsylvania system appears to be the appropriate model.

Finally, it should be noted that in each jurisdiction, the parties and the neutrals tended to prefer their own procedure to those of the other states with which they were not familiar. It seems, therefore, that the ideal solution is the one designed by the parties themselves for their own use. It can be an amalgam of the various features of the systems used elsewhere, but if self-designed, it will have a better chance for a longer life.

Notes

1. *Wisconsin State Journal,* September 10, 1974.

2. Harry H. Wellington and Ralph K. Winter, Jr., *The Unions and the Cities* (Washington: The Brookings Institution, 1971).

3. Statistics on arbitration were reported in *The New York Times,* March 3, 1974. A favorable evaluation of the procedure by one of the arbitrators who participated in it was written by Peter Seitz, "Footnotes to Baseball Salary Arbitration," *Arbitration Journal* (June 1974), pp. 98-103.

4. Herbert L. Haber, "Exploring Alternatives to the Strike," *Monthly Labor Review* (September 1973), p. 43.

Appendixes

Appendix A
Pennsylvania Act 111 of 1968

SECTION 1. Policemen or firemen employed by a political subdivision of the Commonwealth or by the Commonwealth shall, through labor organizations or other representatives designated by fifty percent or more of such policemen or firemen, have the right to bargain collectively with their public employers concerning the terms and conditions of their employment, including compensation, hours, working conditions, retirement, pensions and other benefits, and shall have the right to an adjustment or settlement of their grievances or disputes in accordance with the terms of this act.

SEC. 2. It shall be the duty of public employers and their policemen and firemen employees to exert reasonable effort to settle all disputes by engaging in collective bargaining in good faith and by entering into settlements by way of written agreements and maintaining the same.

SEC. 3. Collective bargaining shall begin at least six months before the start of the fiscal year of the political subdivision or of the Commonwealth, as the case may be, and any request for arbitration, as hereinafter provided, shall be made at least one hundred ten days before the start of said fiscal year.

SEC. 4. (a) If in any case of a dispute between a public employer and its policemen or firemen employees the collective bargaining process reaches an impasse and stalemate, or if the appropriate lawmaking body does not approve the agreement reached by collective bargaining, with the result that said employers and employees are unable to effect a settlement, then either party to the dispute, after written notice to the other party containing specifications of the issue or issues in dispute, may request the appointment of a board of arbitration.

For purposes of this section, an impasse or stalemate shall be deemed to occur in the collective bargaining process if the parties do not reach a settlement of the issue or issues in dispute by way of written agreement within thirty days after collective bargaining proceedings have been initiated.

In the case of disputes involving political subdivisions of the Commonwealth, the agreement shall be deemed not approved within the meaning of this section if it is not approved by the appropriate lawmaking body within one month after the agreement is reached by way of collective bargaining.

In the case of disputes involving the Commonwealth, the agreement shall be deemed not approved within this meaning of this section if it is not approved by the legislature within six months after the agreement is reached by way of collective bargaining.

(b) The board of arbitration shall be composed of three persons, one appointed by the public employer, one appointed by the body of policemen or firemen involved, and a third member to be agreed upon by the public employer and such policemen or firemen. The members of the board representing the public employer and the policemen or firemen shall be named within five days from the date of the request for the appointment of such board. If, after a period of ten days from the date of the appointment of the two arbitrators appointed by the public employer and by the policemen or firemen, the third arbitrator has not been selected by them, then either arbitrator may request the American Arbitration Association, or its successor in function, to furnish a list of three members of said association who are residents of Pennsylvania from which the third arbitrator shall be selected. The arbitrator appointed by the public employer shall eliminate one name from the list within five days after publication of the list, following which the arbitrator appointed by the policemen or firemen shall eliminate one name from the list within five days thereafter. The individual whose name remains on the list shall be the third arbitrator and shall act as chairman of the board of arbitration. The board of arbitration thus established shall commence the arbitration proceedings within ten days after the third arbitrator is selected and shall make its determination within thirty days after the appointment of the third arbitrator.

SEC. 5. Notice by the policemen or firemen involved under section 4 shall, in the case of disputes involving the Commonwealth, be served upon the Secretary of the Commonwealth and, in the case of disputes involving political subdivisions of the Commonwealth, shall be served upon the head of the governing body of the local governmental unit involved.

SEC. 6. Each of the arbitrators selected in accordance with section 4 hereof shall have the power to administer oaths and compel the attendance of witnesses and physical evidence by subpoena.

SEC. 7. (a) The determination of the majority of the board of arbitration thus established shall be final on the issue or issues in dispute and shall be binding upon the public employer and the policemen or firemen involved. Such determination shall be in writing and a copy thereof shall be forwarded to both parties to the dispute. No appeal therefrom shall be allowed to any court. Such determination shall constitute a mandate to the head of the political subdivision which is the employer, or to the appropriate officer of the Commonwealth if the Commonwealth is the employer, with respect to matters which can be remedied by administrative action, and to the lawmaking body of such political subdivision or of the Commonwealth with respect to matters which require legislative action, to take the action necessary to carry out the determination of the board of arbitration.

(b) With respect to matters which require legislative action for implementation, such legislation shall be enacted, in the case of the Commonwealth, within six months following publication of the findings, and, in the case of a political subdivision of the Commonwealth, within one month following publication of the findings. The effective date of any such legislation shall be the first day of the fiscal year following the fiscal year during which the legislation is thus enacted.

SEC. 8. The compensation, if any, of the arbitrator appointed by the policemen or firemen shall be paid by them. The compensation of the other two arbitrators, as well as all stenographic and other expenses incurred by the arbitration panel in connection with the arbitration proceedings, shall be paid by the political subdivision or by the Commonwealth, as the case may be.

SEC. 9. The provisions of this act shall be applicable to every political subdivision of this Commonwealth notwithstanding the fact that any such political subdivision, either before or after the passage of this act, has adopted or adopts a home rule charter.

SEC. 10. If any provision of this act or the application thereof to any person or circumstances is held invalid, the remainder of this act, and the application of such provision to other persons or circumstances, shall not be affected thereby, and to this end the provisions of this act are declared to be severable.

SEC. 11. All acts or parts of acts inconsistent herewith are hereby repealed.

Appendix B
Act 127 of Michigan Public
Acts of 1972

Michigan Police-Fire Fighters Arbitration Act

Act 312 of Public Acts of 1969, as amended by Pub. Acts 1972, No. 127

An act to provide for compulsory arbitration of labor disputes in municipal police and fire departments; to define such public departments; to provide for the selection of members of arbitration panels; to prescribe the procedures and authority thereof; and to provide for the enforcement and review of awards thereof.

The People of the State of Michigan Enact:

SECTION 1. It is the public policy of this state that in public police and fire departments, where the right of employees to strike is by law prohibited, it is requisite to the high morale of such employees and the efficient operation of such departments to afford an alternate, expeditious, effective and binding procedure for the resolution of disputes, and to that end the provisions of this act, providing for compulsory arbitration, shall be liberally construed.

SEC. 2. Public police and fire departments means any department of a city, county, village or township having employees engaged as policemen or in fire fighting or subject to the hazards thereof.

SEC. 3. Whenever in the course of mediation of a public police or fire department employee's dispute, the dispute has not been resolved to the agreement of both parties within 30 days of the submission of the dispute to mediation and factfinding, or within such further additional periods to which the parties may agree, the employees or employer may initiate binding arbitration proceedings by prompt request therefor, in writing, to the other, with copy to the labor mediation board.

SEC. 4. Within 10 days thereafter, the employer shall choose a delegate and the employees' designated or selected exclusive collective bargaining representative, or if none, their previously designated representative in the prior mediation and factfinding procedures, shall choose a delegate to a panel of arbitration as provided in this act. The employer and employees shall forthwith advise the other and the mediation board of their selections.

SEC. 5. Within 5 days thereafter, or within such further additional periods to which they may agree, the delegates shall designate an impartial, competent and reputable person to act as an arbitrator, hereafter called the arbitrator or chairman of the panel of arbitration, and with them to constitute an arbitration panel to further consider and order a settlement of all matters. Upon their failure to agree upon and appoint the arbitrator within such time, or mutually extended time, either of them may request the chairman of the state labor mediation board to appoint the arbitrator, and the chairman of the state mediation board shall appoint, in not more than 7 days, an impartial, competent and reputable citizen as the arbitrator.

SEC. 6. Upon the appointment of the arbitrator, he shall proceed to act as chairman of the panel of arbitration, call a hearing to begin within 15 days and give reasonable notice of the time and place of the hearing. The chairman shall preside over the hearing and shall take testimony. Upon application and for good cause shown, and upon such terms and conditions as are just, a person, labor organization, or governmental unit having a substantial interest therein may be granted leave to intervene by the arbitration panel. Any oral or documentary evidence and other data deemed relevant by the arbitration panel may be received in evidence. The proceedings shall be informal. Technical rules of evidence shall not apply and the competency of the evidence shall not thereby be deemed impaired. A verbatim record of the proceedings shall be made and the arbitrator shall arrange for the necessary recording service. Transcripts may be ordered at the expense of the party ordering them but the transcripts shall not be necessary for a decision by the arbitration panel. The expense of the proceedings, including a fee to the chairman, established in advance by the labor mediation board shall be borne equally by each of the parties to the dispute and the state. The delegates, if public officers or employees, shall continue on the payroll of the public employer at their usual rate of pay. The hearing conducted by the arbitration panel may be adjourned from time to time, but, unless otherwise agreed by the parties, shall be concluded within 30 days of the time of its commencement. Its majority actions and rulings shall constitute the actions and rulings of the arbitration panel.

SEC. 7. The arbitration panel may administer oaths, require the attendance of witnesses, and the production of such books, papers, contracts, agreements and documents as may be deemed by it material to a just determination of the issues in dispute, and for such purpose may issue subpoenas. If any person refuses to obey a subpoena, or refuses to be sworn or to testify, or if any witness, party or attorney is guilty of any contempt while in attendance at any hearing, the arbitration panel may, or the attorney general if requested shall, invoke the aid of any circuit court within the jurisdiction in which the hearing is being held, which court shall issue an appropriate order. Any failure to obey the order may be punished by the court as contempt.

SEC. 7a. At any time before rendering of an award, the chairman of the arbitration panel, if he is of the opinion that it would be useful or beneficial to do so, may remand the dispute to the parties for further collective bargaining for a period not to exceed 3 weeks. If the dispute is remanded for further collective bargaining the time provisions of this act shall be extended for a time period equal to that of the remand. The chairman of the panel of arbitration shall notify the employment relations commission of the remand.

SEC. 8. At or before the conclusion of the hearing held pursuant to section 6, the arbitration panel shall identify the economic issues in dispute, and direct each of the parties to submit, within such time limit as the panel shall prescribe, to the arbitration panel and to each other its last offer of settlement on each economic issue. The determination of the arbitration panel as to the issues in dispute and as to which of these issues are economic shall be conclusive. The arbitration panel, within 30 days after the conclusion of the hearing, or such further additional periods to which the parties may agree, shall make written findings of fact and promulgate a written opinion and order upon the issues presented to it and upon the record made before it, and shall mail or otherwise deliver a true copy thereof to the parties and their representatives and to the employment relations commission. As to each economic issue, the arbitration panel shall adopt the last offer of settlement which, in the opinion of the arbitration panel, more nearly complies with the applicable factors prescribed in section 9. The findings, opinions and order as to all other issues shall be based upon the applicable factors prescribed in section 9. This section as amended shall be applicable only to arbitration proceedings initiated under section 3 on or after January 1, 1973.

SEC. 9. Where there is no agreement between the parties, or where there is an agreement but the parties have begun negotiations or discussions looking to a new agreement or amendment of the existing agreement, and wage rates or other conditions of employment under the proposed new or amended agreement are in dispute, the arbitration panel shall base its findings, opinions and order upon the following factors, as applicable:

(a) The lawful authority of the employer.

(b) Stipulations of the parties.

(c) The interests and welfare of the public and the financial ability of the unit of government to meet those costs.

(d) Comparison of the wages, hours and conditions of employment of the employees involved in the arbitration proceeding with the wages, hours and conditions of employment of other employees performing similar services and with other employees generally:

(i) In public employment in comparable communities.

(ii) In private employment in comparable communities.

(e) The average consumer prices for goods and services, commonly known as the cost of living.

(f) The overall compensation presently received by the employees, in-

208

cluding direct wage compensation, vacations, holidays and other excused time, insurance and pensions, medical and hospitalization benefits, the continuity and stability of employment, and all other benefits received.

(g) Changes in any of the foregoing circumstances during the pendency of the arbitration proceedings.

(h) Such other factors, not confined to the foregoing, which are normally or traditionally taken into consideration in the determination of wages, hours and conditions of employment through voluntary collective bargaining, mediation, factfinding, arbitration or otherwise between the parties, in the public service or in private employment.

SEC. 10. A majority decision of the arbitration panel, if supported by competent, material and substantial evidence on the whole record, shall be final and binding upon the parties, and may be enforced, at the instance of either party or of the arbitration panel in the circuit court for the county in which the dispute arose or in which a majority of the affected employees reside. The commencement of a new municipal fiscal year after the initiation of arbitration procedures under this act, but before the arbitration decision, or its enforcement, shall not be deemed to render a dispute moot, or to otherwise impair the jurisdiction or authority of the arbitration panel or its decision. Increases in rates of compensation awarded by the arbitration panel under section 10 may be effective only at the start of the fiscal year next commencing after the date of the arbitration award. If a new fiscal year has commenced since the initiation of arbitration procedures under this act, the foregoing limitation shall be inapplicable, and such awarded increases may be retroactive to the commencement of such fiscal year any other statute or charter provisions to the contrary notwithstanding. At any time the parties, by stipulation, may amend or modify an award of arbitration.

SEC. 11. Where an employee organization recognized pursuant to Act No. 336 of the Public Acts of 1947, as amended, as the bargaining representative of employees subject to this act, willfully disobeys a lawful order of enforcement by a circuit court pursuant to section 10, or willfully encourages or offers resistance to such order, whether by a strike or otherwise, the punishment for each day that such contempt persists, may be a fine fixed in the discretion of the court in an amount not to exceed $250.00 per day. Where an employer, as that term is defined by Act No. 336 of the Public Acts of 1947, as amended, willfully disobeys a lawful order of enforcement by the circuit court or willfully encourages or offers resistance to such order, the punishment for each day that such contempt persists may be a fine, fixed at the discretion of the court, an amount not to exceed $250.00 per day to be assessed against the employer.

SEC. 12. Orders of the arbitration panel shall be reviewable by the circuit court for the county in which the dispute arose or in which a majority of the affected employees reside, but only for reasons that the arbitration panel was without or exceeded its jurisdiction; the order is unsupported by competent, material and substantial evidence on the whole record; or the order was procured by fraud, collusion or other similar and unlawful means. The pendency of such proceeding for review shall not automatically stay the order of the arbitration panel.

SEC. 13. During the pendency of proceedings before the arbitration panel, existing wages, hours and other conditions of employment shall not be changed by action of either party without the consent of the other but a party may so consent without prejudice to his rights or position under this act.

SEC. 14. This act shall be deemed as supplementary to Act No. 336 of the Public Acts of 1947, as amended, being sections 423.201 to 423.216 of the Compiled Laws of 1948, and does not amend or repeal any of its provisions; but any provisions thereof requiring factfinding procedures shall be inapplicable to disputes subject to arbitration under this act.

SEC. 15. This act shall expire June 30, 1975. Cases pending under negotiations on June 30, 1975 shall be completed under the provisions of this act.

SEC. 16. No person shall be sentenced to a term of imprisonment for any violation of the provisions of this act or an order of the arbitration panel.

SEC. 17. This act shall become effective on October 1, 1969.

SECTION 111.77 Settlement of disputes in collective bargaining units composed of law enforcement personnel and firefighters. In fire departments and city and county law enforcement agencies municipal employers and employees have the duty to bargain collectively in good faith including the duty to refrain from strikes or lockouts and to comply with the procedures set forth below:

(1) If a contract is in effect, the duty to bargain collectively means that a party to such contract shall not terminate or modify such contract unless the party desiring such termination or modification:

(a) Serves written notice upon the other party to the contract of the proposed termination or modification 180 days prior to the expiration date thereof or, if the contract contains no expiration date, 60 days prior to the time it is proposed to make such termination or modification. This paragraph shall not apply to negotiations initiated or occurring in 1971.

(b) Offers to meet and confer with the other party for the purpose of negotiating a new contract or a contract containing the proposed modifications.

(c) Notifies the commission within 90 days after the notice provided for in par. (a) of the existence of a dispute.

(d) Continues in full force and effect without resorting to strike or lockout all terms and conditions of the existing contract for a period of 60 days after such notice is given or until the expiration date of the contract, whichever occurs later.

(e) Participants in mediation sessions by the commission or its representatives if specifically requested to do so by the commission.

(f) Participates in procedures, including binding arbitration, agreed to between the parties.

(2) If there has never been a contract in effect the union shall notify the commission within 30 days after the first demand upon the employer of the existence of a dispute provided no agreement is reached by the time, and in such case sub. (1) (b), (e) and (f) shall apply.

(3) Where the parties have no procedures for disposition of a dispute and an impasse has been reached, either party may petition the commission to initiate compulsory, final and binding arbitration of the dispute. If in determining whether an impasse has been reached the commission finds that any of the procedures set forth in sub (1) have not been complied with and that compliance would tend to result in a settlement, it may require such compliance as a prerequisite to ordering arbitration. If

after such procedures have been complied with or the commission has determined that compliance would not be productive of a settlement and the commission determines that an impasse has been reached, it shall issue an order requiring arbitration. The commission shall in connection with the order for arbitration submit a panel of 5 arbitrators from which the parties may alternately strike names until a single name is left, who shall be appointed by the commission as arbitrator, whose expenses shall be shared equally between the parties.

(4) There shall be 2 alternative forms of arbitration:

(a) *Form 1*. The arbitrator shall have the power to determine all issues in dispute involving wages, hours and conditions of employment.

(b) *Form 2*. Parties shall submit their final offer in effect at the time that the petition for final and binding arbitration was filed. Either party may amend its final offer within 5 days of the date of the hearing. The arbitrator shall select the final offer of one of the parties and shall issue an award incorporating that offer without modification.

(5) The proceedings shall be pursuant to form 2 unless the parties shall agree prior to the hearing that form 1 shall control.

(6) In reaching a decision the arbitrator shall give weight to the following factors:

(a) The lawful authority of the employer.

(b) Stipulations of the parties.

(c) The interests and welfare of the public and the financial ability of the unit of government to meet these costs.

(d) Comparison of the wages, hours and conditions of employment of the employees involved in the arbitration proceeding with the wages, hours and conditions of employment of other employees performing similar services and with other employees generally:

    1. In public employment in comparable communities.

    2. In private employment in comparable communities.

(e) The average consumer prices for goods and services, commonly known as the cost of living.

(f) The overall compensation presently received by the employees, including direct wage compensation, vacation, holidays and excused time, insurance and pensions, medical and hospitalization benefits, the continuity and stability of employment, and all other benefits received.

(g) Changes in any of the foregoing circumstances during the pendency of the arbitration proceedings.

(h) Such other factors, not confined to the foregoing, which are normally or traditionally taken into consideration in the determination of wages, hours and conditions of employment through voluntary collective bargaining, mediation, factfinding, arbitration or otherwise between the parties, in the public service or in private employment.

(7) Proceedings, except as specifically provided in this section, shall be governed by ch. 298.

(8) This section shall not apply to cities having a population of 500,000 or more nor to cities, villages or towns having a population of 2,500 or less.

(9) Section 111.70 (4) (c) 3 shall not apply to employments covered by this section.

History: 1971 c. 247, 307 as amended by ch. 64, Laws of 1973, published July 18, 1973.

Appendix D
Definition of Variables
Used in Models Measuring
the Effect of Final-Offer
Arbitration on Salaries

A Land area of city, in square miles, 1970.

B Base salary, monthly, in dollars.

C Urban city.

D Percent of families in poverty in city, 1970.

D' Ratio of percent of families in city with incomes in excess of \$15,000 to the percent of families with poverty incomes in city, 1970.

E Police and fire salaries set by parity arrangement, 1973.

F_1 Wisconsin salary, 1973.

F_2 Wisconsin salary, 1974.

F_3 Michigan salary, 1972.

F_4 Michigan salary, 1973.

F_5 Michigan salary, 1974.

G Percent of employed persons in manufacturing in city, 1970.

H Scheduled hours of work.

I Median family income in city, in dollars, 1970.

L Percent of civilian labor force unemployed.

M Maximum salary, monthly, in dollars.

N 1970 population in city divided by the number of persons employed by the city in 1973.

O Proportion of eligible employees who are members of the bargaining unit.

P Negotiations were considered pattern-setting, 1973.

R Full value of general property, in thousands of dollars, 1971.

S Population in city, 1970.

T Mill rate of property tax in city, in thousandths of a mill, 1971.

U Ratio of city's population to land area, 1970.

W Municipal truck drivers' hourly wage, in dollars.

W' Average weekly wages in manufacturing in city, in dollars.

Index

Index

Act 111 (Pennsylvania): amendments to, 25; attitude of parties to, 25-29; compliance with awards, 26-28; cost of arbitration, 25-26; criticisms of, 24; grounds for appeal of arbitration decision, 24; legal challenges to, 22-23; legislative efforts to amend, 24-25; public employee attitude, 28; public employer attitude to, 28-29; purpose of act, 32; review of act, 5-6; scope of act, 6-7. *See also* Senate Act 372

Act 195 (Pennsylvania), 26

Allegheny County, 7; police and firefighter, 14

Amending final-offers. *See* Finality question in Wisconsin arbitration statute

American Arbitration Association, 12, 16

American Federation of State, County, and Municipal Employees (AFSCME), 38

Arbitration: attitude of arbitrators to, 176-177; compliance with awards, 189-191; comparison between arbitration in Michigan, Pennsylvania, and Wisconsin, 134-135; conference on arbitration (Wingspread conference), 126-136; as equalizer of bargaining power, 143-144; issue-by-issue, 134. *See also* awards (arbitration); final-offer arbitration; Michigan; Pennsylvania; wages; Wisconsin
—cost of: 177-179; in Wisconsin, 177; in Michigan, 178; in Pennsylvania, 177-178
—dependency: 99-101, 182-183; role of firefighter and chiefs and sheriffs in, 97-98
—effect on bargaining outcomes: 187-189; on catch-up effect, 187
—Michigan: awards, 48; court review of awards, 49; criteria for awards, 47; frequency of use, 51-53; scope of, 127-128; selection of neutral, 45
—Pennsylvania: awards, 18-19; compliance with awards, 19-21, 27-28; cost of, 25-26; duration of awards, 18; economic effect of awards, 29-31; effect on wages, 18-19, 29-31; issues in awards, 17; as means to settle negotiations, 13; process of, 6; unanimous awards, 18-19; use of, 12-13, 14-15

—Wisconsin: cost of arbitration, 95; effect of political factors, 99-101; frequency of use, 81-82; frequency of use by suburbs, 95-96; impact on bargaining outcomes, 102-106; purpose of, 69-70; use of economic factors in awards, 98-99

Arbitrators: acting as mediators, 64, 139-140; attitude to final-offer arbitration on narrowing issues between parties, 139-140; selection of (Wisconsin), 81
—attitude to arbitration: in Michigan, 138; Pennsylvania, 138-139; Wisconsin, 138; summary of, 176-177

Ashenfelter, Orley, 171n

Attorneys. *See* lawyers

Awards: arbitration, 111-112; court review of, 49; criteria for, 80-81. *See also* final-offer arbitration; individual states

Bargaining process (Pennsylvania), 9-11

Baseball, arbitration in, 194-195

Bowers, Mollie, 34n, 74n, 75n

Canada, mediation in, 119-120

Canadian system of public employee bargaining, 191-192

Catch-up wage increases, 98, 187

Collective bargaining: extent of, Michigan, 50-51; influence of final-offer arbitration on, 125-126; legislation, 5-6; in Pennsylvania, 10-11; problems with, 33; in self-reliant cities, 93-94; in Wisconsin, in rural counties, 93-94. *See also* arbitration; individual states; final-offer arbitration; factfinding; mediation

Compliance with arbitration awards. *See* arbitration; awards; individual states

Compulsory arbitration, 30. *See also* arbitration; final-offer arbitration

Constitutional Amendment 9-A (Pennsylvania), 5-6

Control group in regression analysis, 143. *See also* regression analysis

Conventional arbitration: Michigan, 67-68; Wisconsin, 80. *See also* arbitration; final-offer arbitration

Corbett, Lawrence P., 75n

Cost of living, effect on arbitration, 98-99

219

About the Authors

James L. Stern received the B.S. degree in Engineering from Antioch College and the Ph.D. in economics from the University of California, Berkeley. A professor of economics at the University of Wisconsin since 1962, he teaches collective bargaining and arbitration courses as well as arbitrating both grievance and interest disputes in Wisconsin and neighboring states. In 1971-1972, while a Fulbright research fellow at the University of Warwick, Dr. Stern studied dispute settlement procedures in the United Kingdom.

Charles M. Rehmus is co-director of the Institute of Labor and Industrial Relations and professor of political science at the University of Michigan. He has served as a consultant for federal, state, and local government units, and his arbitration experience extends over many years. His most recent publications have been on public sector and on transportation industry bargaining and dispute settlement. He received the Ph.D. from Stanford University.

J. Joseph Loewenberg, who holds the D.B.A. degree from Harvard Graduate School of Business Administration, is associate professor at Temple University School of Business Administration. In 1970-1971 he was visiting senior lecturer, Department of Labor Studies, Tel Aviv University. He is co-author of two books and a number of articles on collective bargaining in public employment and has extensive experience as an arbitrator of labor-management disputes.

Hirschel Kasper is professor of economics at Oberlin College where his areas of special interest are labor economics, economic theory, and public policy. His most recent research and writing have been on collective bargaining and salary determination in the public schools and on work effort responses to income maintenance programs. Dr. Kasper received the Ph.D. from the University of Minnesota and was a senior research fellow at the University of Glasgow in 1970-1971.

Barbara D. Dennis is project associate at the Industrial Relations Research Institute, University of Wisconsin, and managing editor of the *Journal of Human Resources.* Currently she also is co-editor of publications of the Industrial Relations Research Association and of the Proceedings of the National Academy of Arbitrators. She received both the B.S. and M.S. degrees in journalism from the University of Illinois.